Instant Revit!:
Commercial Drawing Using Autodesk® Revit® 2021

David Martin

Dedication

I would like to dedicate this book to my friends and co-workers.
Without their constant support and friendship this book would not be possible.

Table of Contents

Introduction

Welcome to: **Commercial Drawing Using Autodesk® Revit® 2021.**

The purpose of this book is to guide the student through the process of drawing a two-story commercial building. This project was originally designed as a one-story building using the Revit 2014 program and was used in the Revit 2015 version of the book.

Please Note:
This project is meant for students that have a basic understanding of Revit. If you have never used Revit before, you may wish to first purchase my other book: **Instant Revit!: A Quick and Easy Guide to Learning Autodesk® Revit ® 2021.** This book goes into more depth and covers the basic commands and techniques of the Revit 2021 software.

The tutorials will guide you through the completion of a two-story commercial building. Each tutorial is divided into parts that will have you accomplish a portion of the project. There is also an Appendix procedure that will instruct the student in adding stacked walls and keynotes the completed project.

Use this link to access the Tutorial Videos.
http://tinyurl.com/2vk9wxr2

Use this link to access the Support Files.
http://tinyurl.com/3rsrfys6

There is a companion website for this book at www.instantrevit.com. You may refer to this site for the PDF portfolio of the projects and other information.

Each of the tutorials is divided into parts that will have the student accomplish a portion of the project. To save your progress through the tutorials, it is recommended that you save your drawing file at the completion of each part of the tutorial. You may refer to the PDF portfolio on the companion website for the finished version of the project.

It is my hope that you find the process of completing the project an enjoyable and valuable experience. Once you have completed the book please feel free to email me with your experiences, suggestions, and compliments.

Enjoy,

David Martin
instantrevit@gmail.com
www.instantrevit.com

Tutorial 1   Creating the Commercial Building Layout

Part 1	Adding the Grids and Levels, Deleting the Sheets
Part 2	Adding the Exterior Walls and First Floor Interior Walls
Part 3	Adding the First Floor Doors and Windows
Part 4	Adding the Second Floor Interior Walls, Doors, and Windows
Part 5	Adding the Stairway and Elevator Shaft Walls
Part 6	Adding the Remaining Doors and Windows, Break Room, Stairs, Stairway Floor, Guardrails, and Elevator
Part 7	Tagging and Dimensioning the First and Second Floor Doors and Windows
Part 8	Modifying the Exterior and Elevator Shaft Walls
Part 9	Creating the Footers, First and Second Floors, and Longitudinal Section
Part 10	Adding the Tower Walls and Roof
Part 11	Creating the Roofs

Note: All screenshots are from the Autodesk® Revit® software.

Starting the Tutorial

1. Before starting the Revit program, create a file structure on your flash drive or hard drive to store your files.

2. Create a folder called Commercial Project.

   You will store your drawings in this folder.

3. Open the folder and create three subfolders called 1 - Revit Drawing Files, 2 - PDF Files, and Renderings.

4. Download the Custom Family files from the Instant Revit website at **www.instantrevit.com**.

5. The families are located under the Support Files page.

   Extract the zip file or download the individual family files to your Family Files folder on your local drive. Copy the entire folder to your Commercial Project folder.

Project Folders

<u>Starting the First Drawing</u>

1. Start Revit 2021.

2. Create a new drawing file.

   Use the Commercial-Default.rte file for the template.

3. Save the file as CL1-1. (CL = Commercial Lesson, Tutorial 1, Part 1)

Note: As you complete each Tutorial it is recommended to save the file with the current Tutorial Number and Part Number in the file name. This way you may return to a previous version of the project.

CL1-1   Adding the Grids and Levels, Deleting the Sheets

Grids are used to align major features of the building to a set of grid lines. For this project, you will use the grid lines to locate the exterior walls of the project.

Levels will be used to locate the vertical height of horizontal planes of the building. Building levels such as: Top of Footers, Top of Floors, Roofs, Ceilings, and Top of Walls will be in relation to a level.

<u>Adding the Grids</u>

1. Open the CL1-1 file created in the last section.

2. Open the Level 1 view in the Project Browser.

3. Unhide the Basepoint of the project using the Reveal Hidden Elements tool in the View Control Bar.

   It will appear in the middle of your elevation markers.

4. Begin by placing grids in their approximate location on the drawing. The grids will be centered on the elevation markers and the base & survey points

   The Grid tool is in the Architecture tab, Datum panel.

   These will be used to locate the outside face of the exterior walls.

Grid Tool

5. To change the Grid letter/number, click on the grid line and then the bubble.

   Type in the correct letter or number.

Changing the Grid Letter

6. To turn on/off the grid bubble, click on the line and then click
    inside the checkbox.

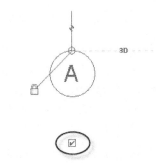

**Hide/Show Grid Bubble
Checkbox**

7. Your grid layout should look like this when finished...

    Use dimensions to locate the grid lines.

    The scale of the view has been changed to 1/16" = 1'-0" for clarity.

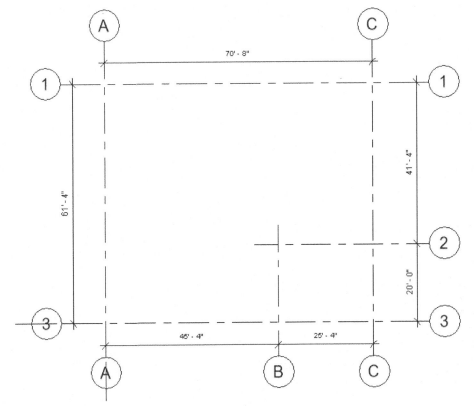

First Floor Grid Layout

8. Set up the location of the base & survey points in relation to the grids as shown.

   Locate the bottom and left gridlines 50 feet from the center of the basepoint. Do not move the gridlines during this step.

   You may wish to use reference planes to assist in locating the grids from the base point.

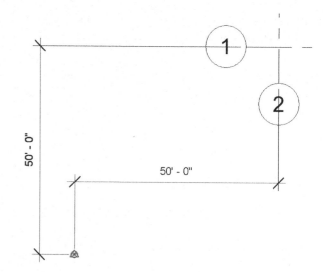

Basepoint & Survey Points Located from Grids

9. You may note that the Survey Point remains at zero regardless of position. If you click on the paperclip icon the position will update as the icon is moved

   The Project Base shows the relative position in relation to the Survey Point

Survey Point   **Base Point**

10. Hide the basepoint, location dimensions, and reference planes if used to locate the grids.

11. After placing the grids, move the elevation markers so that they surround the grids.

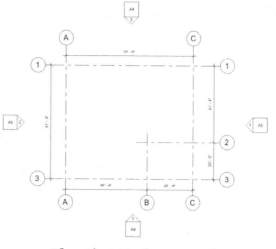

Elevation Marker Moved

Adding and Modifying the Levels.

1. Open the South Elevation view.

2. Hide the reference planes (if applicable). Move the level markers to the right of gridline C.

   Note: This will need to be done in the other three elevation views.

3. Create the levels at the heights shown in the example.

   You may either copy an existing level using the copy tool or create a new level using the Level tool in the Architecture tab, Datum panel.

   Some of the level markers will be blue. This indicates that there is a view associated with it.

   Not all levels with have an associated view.

   You will need to click on the elbow symbol to bend the level line.

   Notes:
   The level named: T.O. SHFT. FTR. Will be for the top of the elevator shaft footer.

   The level named 1ST FLOOR CLG. is for the height of the ceiling.

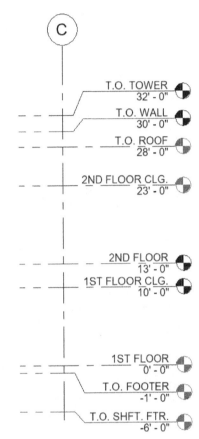

Levels Needed for Project

4. Open the other three elevations views and set up the Grid Line bubble heights and the location of the level text.

5. Create views for the levels that do not have a view.

   Do not create plans for the two ceiling levels.

6. Click on the Plan Views tool in the View tab, Create panel.

   Select the Floor Plan option.

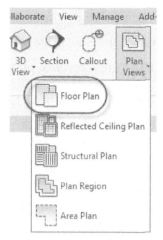

Floor Plan Selected

7. In the New Floor Plan dialog box, select the levels that appear in the example.

   Your list may have different levels shown depending on the method that you used to create the additional levels.

   New floor plan views will appear in the Project Browser.

Levels Selected

New Views Added to the Floor Plan View Category

8. Open each of the views that were created and turn off the reference planes (if applicable). Also turn on any missing grid bubbles.

   If you have an extra ceiling plan views you may delete them.
   Leave the 1st FLOOR view as one of the views.

Deleting the Sheets

The reason for deleting the sheets is that you will be creating new sheets at the beginning of Tutorial 8 when you begin the portfolio. You will also create some sheets during the tutorials to see what portions of the project look like.

1. Scroll down to the Sheets section in the Project Browser.

   Click the "+" sign next to the Sheets (all) text.

   This will expand the section to show all the sheets within the project.

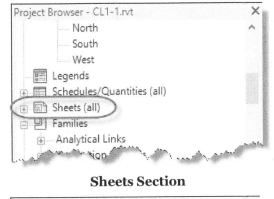

Sheets Section

2. Select the first sheet then scroll down to the last sheet and hold the Shift key.

   Select the last sheet, all the sheets will be selected.

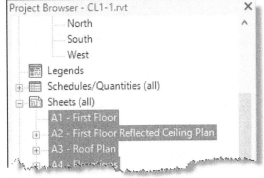

Sheets Selected

3. Press the Delete key to delete the sheets.

4. This is the end of Part 1. Save your file as CL1-1.

CL1-2   Adding the Exterior Walls and First Floor Interior Walls

In this part, you will create the exterior walls for the shell of the building. These walls will extend to the total height of the structure. The interior walls for the first floor will also be added. These walls will extend from floor to a few feet above the ceiling and will end below the second floor level.

1. Open the CL1-1 file and save as CL1-2.

2. Open the 1st Floor View.

3. Create a new wall style called: "Exterior – Concrete on Mtl. Stud". Use the setup shown in the Edit Assembly example for the wall layers.

    When creating the wall type, start with the Generic 8" type.

    The support structure of the wall will consist of 8" Cast-In-Place Concrete. Other layers will be: a Moisture Barrier, Metal Furring, and Gypsum Wall Board.

    When setting the material for the concrete, you will need to create the material: "Concrete, Cast-in-Place". Duplicate the "Concrete, Cast-in-Place gray" to do this.

4. In the Edit Assembly dialog box, click in the material name box, a button will appear next to the name.

    a. Click the button, the Materials dialog box will open.
    b. Search for the "Concrete, Cast-in-Place gray" material.
    c. Right click on the material and choose Duplicate.
    d. Rename the material: "Concrete, Cast-in-Place".
    e. Close the Materials dialog box.

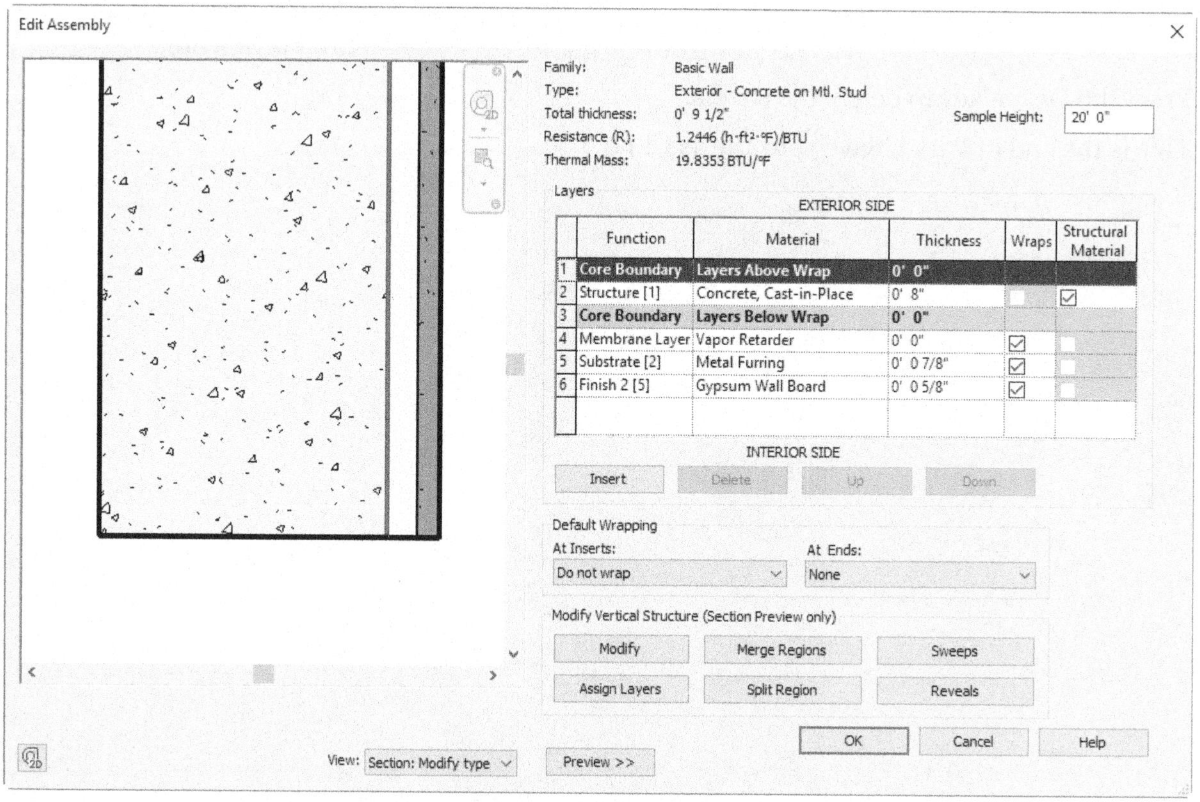

Exterior Wall Setup

5. Add the exterior walls to the project.

    To see the individual layers of the walls, set the
    Detail Level to fine.

    To clearly see each line you will need to turn on the Thin Lines
    toggle. This toggle is in the Quick Access Toolbar above the
    ribbon panel.

    Set the top of the wall to the T.O. Wall level.

6. Use the Align tool in the Modify tab, Modify panel to lock the
    walls to the grid lines.

    Set the location line to Finish Face: Exterior. Draw the walls in
    a clockwise direction so that the exterior side of the wall is
    facing outward.

    You can check which side is facing outward by selecting the
    wall and observing which side the flip arrows are.

    The arrows indicate the exterior face of the wall.

Detail Level Set to Fine

Wall Aligned to Grid Line

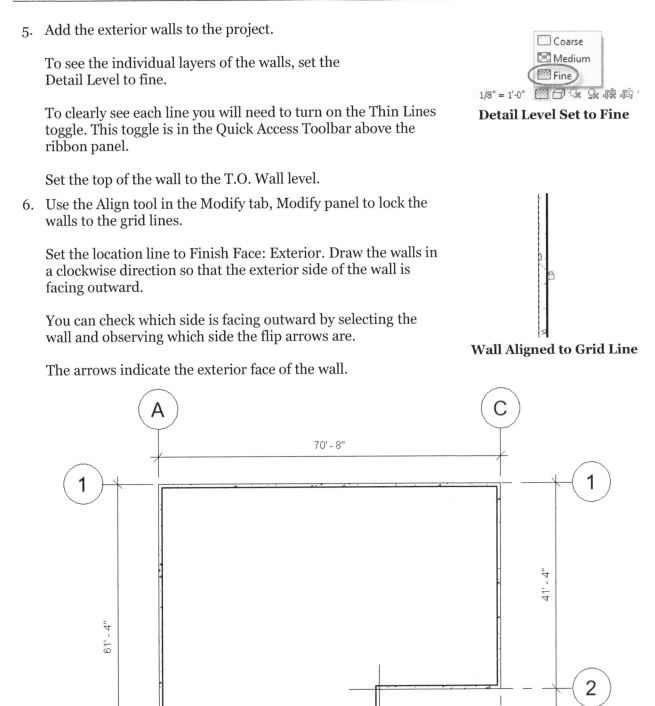

Exterior Walls Added

7. Add the interior walls for the first floor.

8. Refer to the diagram for the location of the walls.

9. Use the Basic Wall – Interior – 5 1/2" Partition (1-Hr) type for the interior walls.

10. The wall that separates the office from the storage area will use the Basic Wall – Interior – 4 7/8" Partition (1-Hr) wall type.

11. Set the height of the walls to the 1st Floor Ceiling Level and the Top Offset to 1'-0". This will give the wall a total height of 11'-0".

Note: The location dimensions are either to the wall faces or to the centerline of the walls.

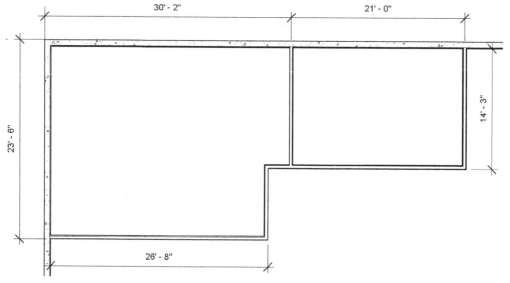

First Floor Interior Wall Properties

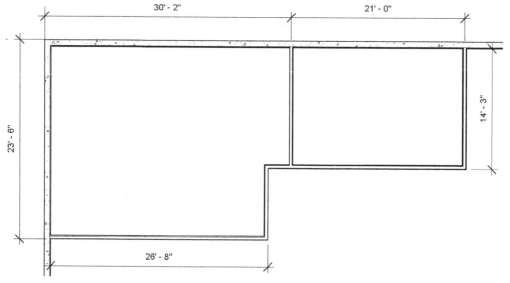

Office and Storage Interior Walls

12. Add the restroom walls.

13. Use the Basic Wall – Interior – 4 7/8" Partition (1-Hr) type for the outside walls. Modify the wall type for the two interior walls.

Note:
The two inside walls are used to enclose the pipes for the restroom fixtures. This is known as a pipe chase.

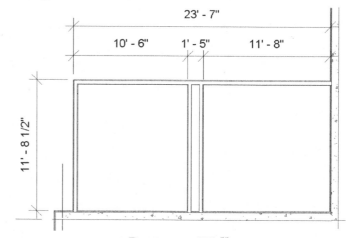

Restroom Walls

14. For the two interior walls for the pipe chase, remove the drywall on the interior side.

    Rename the wall type: Interior – 4 1/4" Wet Wall.

Edit Assembly   ✕

Family: Basic Wall
Type: Interior - 4 1/4" Wet Wall
Total thickness: 0' 4 1/4"   Sample Height: 20' 0"
Resistance (R):   21.0517 (h·ft²·°F)/BTU
Thermal Mass: 0.7230 BTU/°F

Layers   EXTERIOR SIDE

	Function	Material	Thickness	Wraps	Structural Material
1	Finish 2 [5]	Gypsum Wall Boar	0' 0 5/8"	☑	■
2	Core Boundar	Layers Above Wrap	0' 0"		
3	Structure [1]	Metal Stud Layer	0' 3 5/8"		☑
4	Core Boundar	Layers Below Wrap	0' 0"		

                                        INTERIOR SIDE

| Insert | Delete | Up | Down |

Default Wrapping
At Inserts: At Ends:
Do not wrap   ∨   None   ∨

Modify Vertical Structure (Section Preview only)

| Modify | Merge Regions | Sweeps |
| Assign Layers | Split Region | Reveals |

                    | OK | Cancel | Help |

View: Section: Modify type ∨   Preview >>

---

15. These walls will be also be set to the Ceiling level height plus 2'-0" (12'-0").

    Note: The 11'-8 1/2" dimension will change after the north restroom walls are aligned with the elevator shaft wall.

16. This is the end of Part 2. Save your file as CL1-2.

CL1-3   Adding the First Floor Doors and Windows

In this part you will be adding the doors and windows for the first floor of the project. Tags are shown on the drawing example to match the doors and windows to the schedules.

1. Open the CL1-2 file and save as CL1-3.

2. Open the 1st Floor view.

3. Add the First Floor Doors and Windows.

   Refer to the tables for sizes. Some window sizes will need to be created.

   The main entrance Curtain Wall Dbl Glass door and south wall windows will be added later.

   The tags for the doors and windows are for reference. You will add these tags later in the tutorial.

4. When placing the windows, confirm that the head height setting in the Properties dialog box is set to 7'-0".

Door Letter	Door Type and Size	Notes
A	Curtain Wall-Store Front-Dbl Store Front Double Door	This type is included with the template.
B	Single-Flush: 36" x 80"	This type/size is included with the template.
C	Single-Flush: 36" x 84"	This type/size is included with the template.
D	Door-Single-Panel (1HR): 36" x 84"	This size will need to be loaded from the Custom Families.
E	Single-Flush – Womens Room: 36" x 80"	This type will need to be loaded from the Custom Families.
F	Single-Flush – Mens Room: 36" x 80"	This type will need to be loaded from the Custom Families.

Note: The doors for the Women's and Men's have signage on the exterior side of the door.

Window Number	Window Type and Size	Notes
1	Fixed: 36" x 48"	This size is included with the template.
2	Fixed: 36" x 72"	This size is included with the template.
3	Fixed: 48" x 72"	This size will need to be created.
4	Fixed: 48" x 36"	This size will need to be created.
5	Fixed: 16" x 72"	This size is included with the template.

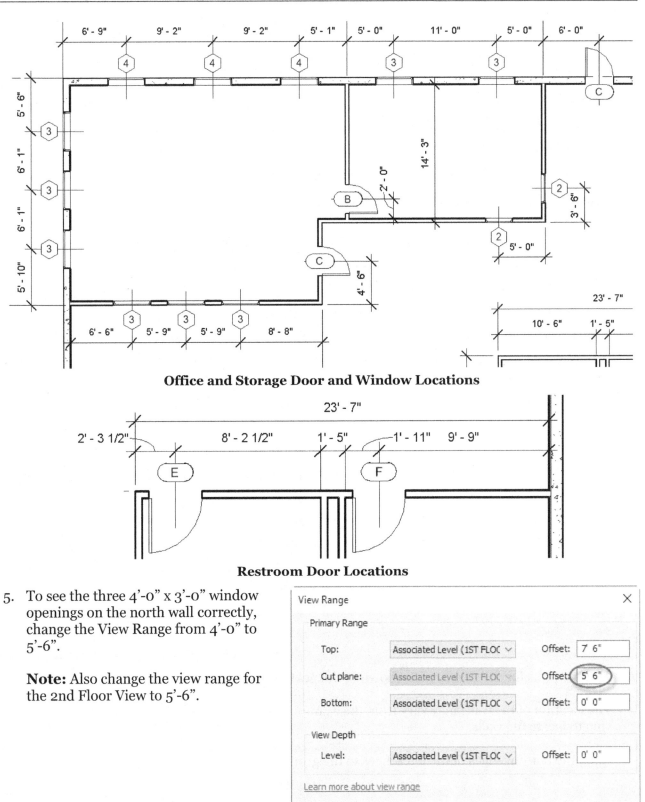

Office and Storage Door and Window Locations

Restroom Door Locations

5. To see the three 4'-0" x 3'-0" window openings on the north wall correctly, change the View Range from 4'-0" to 5'-6".

   Note: Also change the view range for the 2nd Floor View to 5'-6".

6. This is the end of Part 3. Save your file as CL1-3.

CL1-4   Adding the Second Floor Interior Walls, Doors, and Windows

You will be repeating the process that was followed in CL1-3 for adding the interior walls, doors, and windows. Floors will be added later so for now it will appear as if the second floor walls are floating.

Adding the Office Walls

1. Open the CL1-3 file, save the file as CL1-4.

2. Open the 2nd Floor view.

3. Set the Detail Level to Fine and turn on the Thin Lines toggle.

   Note: The detail level should be set to fine for all views.

Thin Lines Toggle

4. Click on the Wall tool and set the wall type to Interior – 4 7/8" Partition (1-hr).

5. Set the height of the wall to the second floor ceiling and the top offset to 2'-0".

Properties		×
	Basic Wall Interior - 4 7/8" Partition (1-hr)	▾
New Walls		▾ Edit Type
Constraints		⌃
Location Line	Wall Centerline	
Base Constraint	2ND FLOOR	
Base Offset	0' 0"	
Base is Attached	☐	
Base Extension Distance	0' 0"	
Top Constraint	Up to level: 2ND FLOOR CLG.	
Unconnected Height	12' 0"	
Top Offset	2' 0"	
Top is Attached	☐	
Top Extension Distance	0' 0"	

Second Floor Interior Wall Properties

6. Add the walls for the 10 offices as shown in the next image.

   The location of the walls may vary from the example. You will be using dimensions in the next step to locate the walls.

   Align the bottom edges of the left offices to the group of offices on the right.

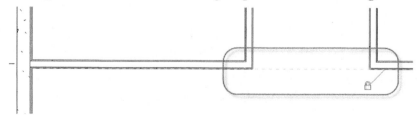

Walls Aligned

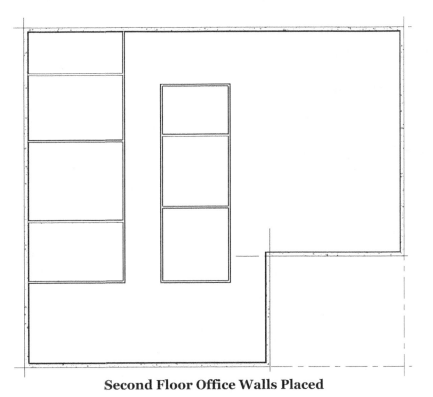

Second Floor Office Walls Placed

7. Add the dimensions for the wall locations and adjust their location.

Use the wall faces when locating the walls to create the 6'-0" hallway widths.

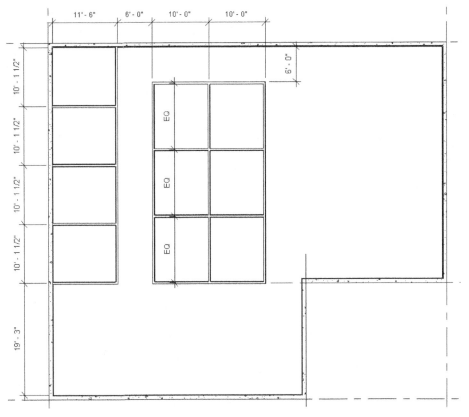

Second Floor Office Walls Added

Modifying the Two Exterior Walls

1. Select the two walls at the lower right corner.

    In the Properties dialog box, set the height of the walls to the second floor level.

    You may need to adjust the corners of the walls in the 1st Floor view so that the ends of the south and east walls end at the grid lines.

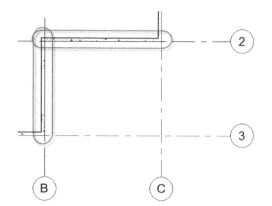

Walls to be Changed

2. The two walls will disappear in the second floor view.

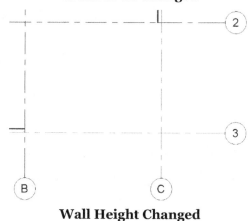

Wall Height Changed

3. The second floor office walls are placed.

4. Go to the 1st Floor view.

5. Select the Bathroom walls and the doors.

6. Click on the Copy to Clipboard tool in the Clipboard panel.

7. Paste the walls and doors to the second floor level using the Aligned to Selected Levels Option.

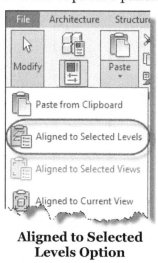

Aligned to Selected Levels Option

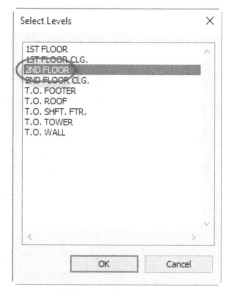

Select Levels Dialog Box

8. Create a new wall type called: Exterior – 9 1/2" Partition.

    Begin with the 4 7/8" Partition wall type and change the Metal Stud Layer to 8 1/4" thick.

    For the Stucco material, start with the Plaster material and duplicate it. The Plaster material will need to be loaded from the AEC Materials folder on the hard drive. Set the color of the stucco material to the gypsum plaster pattern and light gray (RGB 192, 192, 192).

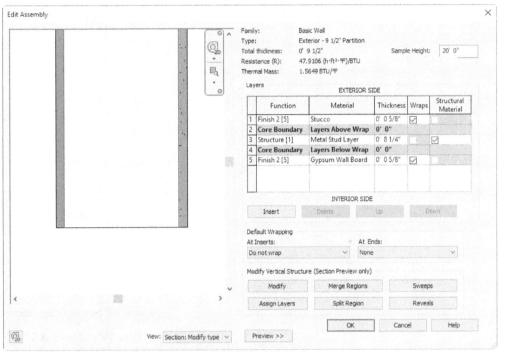

New Wall Properties

9. Open the 2nd Floor view.

    Using the new wall type, drawing the wall across the bottom edge of the bathroom.

    Align the bottom edge of the wall with the grid line.

    Set the top of the wall to the 2ND FLOOR CLG level.

    The 9 1/2" wall thickness will match the first floor exterior wall.

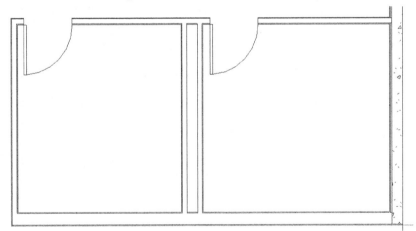

Bathroom Walls Copied and Wall Added

<u>Adding the Second Floor Windows and Doors</u>

1. Select the 36" x 48" fixed window and add to the
    west side of the second floor.

    Center the windows between the inside faces of
    the office walls.

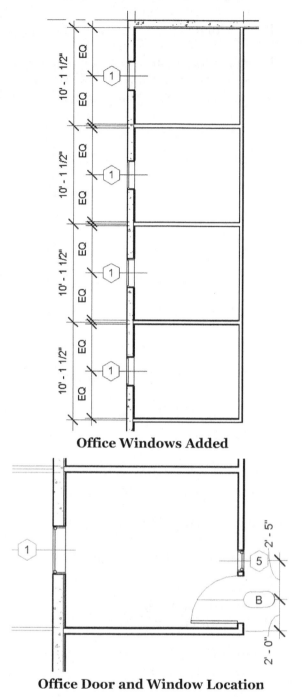

Office Windows Added

2. Add a door and window to the lower left office.

    The door size will be 36" x 80" and the window
    size is 16" x 72".

    Set the window head height to 6'-11" to align with
    the top of the door.

Office Door and Window Location

3. Copy the door and window to each of the offices.

    Use the same relative location as with the first office.

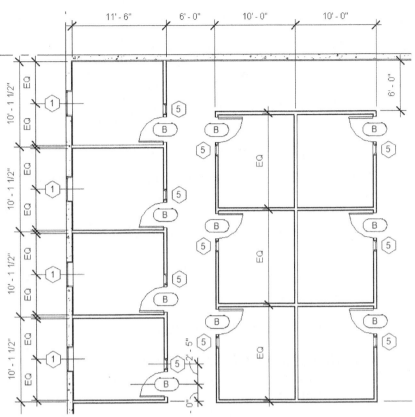

Office Doors and Windows Placed

4. Add three 48" x 36" windows along the north wall.

    Change the view range to 5'-6" to see the windows clearly.

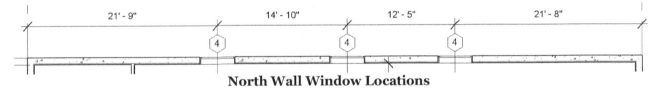

North Wall Window Locations

5. This is the end of Part 4. Save your file as CL1-4.

CL1-5   Adding the Stairway and Elevator Shaft Walls

1. Open the CL1-4 file, save the file as CL1-5.

2. Open the 1st Floor view.

3. Zoom in to the upper right corner of the building.

4. Click on the Wall tool and set the wall type to Generic – 8" Masonry.

    Set the wall height to the T.O Wall level.

5. Add the walls for the stairway enclosure and the elevator shaft.

    The 5'-9" dimension is from the face of core of the exterior wall.

    You may see an error message informing you of a wall overlap.

    This will be resolved in the next step.

    Note: The reason for the wall not following modular dimensions are the size requirements for the elevator shaft from the manufacturer.

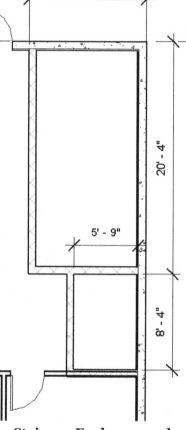

**Stairway Enclosure and
Elevator Shaft Wall Location**

6. Zoom in to the north wall of the restrooms.

    Pull the end of the wall to the edge of the elevator shaft wall.

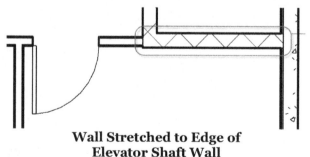

**Wall Stretched to Edge of
Elevator Shaft Wall**

7. Repeat the process for the second floor restroom wall.

8. Switch to a
   Shaded, 3D view.

   At this point your
   model should look
   like this...

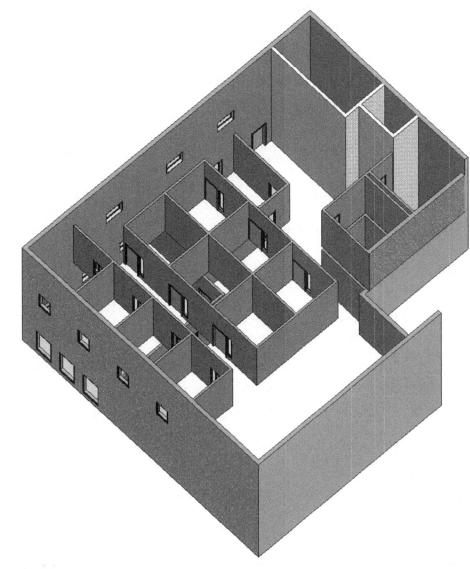

Southwest View of Building

9. This is the end of Part 5. Save your file as CL1-5.

CL1-6   Adding the Remaining Doors and Windows, Break Room, Stairs, Stairway Floor, Guardrails, and Elevator

1. Open the CL1-5 file, save the file as CL1-6.

2. Open the 1st Floor view and zoom in on the Stairway and Elevator area.

3. Load the Door-Single-Panel (1HR) family from the custom family files from the Instant Revit! Website.

4. Add the two doors to the stairway at the first floor.

   Door "D" is the 1 hour door.

   Door "C" is 36"x84" Single-Flush.

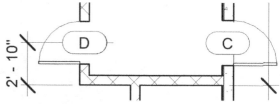

First Floor Doors Locations and Swings

5. Add the door to the stairway at the second floor.

   Note the change in swing between the first and seconds floors. This is due to the direction of travel when exiting the building.

   The second floor door is in the same location.

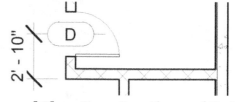

Second Floor Door Location and Swing

6. Load the 2sso.rfa family file from the Schindler Elevator Files folder in the downloaded families.

   This door comes with the Elevator family that will be loaded later. Place the doors on both floor levels at the same location.

   Note: This family will need to be loaded as a component using the Insert tab and is inserted as a component.

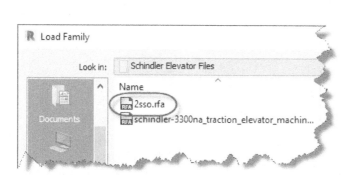

Elevator Door Family File

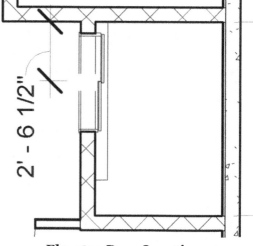

Elevator Door Location

7. Open the second floor view.

    Place the Break Room walls and door as shown.

    Use the 4 7/8" wall type and the 36" x 80" door.

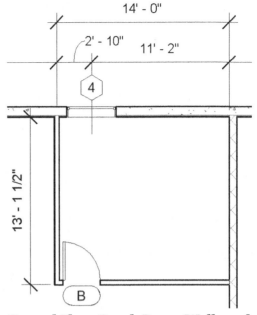

Second Floor Break Room Walls and Door

8. Before adding the stairs, you will need to modify the exterior walls at the north side of the stairway enclosure and the entire east wall.

    The inside wall surfaces of the stairwell and elevator shaft will be bare concrete.

    Create a new wall type starting with the Exterior – Concrete on Mtl. Stud.

    Name the new wall type: Exterior – Concrete.

    Remove the metal furring and gypsum board layers.

New Exterior Wall Type

9. Change the entire east wall to the new wall type.

10. Use the Split Element tool to cut the north wall as shown.

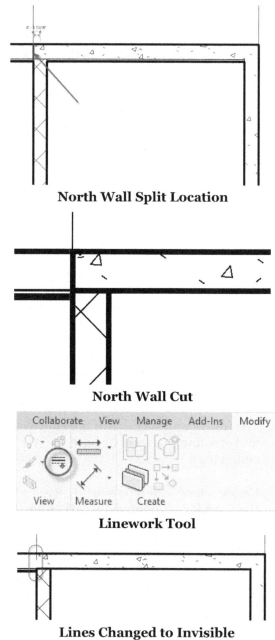

North Wall Split Location

11. After cutting the wall, set the right portion of the wall to the new wall type.

North Wall Cut

12. Use the Linework tool in the Modify tab, View panel to change the vertical cut line to the <Invisible lines> line style.

    You will need to change two overlapping lines.

Linework Tool

Lines Changed to Invisible

Adding the Stairs

1. Click on the Stair tool in the Architecture tab, Circulation panel. Use the Steel Pan Stair type.

2. Add the stair as shown.

   Confirm that the Base Level is set to 1ST FLOOR.

   Set the Top Level to 2ND FLOOR.

   Before clicking the first point, set the Railing type to None.

   The stair run will begin at the left side of the stairwell for 11 risers.

   Then click and begin the return run directly across on the right side.

   Click and drag for another 12 risers for a total of 23.

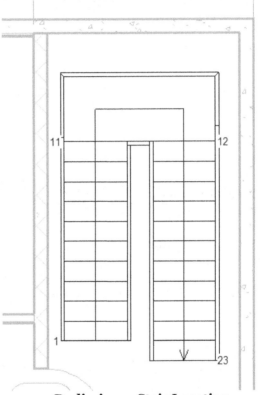

Railing Type Set to None

Preliminary Stair Location

3. Click on the treads and set the actual run width to 44". Do this for both runs and then the landing.

    The width can be adjusted in the Properties dialog box or by changing the temporary dimensions.

Runs and Landing Width Changed to 44"

4. Select the entire stair and move it to the upper left corner of the stairwell.

    Uncheck the Constrain checkbox in the options bar.

    The stringers will be on the face of the wall.

Constrain Unchecked

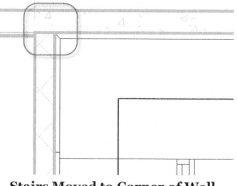

Stairs Moved to Corner of Wall

5. Select the right run of the stair.

    Click the Move tool and move it to the inside edge of the right wall. This will stretch the stairs to fit in the stairwell.

    Snap to the edge of the stringer when moving the run.

Right Side of Stairs Located

6. Click the Green Check to finish the stairs.

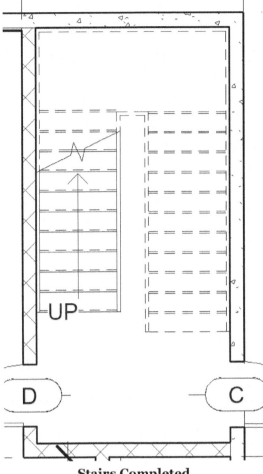

Stairs Completed

Adding the Stairway Floor

In this section you will add a floor landing for the end of the stairs on the second floor. This will be done before adding the floors for the rest of the building.

1. Open the 2nd Floor view. Zoom in on the second floor stair area.

2. Click on the Floor tool.

3. Set the floor type to Generic 12".

    You will change the floor type later when adding the second floor.

4. Draw the floor boundary as shown.

    The notch at the north edge of the floor is 6" up from the beginning of the stairs on the right.

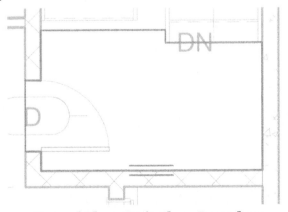

5. Click the green check to complete the floor.

Second Floor Stair Floor Boundary

Adding the Handrails and Guardrails

1.

2. Open the Railing Samples.rvt file in the downloaded families folder.

3. In the Families category in the Project Browser, find the Handrail – Pipe – Wall type.

    You will also need to open the sub-category, Railing to find the family.

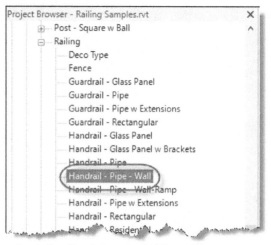

Handrail – Pipe – Wall Railing Type

4. Copy the railing type to the clipboard by right-clicking on the name in the Project Browser.

5. Return to your project file and paste the railing types using the Modify, Paste tool.

    The family type will automatically be inserted and a new railing type.

    Close the Warning Box.

6. After loading this type, also load the Handrail – Pipe w Extensions type.

7. Click on the Railing tool in the Architectural tab, Circulation panel.

8. Select the Handrail – Pipe – Wall type.

Handrail – Pipe – Wall Railing Type

9. Click the Pick New Host tool and then select the stairs.

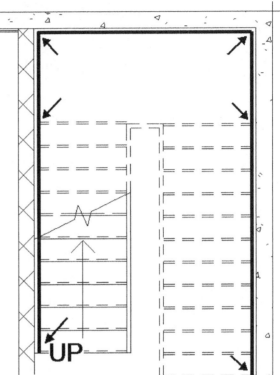

Pick New Host Tool

10. Click the following points for the railing location:

    a. Lower left corner of the stringer.
    b. End of the left stair run.
    c. Upper left corner of the landing.
    d. Upper right corner of the landing.
    e. Start of the right stair run.
    f. End of the right stair run.

    When clicking the points, snap to the inside edge of the stringers.

    Note: Use the Chain option to add the lines one after another.

Railing Points

11. Click the Green check to finish the railing.

    You will need to flip the railing to the outside. Check the end of the railing on the left side to make sure that the rail is facing the right way.

    Note: If you receive an error message that the railing family is corrupt and needs repair, delete the railing and add the railing again.

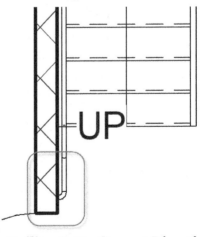

Railing Set to Correct Direction

12. Add the interior railing as shown.

Open the 2nd Floor view.

Use the Handrail – Pipe w Extensions railing type.

Set the host for the rail by picking the stairs.

Pick the inside edge of the stringer for the path starting on the right side of the stringer at the top of the stairs.

Set the offset to 0'-1". This will set up the path so that it is in the middle of the inside stringer.

You may see a warning box that states that the rail is not continuous. You may ignore the message.

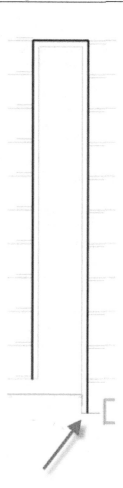

**Railing Path
Start Point**

Offset from Path set to 0'-1"

13. Select the stairs in the plan view.

14. Pick the Selection Box tool in the contextual tab.

Selection Box Tool

15. Name the view: Stairs - Section

    In the 3D view a sectioned area of
    the stairs is shown.

    Hide the east wall to see the stairs
    and railing.

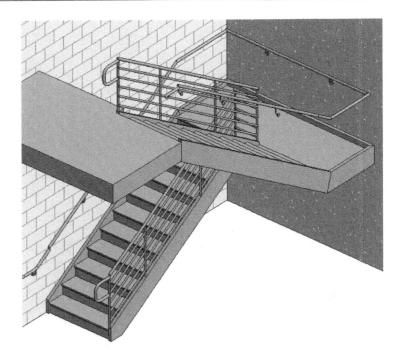

Railing and Stairs

16. Open the 2nd Floor view.

17. Click on the Railing tool.

    Reset the Offset from Path setting to 0'-0".

    Select the Guardrail – Pipe railing type.

    Draw the path as shown from right to left.

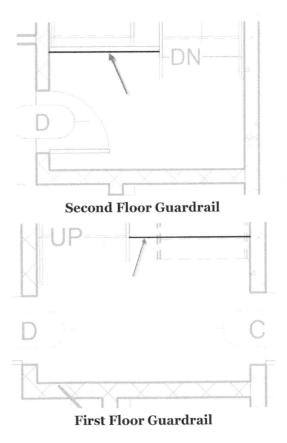

Second Floor Guardrail

18. Add another railing on the first floor.

    Select the Handrail – Pipe railing type.

    The purpose of this railing is to prevent people
    from walking under the stair.

First Floor Guardrail

19. This
completes
the stairs
and
railing.

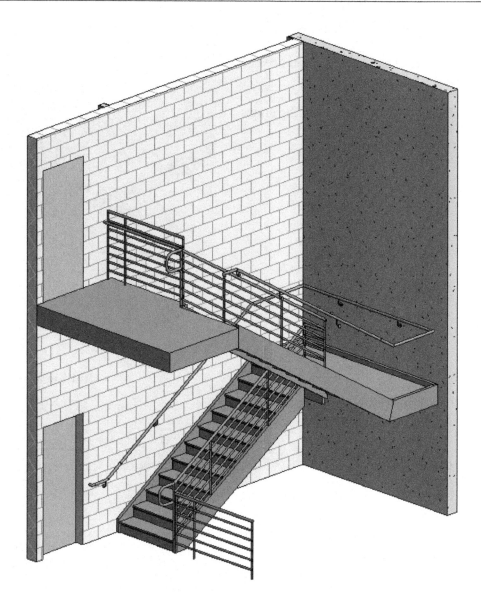

Completed Stair and Railings

Adding the Elevator

1.

2. Open the 1st Floor view and zoom in to the elevator shaft.

3.

4. Load the
Schindler
Elevator
family file
from the
downloaded
families
folder.

The file will be
in the
Schindler
Elevator Files
subfolder.

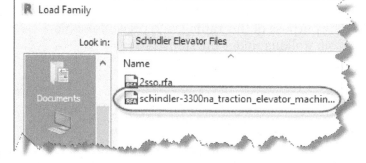

Elevator Family File

Note:

This type of
elevator does
not require a
separate
equipment
room.

5. Choose the 2500 Front family type.

    Place the elevator off to the side of the building.

    Mirror the elevator so that the door is on the left side of the elevator car.

    The red dashed lines are the edges of the envelope of the elevator.

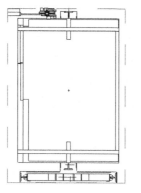

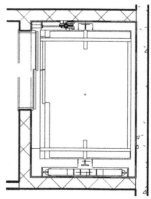

Elevator Mirrored   **Schindler 2500 Front Family Type**

6. Align the edges of the envelope with the inside edge of the elevator shaft walls.

    Confirm that the center of the elevator door is aligned with the center of the door leading into the shaft.

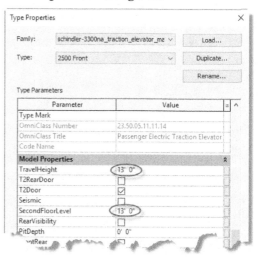

Elevator Placed and Door Centered

7. Click on the elevator and then the Edit Type button in the Properties dialog box.

8. In the Type Properties dialog box set the TravelHeight and SecondFloorLevel parameters to 13'-0".

Type Properties for Elevator

9. This is the end of Part 6. Save your file as CL1-6.

CL1-7   Tagging and Dimensioning the First and Second Floor Doors and Windows

1. Open the CL1-6 file and save as CL1-7.

2. Before tagging the doors and windows you will need to modify the tags so that the numbers/letters will show up with the correct format. You will also need to create a masking region so that the extension lines are broken when they cross over the tags.

3. You will begin by modifying the door tags.

4. Go to the Door Tag family in the Project Browser.

5. It is in the Families Category, Annotation Symbols sub-category, Door Tag family.

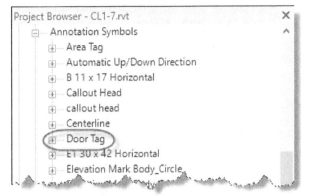

Door Tag Family in Project Browser

6. Right click on the Door tag family and select Edit.

   This will open the family file (Door Tag.rfa).

7. You will need to change the Door Tag family so that the number/letter is based on the type mark and not the mark.

8. Click on the field for the mark. This is the text labeled 101.

9. The text will turn blue. Click on the Edit... button next to Label in the Properties Box.

Edit Label Dialog Box

10. In the Edit Label dialog box click on the 1 next to the Mark in the Parameter Name field.

11. Click the red arrow to remove the parameter.

12. In the Category Parameters area, scroll down to Type Mark. Click the green arrow to add the parameter.

13. Click OK.

14. The text in the bubble has changed to 1t.

Adding the Masking Region

1. Click on the Masking Region tool in the Create tab, Detail panel.

Masking Region Tool

2. Select the Pick Lines option in the Draw panel.

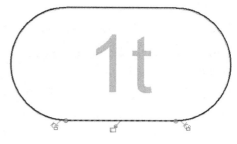

Pick Lines Option

3. Click on the two arcs and two lines the make up the boundary of the symbol.

Boundary Picked

4. Click the Green Check to complete the boundary.

5. Click the Load into Project tool in the ribbon to load the Door Tag into the project.

6. Select "Overwrite the existing version" to replace the original door tag.

   Note:
   This will only affect this drawing.

Family Already Exists Box

7. Repeat the process for the window tag.

   You will not need to change the label, only add the masking region.

Tagging the Doors and Windows

1. Tag and dimension the door and window locations using the Tag All tool.

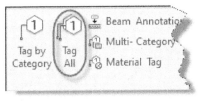

Tag All Tool

   In the Tag All Not Tagged dialog box, choose the Door Tags and Window Tags categories.

   At this point you may also wish to add in missing dimensions and space them the proper distance from the edge of the structure. Use 6'-0" for the first dimension line and 4'-0" for the second and third dimension lines.

   More dimensions will be added later.

   Refer to the drawing for the location of the tags.

   After tagging change them to the correct number or letter.

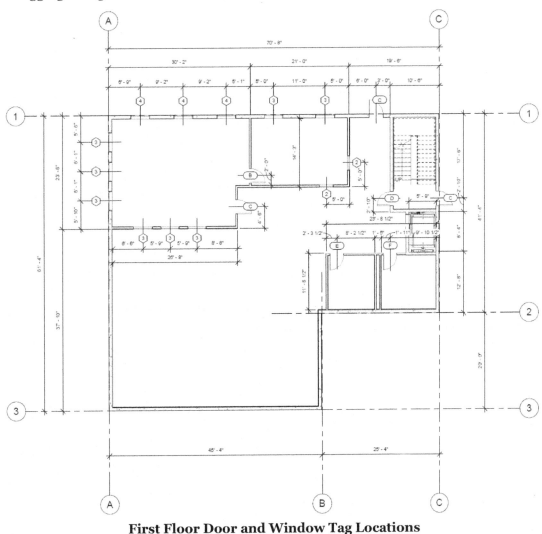

First Floor Door and Window Tag Locations

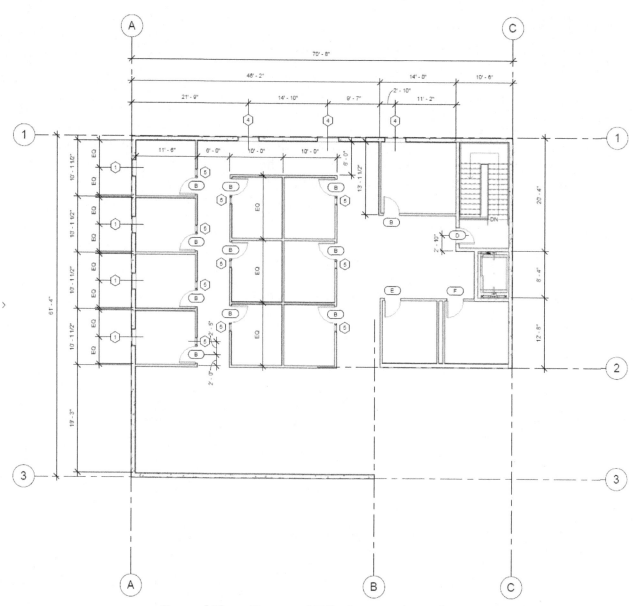

Second Floor Door and Window Tag Locations

2. This is the end of Part 7. Save your file as CL1-7.

CL1-8   Modifying the Exterior, Stairwell, and Elevator Shaft Walls

1. Open the CL1-7 file, save the file as CL1-8.

2. Select all the exterior walls in the 1st Floor view.

3. The bottom constraint of the walls needs to be changed.

   Currently the walls have a base constraint of 1ST FLOOR. Change the base constraint to T.O. FOOTER.

4. Click on the Wall tool and select the Exterior – Concrete on Mtl. Stud wall type.

5. Click on the Edit Type button to open the Type properties dialog box.

6. Click on the Edit... button next to the Structure parameter. This will open the Edit Assembly dialog box for the wall.

7. Switch to the Section view of the wall and zoom in to the top of the wall.

8. Click on the Modify button in the Modify Vertical Structure area of the dialog box.

9. Click on the lines as indicated by the arrows.

10. Unlock the Metal Furring and Gypsum Board layers.

11. Repeat the process for the same layers at the bottom of the wall.

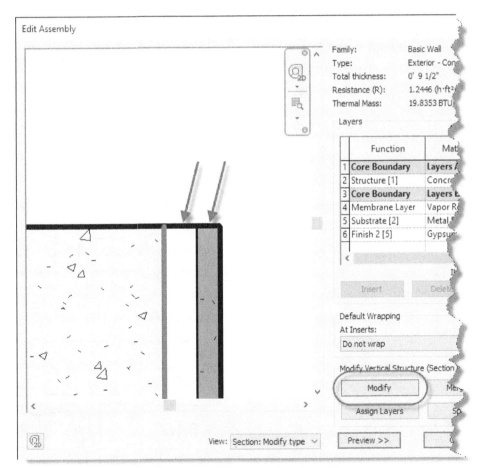

Unlock Top and Bottom Ends of Layers
(Top Portion Shown)

12. Select the longer north, west, and south exterior walls and match the settings to the properties shown.

    Select the two shorter walls at the right corner and change the Base Extension Distance.

    Note:
    The reason for the Top Extension Distance -5'-0" setting is so that the drywall will be below the bottom edge of the roof and above the ceiling.

    The 1'-0" for the Base Extension distance is so the drywall will be at the edge of the first floor slab.

Settings for Exterior Walls

13. Select the interior stairwell walls.
14. Change the Base Constraint to the T.O. Footer level.

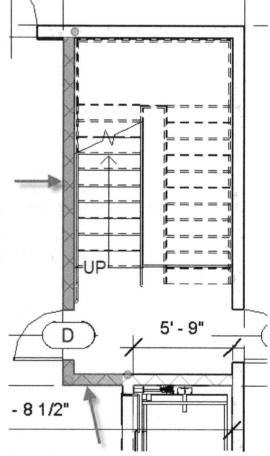

15. In the 1st Floor view, zoom in to the Elevator Shaft walls.

16. You will need to set the Base Constraint of the elevator shaft walls to the top of the shaft footer level.

    Split the north elevator shaft wall as shown. Drag the end of the left side of the wall to detach it from the other wall.

    Position the split at the outside corner of the west elevator shaft wall.

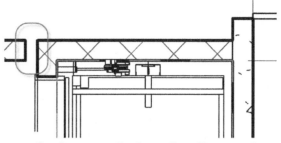

North Elevator Shaft Wall Split Location

17. Set the Base Constraint of the three shaft walls to the T.O. SHFT. FTR. Level.

    Drag the end of the left side wall to reattach it to the corner of the other portion of the wall.

18. Switch to the 3D view and rotate to see under the building in the elevator area.

    Set the Visual Style to Shaded.

    You should see the three walls extend below the other walls.

Shaft Walls Extended

19. Open the East Elevation view.

20. You will adjust the profile of the east exterior wall so that the portion that covers the edge of the shaft that extends down.

    Click on the bottom edge of the wall and select the Edit Profile tool. The edge of the wall shows as a magenta line.

21. Modify the bottom edge of the profile.

    Set the edge to the outside edge of the north and south shaft walls.

    Set the bottom to the level line for the top of the shaft footer.

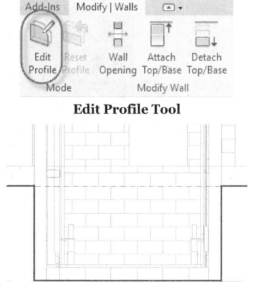

Edit Profile Tool

Modified Profile

22. Click the green check to complete the profile change.

Switch to the 3D view to verify the modification.

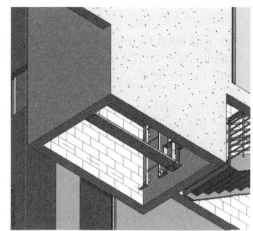

Shaft Walls Completed

23. Rotate the 3D view to show to top of the building.

Your view should look like this...

1/8" = 1'-0"

Shadows On Toggle

Note:
The shadows have been switched on for clarity. You can do this by clicking on the Shadows On toggle at the bottom of the view window.

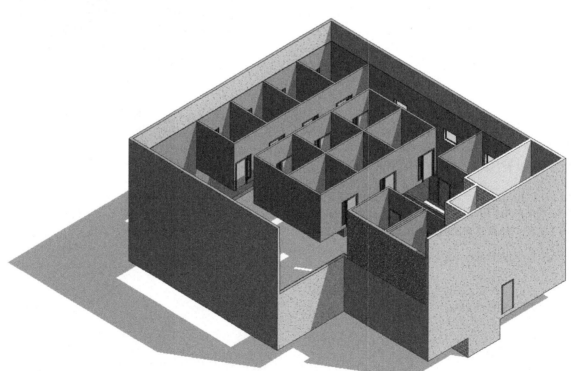

3D Shaded View of Structure

24. This is the end of Part 8. Save your file as CL1-8.

CL1-9   Creating the Footers, First and Second Floors, and Longitudinal Section

Creating the Footers

1. Open the CL1-8 file, save the file as CL1-9.

2. Open the T.O. Footer view.

3. Click the Wall tool and select the "Foundation – 12" Concrete" wall type.

   Duplicate the wall type and name it: "Foundation – 1'-8" Wide".

   Edit the structure and change the wall thickness to 1'-8".

Foundation Wall Type

4. Set the View Range for the view so that the cut plane is 6" and the bottom and the view depth offsets are at -1'-0".

   Turn off the underlay to hide the first floor walls.

   This way you will be able to see the foundation wall as it is placed.

View Range Settings

5. Place the foundation wall centered on the concrete exterior wall.

   Use the following settings for the wall properties.

6. When placing the foundation wall, use the Core Centerline for the center of the wall.

   This way the foundation wall will be centered on the concrete portion of the exterior wall.

Foundation Wall Properties

7.   Zoom in on the lower left corner.

     Center the footer on the center of the
     concrete portion of the wall.

     Note:
     The metal stud and gypsum board layers
     are not visible due to the cut plane
     settings.

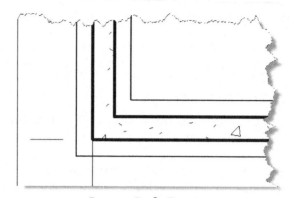

Lower Left Corner

8.   Place the foundation walls as shown.

     Leave gaps at the elevator shaft walls.

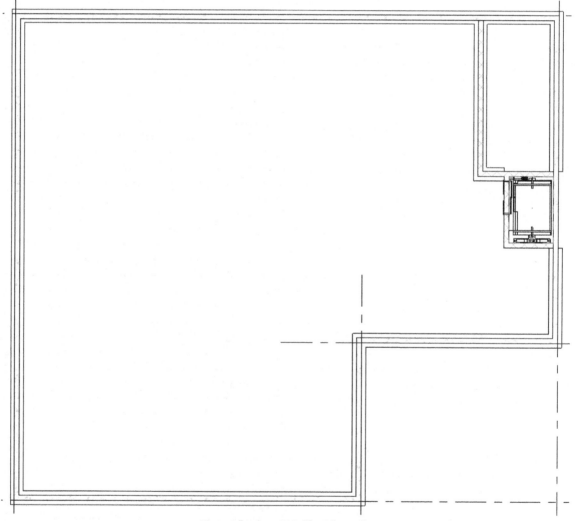

Foundation Walls Placed

9. Open the T.O. SHFT. FTR. view.

10. Set the view range settings to the same as the T.O. FOOTER view.

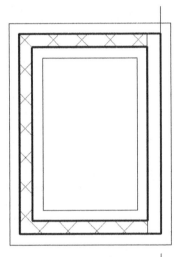

View Range Settings

11. Add another footer at the elevator shaft.

    The Base Constraint will be T.O. SHFT. FTR.

    The other settings will be the same as the other footer.

Footer at Elevator Shaft

12. Open the 3D view to verify the footer placement.

3D Shaded View of Footers

Creating the First Floor Slab

1. Open the 1st Floor view.

2. Create a new floor slab type.

    a. Start with the 4" Concrete Slab and duplicate it.
    b. Name the floor type: "4" Concrete Slab w/Carpet".
    c. Use the Sand material for the Carpet surface pattern. Set the color to light gray (RGB 192 192 192).
    e. Change the Concrete layer to Concrete, Cast-in Place and the cut pattern to light gray.
    f. For the 2" Sand, set the cut pattern to Sand – Dense and the color to light gray. (The sand material will need to be loaded from the AEC Materials folder.)

Family:	Floor
Type:	4" Concrete Slab w/Carpet
Total thickness:	0' 6 1/8" (Default)
Resistance (R):	1.4126 (h·ft²·°F)/BTU
Thermal Mass:	10.5046 BTU/°F

Layers

	Function	Material	Thickness	Wraps	Structural Material
1	Finish 1 [4]	Carpet (1)	0' 0 1/8"		
2	**Core Boundary**	**Layers Above Wrap**	**0' 0"**		
3	Structure [1]	Concrete, Cast-in-Place	0' 4"		☑
4	**Core Boundary**	**Layers Below Wrap**	**0' 0"**		
5	Membrane Layer	Vapor Retarder	0' 0"		
6	Substrate [2]	Sand	0' 2"		

Insert   Delete   Up   Down

OK   Cancel   Help

Modify type ∨   Preview >>

Floor Slab Settings

3. When placing the boundary, pick the inside face of the concrete - not the edge of the drywall furring. This should happen automatically when using the Pick Walls option.

Do not include the stairway and elevators shafts for the floor boundary.

Refer to the diagram below for the boundary.

Note: After picking the boundary and accepting it, answer No when asked if you would like to join the geometry of the floors to the walls. This is done to show that the floor slab and the cast-in-place walls are separate.

Revit ×

The floor/roof overlaps the highlighted wall(s). Would you like to join geometry and cut the overlapping volume out of the wall(s)?

Yes   No

Answer No in Alert Box

First Floor Slab Boundary

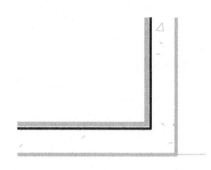

Floor Sketch Boundary

3D View of Footer, Slab, and Wall

4. Add another slab for the stairway shaft.

   Starting with the 4" Concrete Slab w/Carpet floor type, create a new slab type called: 4" Concrete Slab-on-Grade.

   The only change will be to remove the carpet level.

   Use the pick line option to place the floor boundary. The north and east edges of the boundary are on the inside edges of the walls.

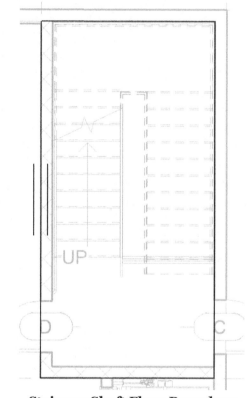

Stairway Shaft Floor Boundary

5. Create a slab for the elevator shaft.

   Use the same slab type as the stairway shaft.

   Set the height of the slab to first floor and the Height Offset From Level setting to -5'-0".

   If you used the Pick Walls option, answer No when the alert box appears.

   This will be the depth of the slab at the bottom of the elevator pit.

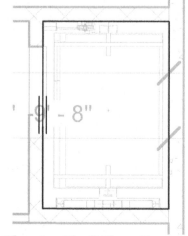

Elevator Shaft Floor Boundary

Creating the Second Floor

1. Open the 2nd Floor view.

2. Add two reference planes.

   One will be 3'-0" below grid line 3. The other will be 3'-0" to the right of grid line C.

   These two lines will be used to locate the lower right corner of the floor boundary. The boundary will be adjusted later to the inside edge of the tower walls.

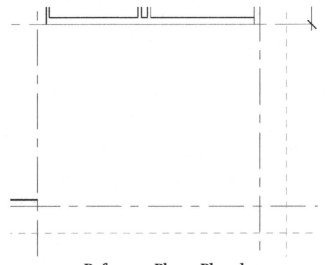

Reference Planes Placed

3. Create a new floor type.

   a. Begin with the 4" Concrete Slab w/Carpet floor type.
   b. The floor type will be named: Steel Bar Joist 14" – Carpet on Concrete.
   c. Match the settings shown below.
   d. Some materials will need to be loaded from the Autodesk Materials.

Family: Floor
Type: Steel Bar Joist 14" - Carpet on Concrete
Total thickness: 1' 7 5/8" (Default)
Resistance (R):   83.5328 (h·ft²·°F)/BTU
Thermal Mass: 10.1460 BTU/°F

Layers

	Function	Material	Thickness	Wraps	Structural Material	
1	Finish 1 [4]	Carpet (1)	0' 0 1/8"			
2	Core Boundary	Layers Above Wrap	0' 0"			
3	Structure [1]	Concrete, Lightweight	0' 4"		☑	
4	Structure [1]	Metal Deck	0' 1 1/2"		☐	
5	Structure [1]	Structure, Steel Bar Joist	1' 2"		☐	
6	Core Boundary	Layers Below Wrap	0' 0"			

Insert   Delete   Up   Down

OK   Cancel   Help

n: Modify type ∨   Preview >>

Second Floor Assembly Properties

4. Draw the boundary as shown.

    Make sure that the Height Offset From
    Level setting is changed back to 0'-0".

    The stairway and elevator shaft will not be
    included.

    Answer Yes when asked if you would like
    for the walls to attach to the floor.

    Answer Yes for the second alert box. This
    will break the drywall at the intersection of
    the second floor and the exterior walls.

Answer Yes in First Alert Box

Answer Yes in Second Alert Box

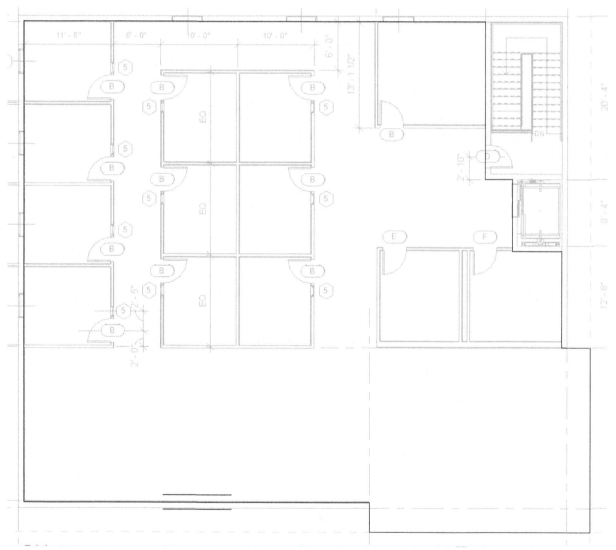

Second Floor Boundary

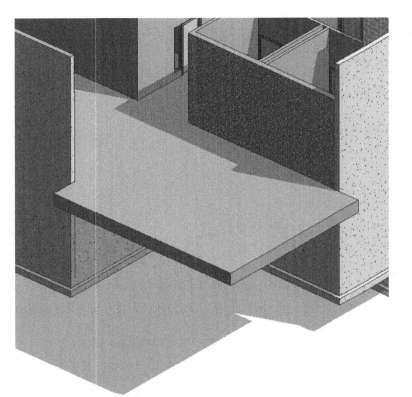

Walls Attached to Second Floor Plate

5. Zoom in to the second floor stair landing inside the stairwell and select the floor.

6. Change the floor type to the Steel Bar Joist 14" – Carpet on Concrete type.

7. Click the Edit Type button.

   Duplicate the floor type and name it: Steel Bar Joist 14" –Concrete.

8. Modify the new floor type.

   Remove the 1/8" carpet level.

   Change the Concrete, Lightweight material surface pattern to light gray.

Creating the Longitudinal Section

1. Open the 1st Floor Plan view.

2. Go to the View tab, Create panel, Section tool. Left-click on the tool.

   In the type selector select the Building Section type.

3. Click on the left side of the floor plan for the start point.

   Drag to the right and click on the other side of the floor plan for the second point.

4. Click on the section view line.

    Select the Split Segment tool.

    Create a split to the left of the elevator shaft.

    Adjust the line to run through the elevator shaft.

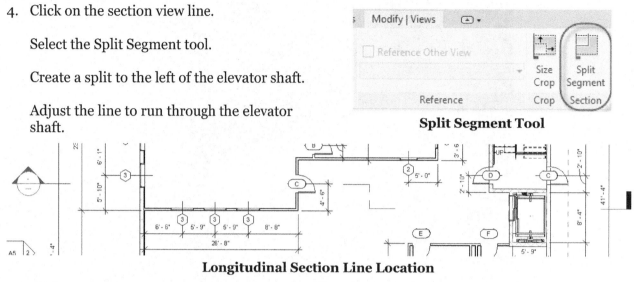

Split Segment Tool

Longitudinal Section Line Location

5. Click on the break control symbol in the middle of the cutting plane line to break it.

    You can adjust the length of the line by dragging the handle point.

6. Open the view named Section 1 and rename it: LONGITUDINAL SECTION.

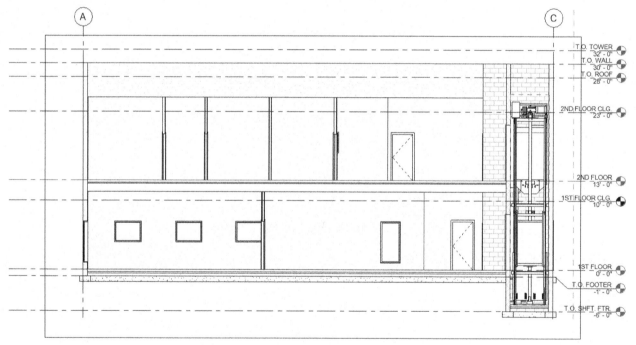

Longitudinal Section View

7. You will need to adjust the crop window and set the detail level of the view to Fine to match the example.

    If the top of the interior wall on the first floor overlaps with the floor, use the Attach Top/Base tool to attach them to the bottom of the floor.

8. You will need to make the material for the gypsum wall board visible.

    To do this, you will need to modify the wall structure. Select one of the interior walls and click on the Edit Type button in the Properties dialog box to begin this process.

    You may also open the material in the Materials dialog box to make the pattern visible.

    Change the Gypsum Wall Board material to show the Gypsum-Plaster pattern and make the pattern light gray in color. Also change the Concrete Cast-in-Place surface pattern to light gray.

Settings for Gypsum Wall Board Material

9. Set the scale of the section view to 3/16" = 1'-0".

    Adjust the location of the level markers so that the text does not overlap.

10. This is the end of Part 9. Save your file as CL1-9.

CL1-10   Adding the Tower Walls

1. Open the CL1-9 file, save the file as CL1-10.

2. Open the 1st Floor view.

3. Delete or hide the reference planes that were used to create the edge of the second floor.

4. Create a new wall type called Exterior – Stucco on Mtl. Stud.

   Begin with the Generic – 8" wall type.

5. Refer to the diagram for the layer materials and sizes.

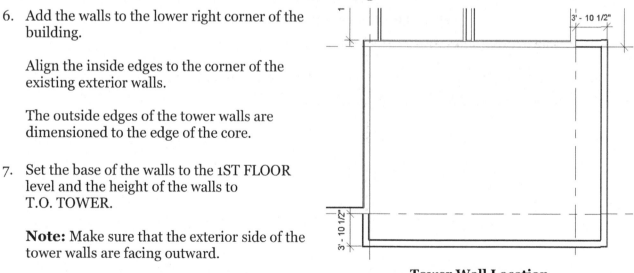

Tower Wall Settings

6. Add the walls to the lower right corner of the building.

   Align the inside edges to the corner of the existing exterior walls.

   The outside edges of the tower walls are dimensioned to the edge of the core.

7. Set the base of the walls to the 1ST FLOOR level and the height of the walls to T.O. TOWER.

   Note: Make sure that the exterior side of the tower walls are facing outward.

Tower Wall Location

8. Open the 2nd Floor view.

    Now you will align the edge of the floor to the tower walls.

9. Select the second floor and click the Edit Boundary tool.

10. Align the edge of the floor in the tower area
    to the inside core of the tower walls.

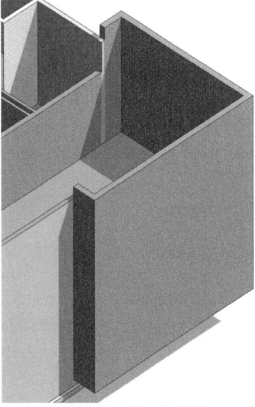

Floor Edge Aligned to Tower Walls

11. This is what you should have so far...

3D View of Tower Walls

Splitting the Tower Walls

Next, you will split the tower walls into three sections. The reason for this is that the portion of the tower walls that are used for the inside of the building will need to have gypsum wall board material for the interior surface material. The tower walls for main entry and the top of the building will have stucco for the inside and the outside material.

1. Open the 1st Floor view.

2. Before separating the walls into individual sections, you will need to change the joins at the corners.

    The walls are currently set as butt joins, you will change them to miter joins.

    Click on the Wall Joins tools in the Modify tab, Geometry panel.

Wall Joins Tool

3. Click on the lower left corner of the tower walls. A square will appear at the join of the two walls.

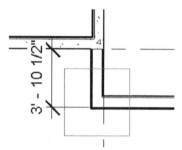

Square at Join

4. In the options bar, click the button next to Miter. You will see a diagonal line appear at the wall join.

    Click to accept the join.

    Repeat the process at the other two corners of the tower.

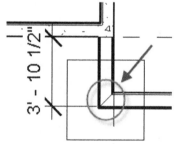

Diagonal Line at Join

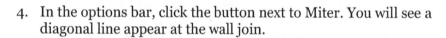

Miter Button

5. Open the South Elevation view.

6. Select the Split tool in the Modify tab, Modify panel.

Split Tool

7. Mouse over the edge of the south tower wall
    and split the wall at the 2ND FLOOR level.

    This will be 13'-0" up from the first floor level.

    When using the Split tool, make sure that the
    outline of the wall highlights in blue.

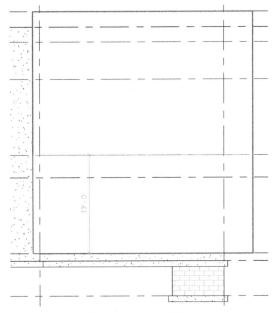

First Split at Second Floor Level

8. Split the wall again 12'-0" up from the 2ND FLOOR level.

    A temporary dimension should appear.

9. Verify the split by picking the upper portion of
    the wall.

    Only the upper portion should highlight.

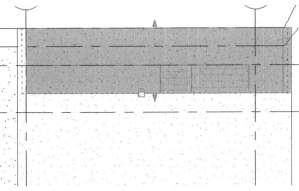

Upper Portion of Split Highlighted

10. Open the East Elevation view and repeat the process for the east tower wall.

11. Open the West Elevation view and split the short tower wall.

    You might need to go back and change the upper portions of the walls to change the wall joins
    back to a miter join.

    If you are having trouble selecting the tower wall, press the Tab key until the entire outline of
    the wall highlights blue.

12. Repeat the process for the short north tower wall.

13. If you are having trouble picking the north wall, temporarily turn off the other tower walls in the
    elevation view.

    Mouse over the edge of the walls and press the tab key to cycle through the choices.

14. Open the 3D view.

15. In the 3D view you may see lines at the split locations.

    There are two options to hide the lines at the split locations.

    The first method is to join the geometry. This is a graphical join and will not affect the structure of the walls. This is the faster of the two methods.

    The second method is to change the linestyle of the split lines to invisible lines.

    Both of these methods will be covered in the next few steps.

16. For the first method click on the Join tool in the Modify tab, Geometry panel.

Join Geometry Tool

17. Click one of the split sections and then the next. You will see the lines between the sections disappear.

18. For the second method, use the Linework tool in the Modify tab, View panel to hide the lines

    Set the lines to the <Invisible Lines> style.

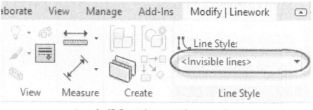

Invisible Lines Linestyle

    You will need to select both lines of the split, one for the top portion of the wall and the other for the bottom portion.

    If you wish to bring the lines back, set the linestyle to Thin Lines and mouse over the location until the line highlights.

19. Click the line to change the linestyle back to Thin Lines.

    Note: Both of these methods are only for the particular view that has been changed. You will need to repeat the process for other views.

Changing the Walls to the New Type

1. Open the 2nd Floor view and click on one of the tower walls.

   This will select the middle section of the tower wall.

2. Click the Edit Type button in the Properties dialog box.

3. Duplicate the Exterior – Stucco on Mtl. Stud wall type.

   Name the new wall type: Exterior Stucco on Mtl. Stud w/Gyp Bd Interior

4. In the Edit Assembly dialog box, change layer 7 to match the settings below. The wall will still be the same thickness.

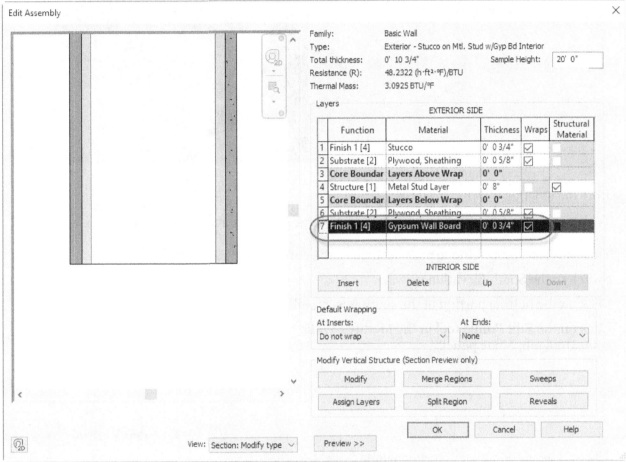

New Exterior Wall Type

5. Change the other three walls to the new wall type.

Adding the Two Additional Tower Walls

1. Switch to the T.O WALL view.

2. If you do not have the view, go to the Plan Views tool in the View menu, Create panel.

3. Select the Floor Plan option and choose the T.O. WALL level.

4. Next you will add two walls to enclose the tower portion.

   Use the Exterior – Stucco on Mtl. Stud wall type.

5. When placing the walls, align the walls with the face of the other tower walls.

6. Set the Base Constraint to T.O. ROOF and the Top Constraint to T.O. TOWER.

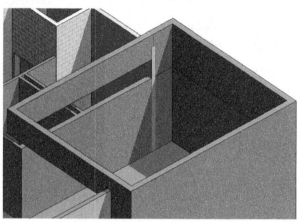

Two Walls Added

Creating the Openings in the Tower Walls

1. To complete the tower walls, you will add two large openings at the base of the walls.

   This will allow foot traffic to pass through to the entrance of the building.

2. Switch to the South Elevation view.

3. Click on the bottom portion of the south tower wall.

4. Click on the Edit Profile tool in the Modify | Walls contextual tab, Mode panel.

Edit Profile Tool

5. The outline of the wall will turn magenta.

   Only the bottom third of the wall will be picked.

Magenta Outline of Base of Tower Wall

6. Modify the outline as shown.

7. You may include dimensions to help with the size and shape.

8. Add reference planes to aid in creating the arched surface.

   Note: To aid in placing the 11'-0" dimension, add a reference plane that matches the top of the arch.

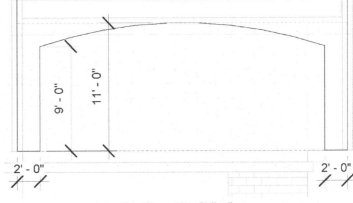

Outline Modified

9. Click the Green Check to create the opening.

10. Repeat the process for the east tower wall.

    Note: The arched portion of the opening will have a different radius due to the wall being shorter.

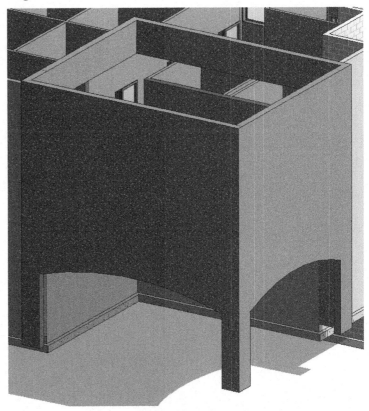

Tower Wall Openings Created

11. This is the end of Part 10. Save your file as CL1-10.

CL1-11   Creating the Roofs

1.   Open the CL1-10 file, save the file as CL1-11.

2.   Open the T.O. ROOF view.

3.   Click on the Roof tool in the Architecture tab, Build panel.

4.   Select the Insulation on Metal Deck – EPDM roof type.

5.   Click on the Edit Type button.

6.   Duplicate the type and rename it Steel Truss – Insulation on Metal Deck – EPDM.

7.   Modify the structure. Refer to the example below for specifications.

8.   Click the OK button twice to complete the process.

Edit Assembly					

Family: Basic Roof
Type: Steel Truss - Insulation on Metal Deck - EPDM
Total thickness: 1' 10 3/4" (Default)
Resistance (R):   113.1759 (h·ft²·°F)/BTU
Thermal Mass: 7.8613 BTU/°F

Layers

	Function	Material	Thickness	Wra
1	Finish 1 [4]	Roofing, EPDM Membrane	0' 0 1/4"	
2	Thermal/Air Layer	Rigid insulation	0' 5"	
3	**Core Boundary**	**Layers Above Wrap**	**0' 0"**	
4	Structure [1]	Metal Deck	0' 1 1/2"	
5	Structure [1]	Structure, Steel Bar Joist Layer	1' 4"	
6	**Core Boundary**	**Layers Below Wrap**	**0' 0"**	

Insert   Delete   Up   Down

View: Section: Modify type   Preview >>   OK   Cancel   Help

New Roof Style

9.   While still in the Place Roof tool, select the Pick Walls option in the Draw panel.

10. Check the Extend into wall (to core) checkbox.

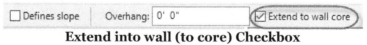

Extend into wall (to core) Checkbox

11. Set the Base Offset from Level to -1' 10 3/4". (This is equal to the thickness of the roof.)

12. Select the inside of the walls for the roof boundary.

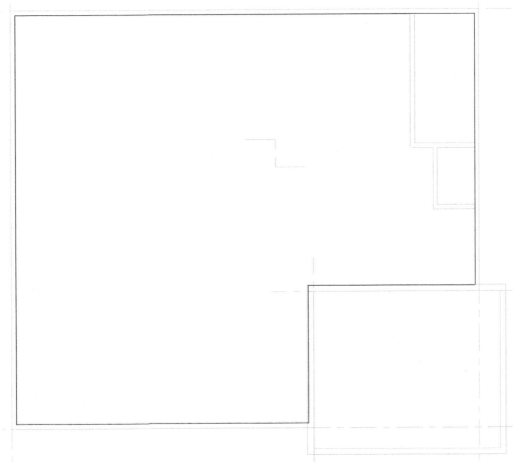

Main Roof Boundary

13. When finished with the boundary click the Green Check.

    Answer Yes to the alert box asking if you would like to join the geometry.

14. Open the 3D view.

    You will see that the stairwell and elevator
    shaft walls extend through the roof.

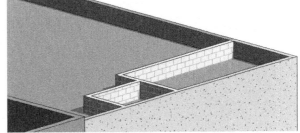

Walls Extending Through Roof

15. Select the five walls.

16. Click on the Attach Top/Base tool and then click on the roof.

    This will lower the tops of the walls so that they are below the roof.

Adding the Roof to the Tower Walls

Next you will add the roof to the Tower. The roof will be higher than the roof for the main building. You will use the same roof type.

1. Open the T.O. ROOF view.

2. If you cannot see the roof in the view, set the view range to the settings in the example.

View Range

Primary Range

Top:	Associated Level (T.O. ROC ⌄	Offset:	20' 0"
Cut plane:	Associated Level (T.O. ROC ⌄	Offset:	20' 0"
Bottom:	Level Below (2ND FLOOR) ⌄	Offset:	0' 0"

View Depth

Level:	Level Below (2ND FLOOR) ⌄	Offset:	0' 0"

Learn more about view range

<< Show   OK   Apply   Cancel

View Range to the T.O. Roof View

3. Click on the Roof tool.

   Set the base level to T.O Tower and the Base Offset From Level is set to -4'-0".

4. Select the Steel Truss - Insulation on Metal Deck – EPDM roof type.

5. When creating the roof footprint, use the Pick Walls option and click the inside face of the walls.

   Check the Extend to wall core checkbox in the options bar.

Tower Roof Boundary

6. Click the Green Check top add the roof.
    Your roof should look like this...

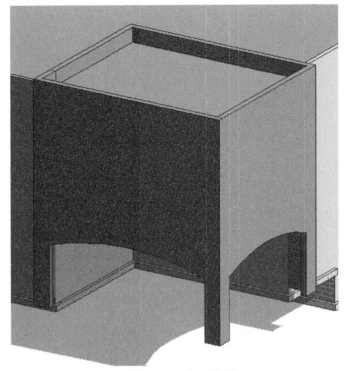

Tower Roof Added

7. This is the end of Part 11 and Tutorial 1. Save your file as CL1-11.

Tutorial 2   Adding Curtain Walls and Mullions

Part 1	Adding the First Floor Curtain Wall
Part 2	Adding the First and Second Floor Curtain Grids and Mullions
Part 3	Adding the Mullions and Curtain Wall Door (East Elevation)
Part 4	Adding the Second Floor Curtain Walls (Tower Walls)

Note: All screenshots are from the Autodesk® Revit® software.

Starting the Tutorial

This tutorial will guide you through the process of adding curtain walls and mullions to the project. Curtain walls are non-structural walls that are usually made of a lightweight material, in this case glass and metal. These walls will be used to add natural light to the south side and a portion of the east of the building.

1. Open the drawing file from Tutorial 1 named CL1-11.

2. Save the file as CL2-1.

CL2-1   Adding the First Floor Curtain Wall

1. Open the 1st Floor view.

2. To locate the ends of the curtain wall, create two reference planes 2'-0" from the centers of each wall.

   Note: Dimensions are not required.

First Floor Curtain Wall Edges

3. Go to the Architecture tab, Wall tool. Select the Curtain Wall wall type.

   Use the settings in the example for the properties.

Properties   ✕

Curtain Wall   ▾

New Walls   ✏ Edit Type

Constraints   ⌃
Base Constraint   1ST FLOOR
Base Offset   0' 6"
Base is Attached   ☐
Top Constraint   Up to level: 1ST FLOOR CLG.
Unconnected Height   9' 6"
Top Offset   0' 0"
Top is Attached   ☐

Curtain Wall Settings

4. When adding the curtain wall:

    a. Pick the center of the concrete wall.
    b. Start the wall from the reference plane on the right and drag to the plane on the left.
    c. After the second point is placed a warning box will appear. It may be ignored.
    d. After adding the wall, check that the flip arrows are on the outside.

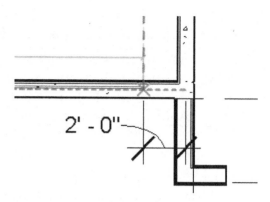

**Snapping on Reference Plane
for Start of Curtain Wall**

5. Once you have added the wall use the Cut Geometry in the Modify tab, Geometry panel to remove the overlapping area.

    Pick the Concrete Wall first and then the Curtain Wall.

Cut Geometry Tool

6. Your wall should look like this...

Curtain Wall Placed

7. Delete or hide the two reference planes.

8. This is the end of Part 1. Save your file as CL2-1.

CL2-2   Adding the First and Second Floor Curtain Grids and Mullions

In this part you will add curtain grids and mullions to the first floor curtain wall. Once this is done, you will copy all of the elements as one group to the second floor level.

1. Open the CL2-1 file, save the file as CL2-2.

2. Open the South Elevation view.

3. Click on the Curtain Grid tool in the Architecture tab, Build panel.

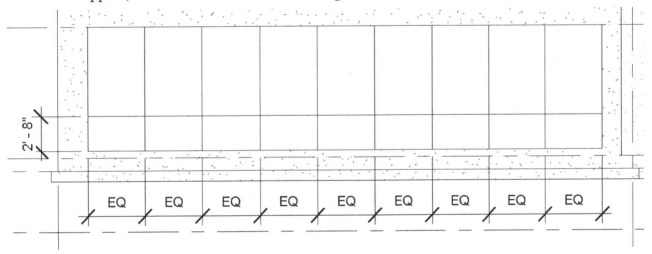

Curtain Grid Tool

4. To add grid lines:

   a. To add vertical grid lines, pick on bottom horizontal edge of the Curtain Wall.
   b. When adding the vertical lines, create eight lines and then add a chain dimension to the edges of the curtain wall and each of the vertical grid lines. To equally space the lines, press the EQ toggle.
   c. To add horizontal grid lines, pick on the right or left edge of the Curtain Wall.
   d. Use the diagram below for the measurements.

5. After the grids are placed, delete or hide the dimensions. If deleting the dimensions, a warning box will appear, click the OK button to leave the grids constrained.

Equally Spaced Grids

6. Click the Mullion tool in the Architecture tab, Build panel.

7. To place mullions on all the grids lines at once, select the
    All Grid Lines option in the Placement panel.

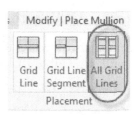

All Grid Lines Option

8. Mouse over one of the grid lines. When they all select, click the mouse.

9. The mullions appear. You will need to modify how they intersect.

    The goal is to make the top and bottom mullions continuous. The vertical mullions will also
    remain continuous.

10. Use the join toggle at the ends of each
    mullion segment.

    When the toggle is clicked the join will
    change.

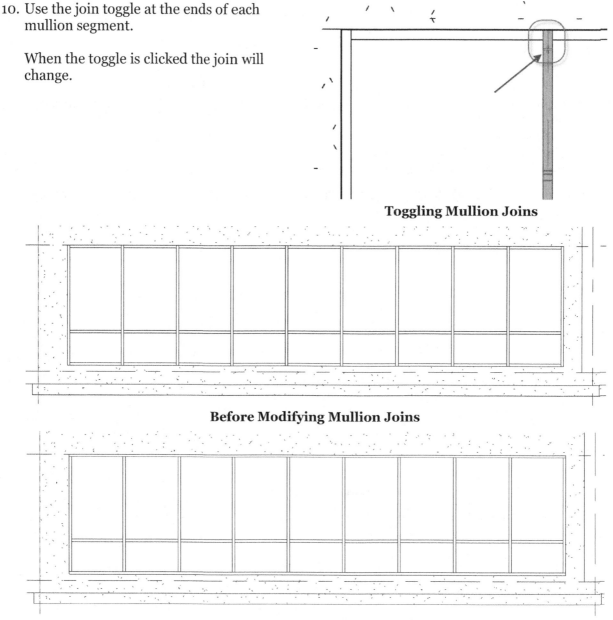

Toggling Mullion Joins

Before Modifying Mullion Joins

After Modifying Mullion Joins

Copying the First Floor Curtain Wall to the Second Floor

1. Select the edge of the curtain wall.

2. Copy the element to the clipboard.

3. Click the arrow beneath the Paste tool and select the Aligned to Selected Levels option.

Aligned to Selected Levels Option

4. In the Select Levels dialog box select the 2ND FLOOR level.

Select Levels Dialog Box

5. The curtain wall has been copied to the second floor level.

   After the curtain wall is copied a warning box will appear. Close the box.

6. Select the Cut tool in the Modify tab, Geometry panel.

7. Select the south wall and then select the curtain wall on the second floor.

8. Click to cut the curtain wall out of the south wall.

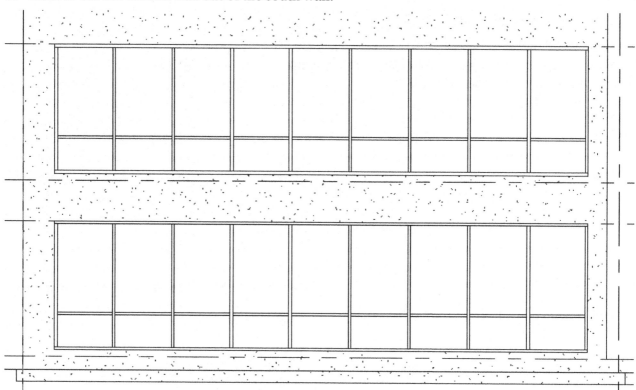

Second Floor Curtain Wall Placed

9. This is the end of Part 2. Save your file as CL2-2.

CL2-3   Adding the Mullions and Curtain Wall Door (East Elevation)

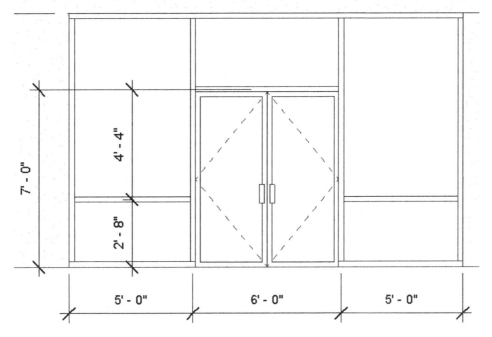

Main Entry Curtain Wall with Door

1. Open the CL2-2 file, save the file as CL2-3.

2. Open the 1st Floor view.

3. Create two horizontal reference planes 2'-0"
    in from the centers of the two walls at grid
    lines 2 and 3.

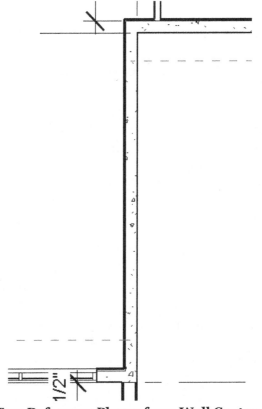

Two Reference Planes from Wall Centers

4. Add the Curtain Wall.

    The size of the wall is 10'-0" high and
    16'-0" long.

    The wall is 2'-0" from the edge and is measured
    from the wall centerline.

    Use the Cut Geometry tool as before.

Main Entry Curtain Wall Settings

5. Next, you will create an interior elevation view facing the curtain wall.

    Click on the Elevation tool in the View tab, Create panel.

6. Choose the Interior Elevation type in the type
    selector.

Interior Elevation Type

7. Place the marker to the right of the curtain wall facing left.

8. Before continuing, turn off the view name
    by selecting the Elevation Tags tool in the
    Manage tab, Settings panel, Additional
    Settings drop-down menu.

9. Name the elevation view,
    STOREFRONT ELEVATION.

Elevation Symbol Changed

10. Open the interior elevation view.

    Set the scale to 1/4" = 1'-0".

11. Locate the grids as shown. (Dimensions are not required.)

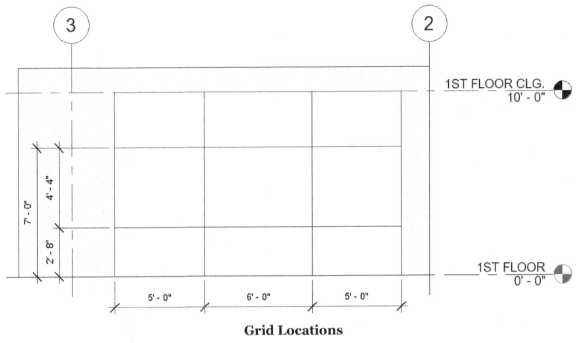

Grid Locations

12. Add the mullions and set up the joins.

    When adding the mullions use the Grid Line Segment setting in the Placement panel.

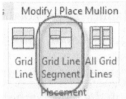

Grid Line Segment Tool

Mullions Added

13. Remove the extra grid segments.

    Click on the 7'-0" high curtain grid and then the Add/Remove Segments tool in the Curtain Grid panel.

Add/Remove Segments Tool

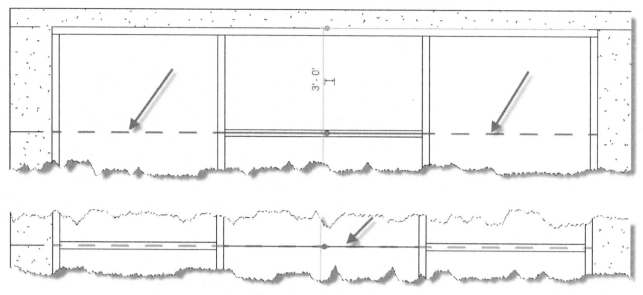

Segments to Remove

14. Next you will add the door to the curtain wall.

    You will use the Curtain Wall-Store Front-Dbl Store Front Double Door type.

    This family is preloaded within the template file.

15. To place the door, you will first need to mouse over the edge of the panel.

    Then press the tab key until the square area turns blue.

16. Click on the panel without moving the mouse.

17. In the Properties window select the Curtain Wall-Store Front-Dbl Store Front Double Door type.

Door Type Selected

Panel Selected

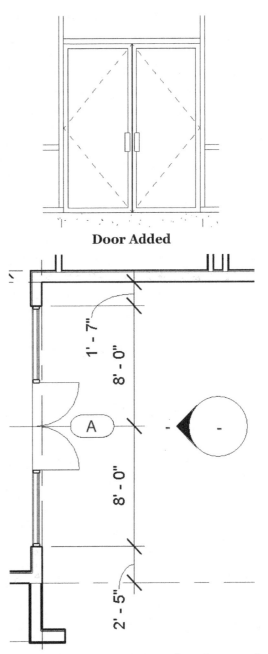

Door Added

18. Switch to the 1st Floor view, dimension the curtain wall and tag the door.

    Hide or delete the two reference planes.

    Note: You will need to adjust the dimensions slightly.

Curtain Wall Dimensioned and Tagged

19. This is the end of Part 3. Save your file as CL2-3.

CL2-4   Adding the Second Floor Curtain Walls (Tower Walls)

1.   Open the CL2-3 file, save the file as CL2-4.

2.   Open the 2nd Floor view.

3.   Add four reference planes located inward 2'-0" from the inside edges of the tower walls. These will be used to locate the ends of the two curtain walls.

4.   Set the curtain wall to the settings as shown.

Properties		✕
Curtain Wall		▾
Walls (1)		⌄ ⊞ Edit Type
Constraints		⊼ ⌃
Base Constraint	2ND FLOOR	
Base Offset	0' 6"	
Base is Attached	☐	
Top Constraint	Up to level: 2ND FLOOR CLG.	
Unconnected Height	9' 6"	
Top Offset	0' 0"	
Top is Attached	☐	
Room Bounding	☑	

Tower Curtain Wall Setting

5.   Add the curtain walls as shown then use the Cut Geometry tool as before to remove the space for the curtain walls.

     After placing the walls delete the reference planes and dimensions.

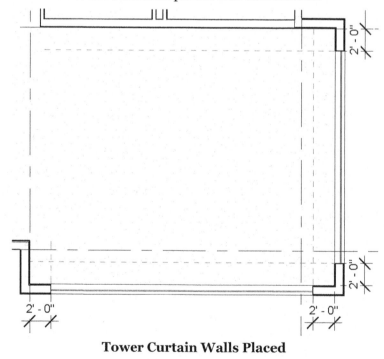

Tower Curtain Walls Placed

6. Open the South elevation view.

7. Add four grid lines for the south tower curtain wall.

   Equally space them over the length of the wall.

8. Add a horizontal grid line 2'-8" up from the bottom.

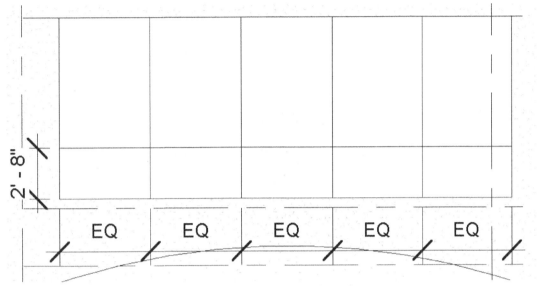

South Grid Lines Placed

9. Add the mullions as shown.

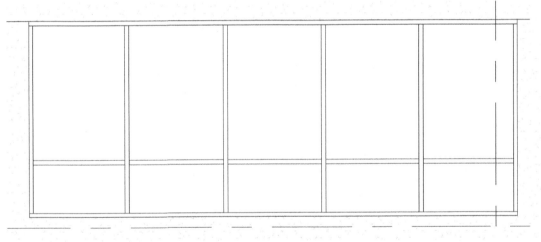

South Curtain Wall Mullions Placed

10. Repeat the process for the east curtain wall.

    Add four mullions and use 4'-6" spacing.

    Use a reference place centered on the curtain wall to center the grids.

    Delete the reference planes and dimensions when finished placing the grids.

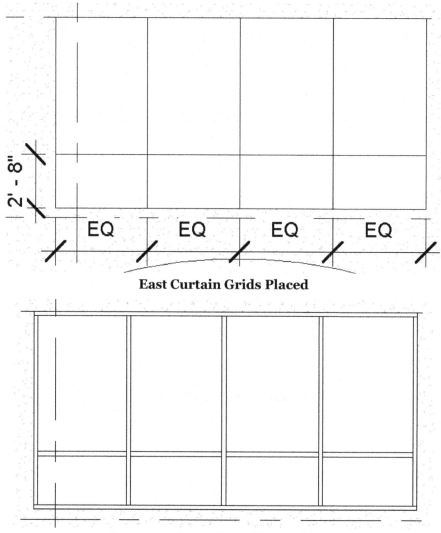

East Curtain Grids Placed

East Curtain Wall Mullions Placed

11. This is the end of Part 4 and Tutorial 2. Save your file as CL2-4.

Tutorial 3   Creating the Commercial Restrooms

Part 1	Inserting the Fixtures and Partitions
Part 2	Changing the Floor Surface Material of the Restrooms and Break Room
Part 3	Creating the Floor Plan Callout and Modifying the Restroom Sinks
Part 4	Creating the Interior Elevation Views of the Restrooms

Note: All screenshots are from the Autodesk® Revit® software.

Starting the Tutorial

1. Open the drawing file from Tutorial 2 named CL2-4.

2. Save the file as CL3-1.

CL3-1   Inserting the Fixtures and Partitions

In Tutorial 1 you laid out the walls for the restrooms. Now you will add the fixtures and partitions.

1. Open the 1st Floor view.

2. Add the two walls in the Men's Restroom from the diagram on the next page,

3. Refer to the diagram below for the fixtures and partitions you will need.

    All of the files that you need are available on the Instant Revit! website.

    You should load all of the family files from the Restroom folder in the Commercial Families website.

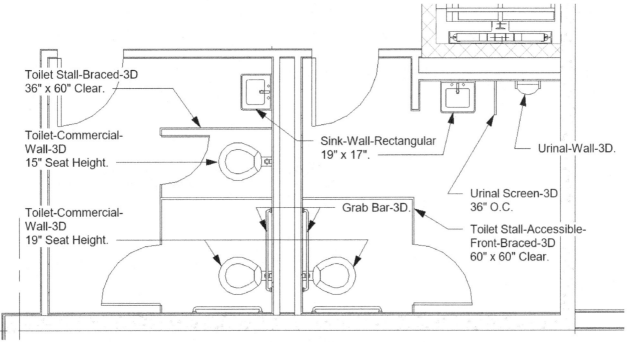

Commercial Restrooms Fixtures and Partitions

4. Refer to the next diagram for placement.

    The view scale has been changed to 1/4" = 1'-0" to show the dimensions clearly.

    When placing the fixtures update the dimension style to the nearest 1/2".

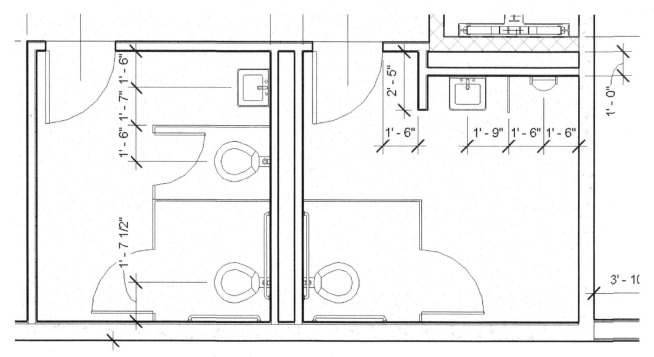

Location of Restroom Fixtures and Partitions

5. Align the north restroom wall with the edge
    of the elevator shaft wall.

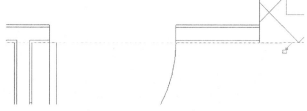

North Restroom Wall Aligned

6. Add the vertical partition wall. Use the 4 7/8 Partion Wall.

   After placing the wall, edit the type so that the Wrapping at Ends setting is set to Exterior.

Type Properties   ✕

| Family: | System Family: Basic Wall | ⌄ | Load... |

| Type: | Interior - 4 7/8" Partition (1-hr) | ⌄ | Duplicate... |

| | | | Rename... |

Type Parameters

Parameter	Value	=	^
Construction		☆	
Structure	Edit...		
Wrapping at Inserts	Do not wrap		
Wrapping at Ends	Exterior		
Width	0 4 7/8"		
Function	Interior		

Wrapping at Ends Setting

7. Add the wet wall in the Men's Restroom at the upper right corner of the room. Set the walls to a height of the respective ceiling height plus 2'-0". Use the Interior – 4 1/4 Wet Wall wall type.

8. After placing the first floor fixtures and wet wall, copy the elements to the clipboard.

9. Paste the elements to the second floor.

10. Save the dimensions from the first floor fixtures, you will need them for the callout view.

11. This is the end of Part 1. Save your file as CL3-1.

CL3-2   Changing the Floor Surface Material of the Restrooms and Break Room

The floor of the restroom is different from the rest of the building. Rather than create a new floor, you will change the surface pattern of the restroom floor.

1. Open the CL3-1 file, save the file as CL3-2.

2. Open the 1st Floor view.

3. Zoom in on the Men's and Women's restrooms.

4. If you can't see the surface pattern of the carpet, turn on the surface pattern toggle in Visibility/Graphic Overrides.

Visibility/Graphic Overrides

5. Click on the Split Face tool.

    The tool is in the Modify tab, Geometry panel.

Split Face Tool

6. Mouse over the edge of the floor boundary.

    The easiest way to select the floor boundary is to mouse of the edge of the floor at the main entry door.

Floor Type Description

    When it highlights, click to select.

    You will know that you have selected it when it gives the description of the floor slab at the bottom left side of the screen.

7. After you have clicked on the boundary the walls will turn gray and the boundary will turn light orange.

8. In the Draw panel, click on the pick lines tool.

    Click on the inside edge of the sets of walls that make up the Women's restrooms.

9. As you are clicking on the walls you will need to use the Trim/Extend tool to join the magenta lines together.

    Note: If you wish to delete the face, mouse over of the boundary and click to select then press the delete key.

10. The final version will look like this...

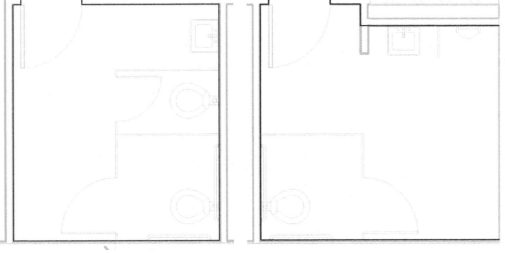

Face Boundaries(Women's and Men's Restrooms)

11. Click the green check when finished.

12. Repeat the process for the other restroom.

    Note that the lines do not extend all the way around the room edge. The lines will stop when they meet the edge of the face.

    Note: If you have difficulty at the north edge of the floor, switch to thin lines and make sure you do not have a small gap between the magenta line and the orange edge.

13. Once you have completed the two faces you will then paint the surface with a tile pattern.

    You will need to set up the material.

14. Go to the Manage tab, Setting panel and click on the Materials tool.

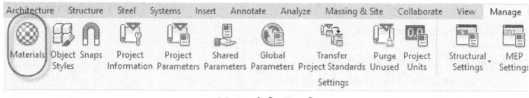

Materials Tool

15. The Material Browser dialog box will open.

    Search for the Tile material.

    Select the Tile, Porcelain, 4in material.

16. After selecting the material, right click and pick Duplicate.

    Rename the material, Tile, Porcelain, 8in.

17. Edit the material in the area to the right.

    Select the pattern in the Surface Pattern area and select 8" Tile for the pattern.
    Set the color to light gray.

Material Browser Dialog Box

18. Click on the Appearance tab at the top right.

    Click on the arrow next to Information.

    Click on the icon at the top right to duplicate the asset for the material. Name the asset 8in Squares – White. Also update the description.

    Note: By creating a new asset, when the material is changed it will not change the original material.

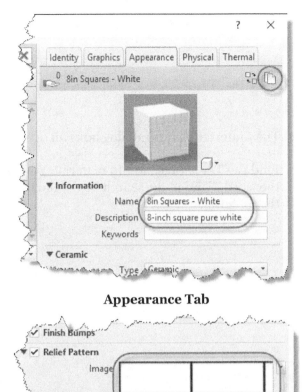

Appearance Tab

19. Click on the arrow next to Relief Pattern and then the sample image of the material pattern.

Relief Pattern

20. The Texture Editor box opens.

    Scroll down and change the Size X and Size Y settings to 1'-4".

    This will change the rendered size of the tiles to 8".

    Click Done and then OK in the Material Browser dialog box.

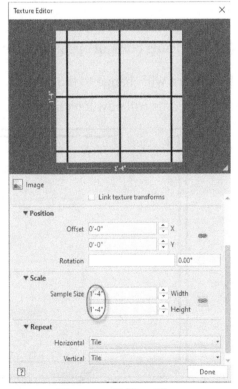

Texture Editor Box

21. Click on the Paint tool in the Modify tab, Geometry panel.

Paint Tool

22. The Material Browser dialog box will open.

Find the Tile, Porcelain 8in material. You may need to type the word "Tile" in the search box at the top and then select the material.

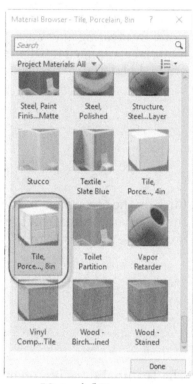

Material Browser

23. With the dialog box still open, click inside each restroom.

The pattern will change to the 8" tile pattern. Press the Done button when finished.

24. The restrooms will now look like this...

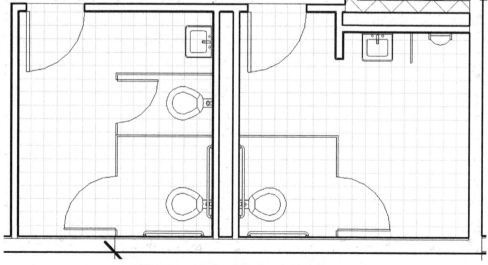

Tile Material Added to Restrooms

25. Copy the split face elements from the first floor to the second floor.

    Paint the restrooms floors on the second floor.

    Create a split face element for the second floor break room use a different material for the floor.

    Note: When creating the boundary and paintings the break room floor, the entire floor may change to the 8 inch tile material. If this happens, continue with the procedure and remove the painted surface on the main floor with the Remove Paint tool.

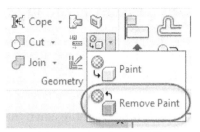

Remove Paint Tool

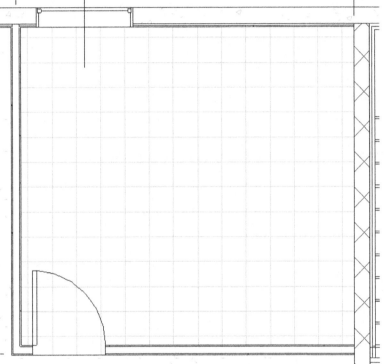

Break Room Boundary

26. This is the end of Part 2. Save your file as CL3-2.

CL3-3   Creating the Floor Plan Callout and Modifying the Restroom Sinks

Since the restrooms are detailed it would be difficult to show the dimensions for the fixture locations at 1/8"=1'-0" scale. You will create a callout that will allow you to show the restrooms as a separate view.

1. Open the CL3-2 file, save the file as CL3-3.

2. Open the 1st Floor view.

    Zoom in on the two restrooms.

3. Click on the Callout tool.

    The tool is located in the View tab, Create panel.

4. Click above and to the left of the restrooms then drag down and to the right to enclose the area.

    A callout boundary will appear as you do this.

5. Click on the edge of the boundary. Handles will appear.

    Use these to drag the bubble up to the top, left corner.

6. The callout area will look like this...

    Note: The restroom wall and fixture dimensions have been hidden.

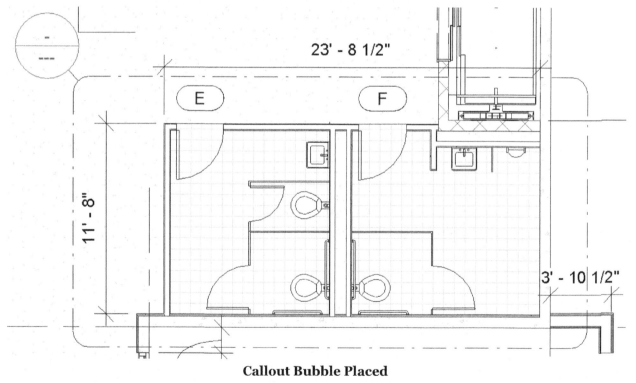

Callout Bubble Placed

7. A new Floor Plan view is created called 1ST FLOOR – Callout 1.

   Later you will drag the view onto a sheet. The bubble will fill in automatically.

8. Open the Callout of 1ST FLOOR – Callout 1 view.

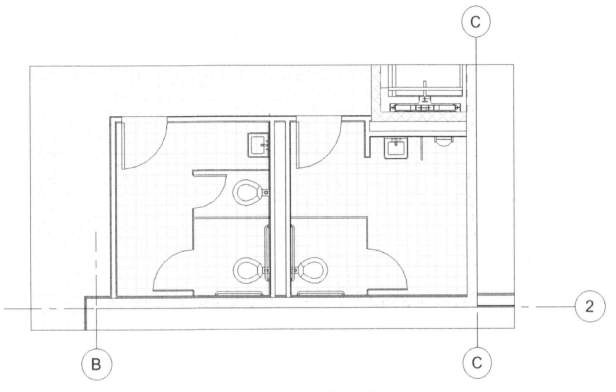

Callout of First Floor View

Note: You may notice that the material under the sinks is not masked. You will modify the sinks to mask the material.

9. Right click on one of the sinks and click on Edit Family. This will open the family file for the sink.

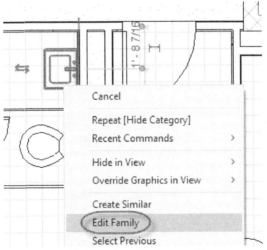

Editing the Sink Family

10. In the family file, open the Floor Line view.

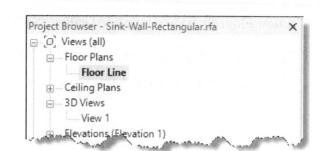

Floor Line View

11. The view opens.

    Zoom in on the sink.

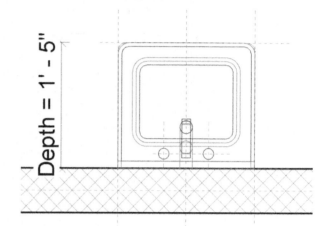

Plan View of Sink

12. Click on the Masking Region tool in the Annotate tab, Detail panel.

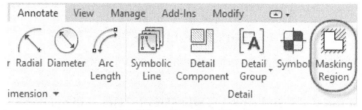

Masking Region Tool

13. The view will turn gray. Click on the Pick Lines option in the Draw panel.

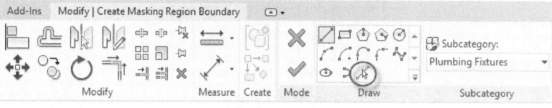

Pick Lines Option

14. Click on the lines that make up the outside edges of the sink.

    The lines will appear as thin and dark. (Not magenta.)

Masking Region Boundary Picked

15. Click the Green Check.

    If you get an error message you will need to continue with the sketch and trim the corners.

16. Click on the Load into Project tool.

    You may also click the Load into Project and Close tool.

    This will prompt you to save the updated family if you wish.

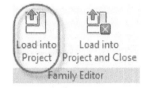

Load into Project Tool

17. When the Family Already Exists alert box opens, click on the "Overwrite the existing version" option.

> Family Already Exists   ×
>
> You are trying to load the family Sink-Wall-Rectangular, which already exists in this project. What do you want to do?
>
> → Overwrite the existing version
>
> → Overwrite the existing version and its parameter values
>
> Cancel
>
> Click here to learn more

Family Already Exists Alert Box

18. The material beneath the two sinks is now masked.

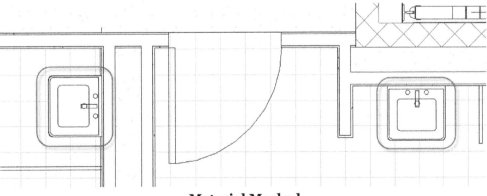

Material Masked

Dimensioning the Callout View

1. Open the 1st Floor view.

2. Zoom in on the restroom area.

3. Unhide the dimensions that you used to locate the fixtures.

4. Select the dimensions and copy them to the clipboard. Include the dimensions that locate the doors as well as the door tags.

5. If the dimensions do not appear in the callout view, they may be turned off.

    Click the Reveal Hidden Element toggle in the view control bar to turn on the dimensions.

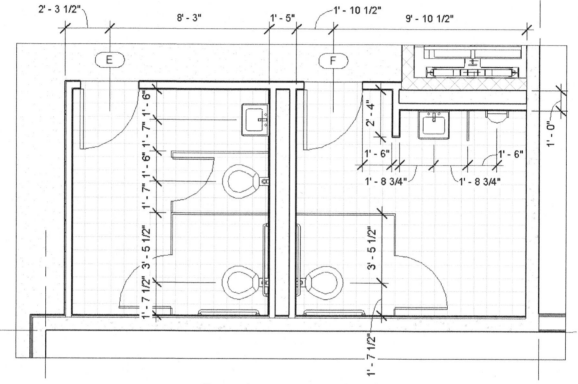

Callout View with Dimensions

6. Open the 1st Floor view and delete or hide the dimensions.

   Keep the dimensions that show the overall size of the restroom area.

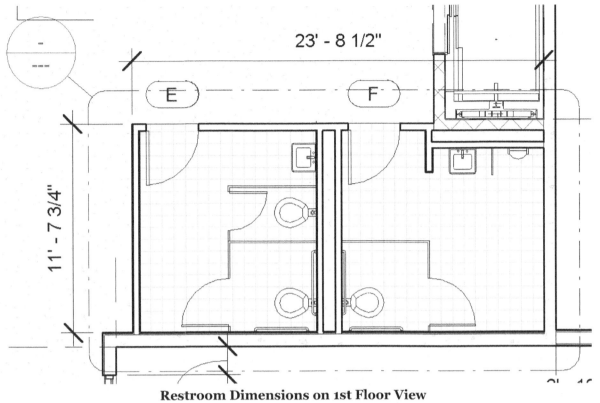

Restroom Dimensions on 1st Floor View

7. This is the end of Part 3. Save your file as CL3-3.

CL3-4   Creating the Interior Elevation Views of the Restrooms

1. Open the CL3-3 file, save the file as CL3-4.

2. Open the 1ST FLOOR – Callout 1 view.

3. Go to the View tab, Create panel, Elevation tool.

    Left-click on the tool.

    In the type selector verify the Interior Elevation type is selected.

4. Click inside the Women's Restroom and drag towards the right wall until the arrow is pointing to the right.

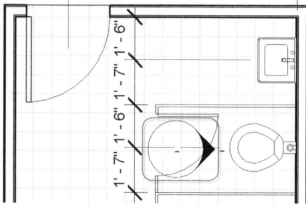

Placing the Elevation Marker

5. Click to place the marker.

    A new view is created called Elevation 2-a. Rename the view, WOMEN'S RESTROOM - EAST.

6. After placing the marker, you will need to adjust the location.

7. Click on the arrow to show the crop window.

    Adjust the crop window of the view to match the example.

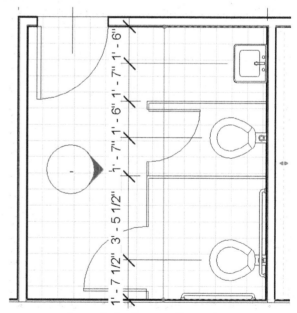

Crop Window - Plan View

8. Repeat the process for the Men's Restroom.

    This time you will create two views.

    Name the views:

    MEN'S RESTROOM – WEST
    MEN'S RESTROOM – NORTH

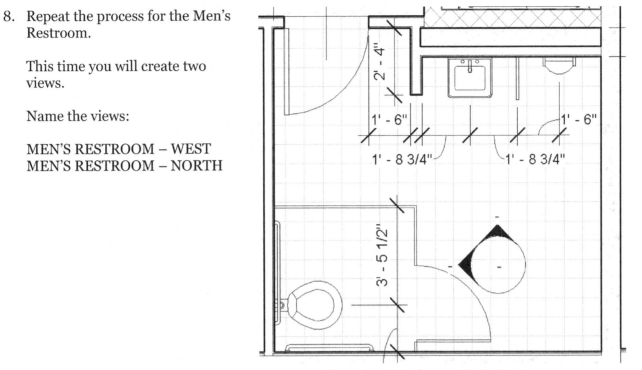

Elevation Marker – Men's Restroom

9. Open the Women's Restroom interior elevation view.

    If the Gypsum Wall Board material is not gray, go to Manage, Materials, and find the material in the Material Browser.

    Set the Surface Pattern setting as shown.

    If the restroom wall is too short, set the height to the 1ST FLOOR CLG level with a top offset of 1'-0".

10. Verify that the scale of the Interior Elevation views is set to 1/4"=1'-0".

11. At this point you will add the Mirror family to the views. You will need to create the size.

12. Add the notes and dimensions as shown.

    a. Modify the text style so that the arrow style is Arrow Filled 30 degree.
    b. Change the lineweight of the ticks to 7 and their size to 3/32".

13. You will also need to adjust the crop window to the floor and ceiling heights.

14. Adjust the height of the urinal to 1'-5" (17") height.

    Note: The urinal height measurement is an ADA (American with Disabilities Act) requirement.

15. To show the grab bar and toilet in the views, right click on the partition, select "Override Graphics in View" and set the transparency to 40

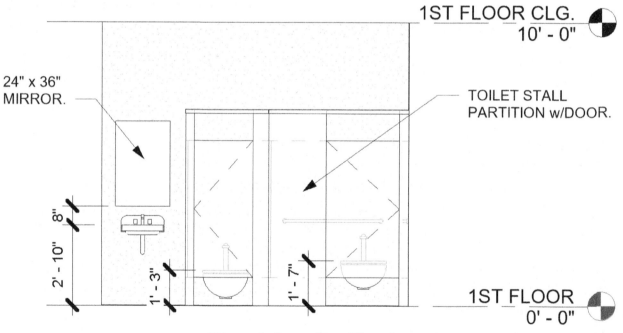

Transparency Set to 40

Women's Room East Elevation

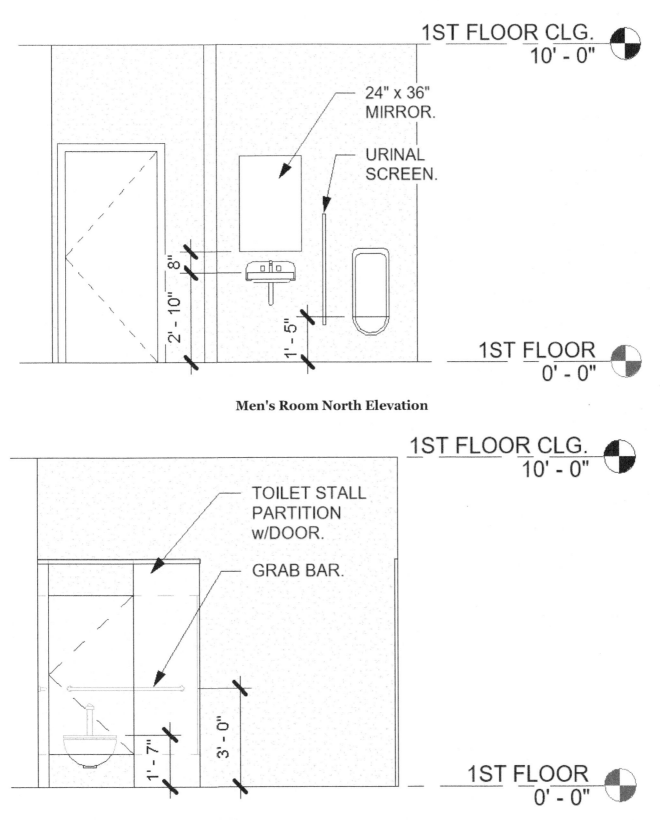

1ST FLOOR CLG.
10' - 0"

24" x 36"
MIRROR.

URINAL
SCREEN.

8"

2' - 10"

1' - 5"

1ST FLOOR
0' - 0"

Men's Room North Elevation

1ST FLOOR CLG.
10' - 0"

TOILET STALL
PARTITION
w/DOOR.

GRAB BAR.

1' - 7"

3' - 0"

1ST FLOOR
0' - 0"

Men's Room West Elevation

Changing the Wall Surface Materials of the Restrooms

Now that you have set up interior elevation views in the restrooms, you can now change the wall material to tile. The same technique that you used for the floors will be used to change the wall material.

1.   Open the 1st Floor – Callout 1 view.

2.   In both restrooms, click on the edge of the interior elevation marker and click the remaining checkboxes to create a total of four interior elevation views in each room.

     These additional views will only be turned on temporarily.

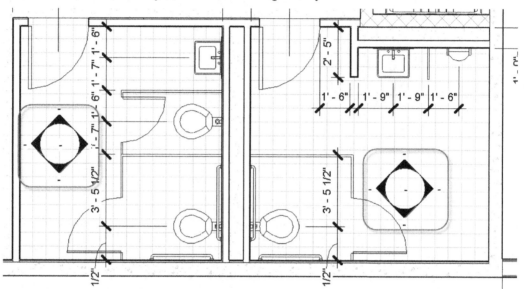

Additional Interior Elevation Views Created

3.   Double click on the north arrow in the Women's Restroom to open the view.

4.   Click on the Split Face tool and then the edge of the wall.

     The view will gray out and the wall edges will turn orange.

5.   Add a line 6'-0" up from the bottom to divide the wall into two faces.

     You can use the Pick Line option set to 6'-0" and pick the bottom edge of the wall.

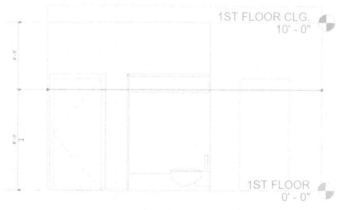

Line Added to Wall

6. Click the green check to finish.

7. Click the Paint tool in the Modify tab, Geometry panel.

   Select the "Tile, Porcelain, 4in" material and click inside the lower portion of the wall.

   Click the Done button when finished.

8. Change the surface color of the tile material to light gray.

9. Repeat the procedure for the other seven views in both restrooms.

   In the east and north elevation views of the Men's restroom you will also need to change the top portion of the concrete block wall to the Gypsum Wall Board material.

   In some views it may help to expand the crop window if the view to see the edge of the walls. For the east view of the women's and the west view of the men's restrooms, move the far clip plane so that it doesn't cross the two walls between the restrooms.

10. After the views are completed, delete the five views not needed for the project. The tile pattern will remain on all the walls.

11. If desired, repeat the process for the second floor restrooms.

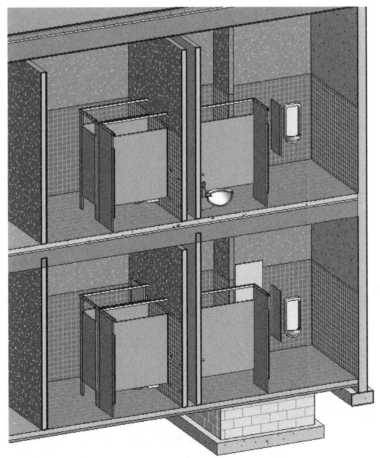

3D Section View of 1st and 2nd Floor Restrooms

12. This is the end of Part 4 and Tutorial 3. Save your file as CL3-4.

Tutorial 4 Creating the Schedules and Room Legend

Part 1	Creating the Door Schedule
Part 2	Creating the Window Schedule
Part 3	Adding the First and Second Floor Room Tags
Part 4	Creating the Room Finish Schedule
Part 5	Creating the Room Legends
Part 6	Creating the Wall Schedule
Part 7	Creating the Path of Travel Schedule

Note: All screenshots are from the Autodesk® Revit® software.

Starting the Tutorial

1. Open the drawing file from Tutorial 3 named CL3-4.

2. Save the file as CL4-1.

CL4-1 Creating the Door Schedule

1. In the Project Browser double-click on the Door
  Schedule view under the Schedules/Quantities
  category.

Door Schedule in Project Browser

2. The Door Schedule view will open.

  Some of the fields will already be filled out.

		Door							
A	B	C	D	E	F	G	H	I	J
Door Number	Type	Width	Height	Thickness	Material	Finish	Under Cut	Fire Rating	Hardware
1	C	3' - 0"	7' - 0"	0' - 2"					
2	C	3' - 0"	7' - 0"	0' - 2"					
3	B	3' - 0"	6' - 8"	0' - 2"					
4	F	3' - 0"	6' - 8"	0' - 2"					
5	E	3' - 0"	6' - 8"	0' - 2"					
6	F	3' - 0"	6' - 8"	0' - 2"					
7	E	3' - 0"	6' - 8"	0' - 2"					
8	B	3' - 0"	6' - 8"	0' - 2"					
9	B	3' - 0"	6' - 8"	0' - 2"					
10	B	3' - 0"	6' - 8"	0' - 2"					

Default Door Schedule

3. Instead of modifying this Door Schedule, you will delete the existing schedule and create a new
  one.

  Right click on the Door Schedule view and select Delete.

4. Click on the Schedules/Quantities tool in the View tab, Create panel.

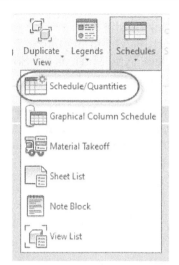

Schedule/Quantities Tool

5. In the New Schedule dialog box select Doors in the Category window.

New Schedule Dialog Box

6. In the New Schedule dialog box add these fields:

   Type Mark
   Count
   Family and Type
   Width
   Height
   Thickness
   Fire Rating

Schedule Properties Dialog Box

7. Click on the Sorting/Grouping tab and select Type Mark as the Sort by: setting.

   Uncheck the "Itemize every instance" checkbox at the bottom left side of the dialog box.

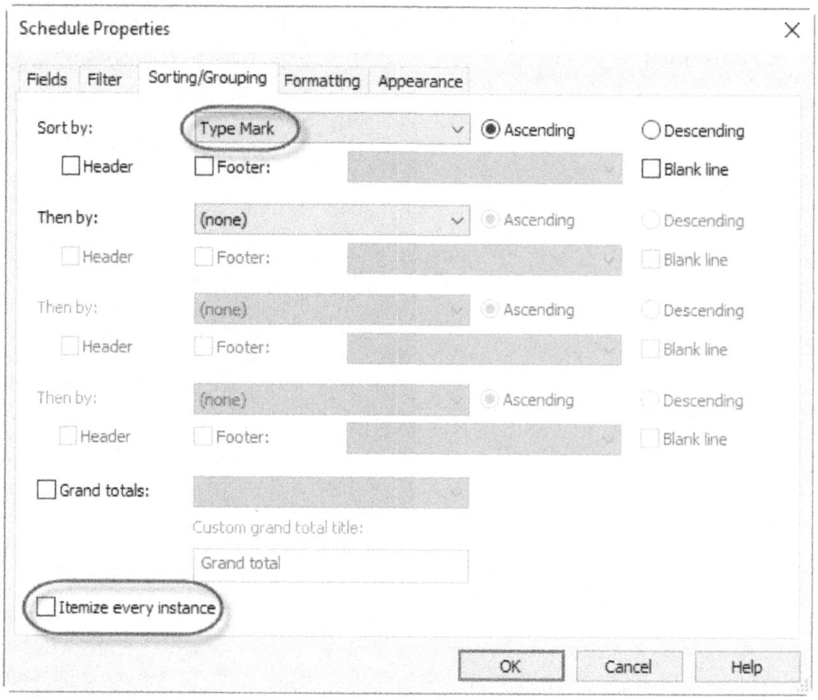

Sort by: Type Mark

8. Click on the Formatting tab and set the Type Mark, Width, Count, Height, Thickness, and Fire Rating fields to Center alignment.

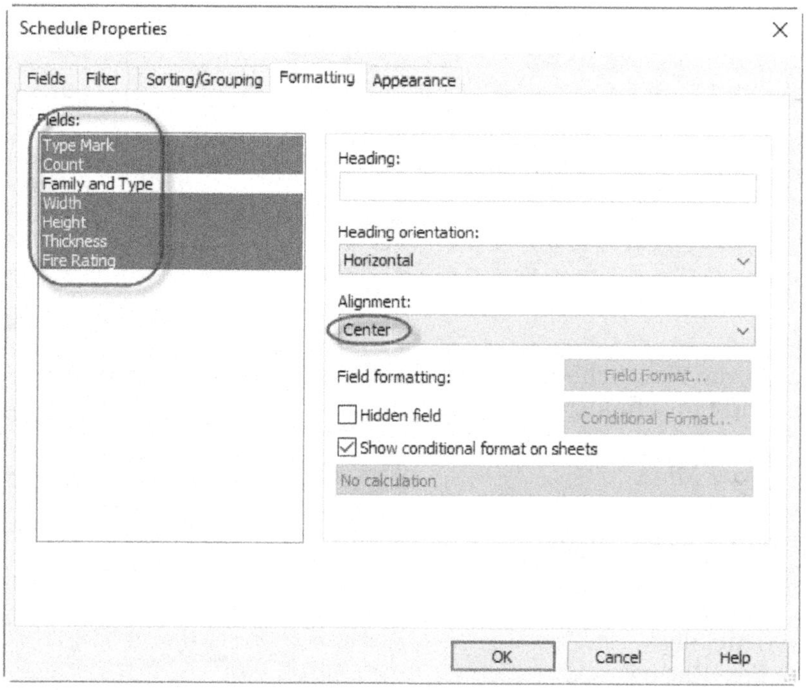

Center Alignment

9. Click on the Appearance tab and uncheck the Blank row before data checkbox.

    a. Check the Outline: checkbox and set the lines to Wide Lines.
    b. Check the Stripe Rows checkbox. This will make every other row light gray.
    c. Click OK to close the   dialog box.

Appearance Settings

10. Click on the Edit... button next to Fields in the Properties box.

11. Create a new field called Name on Schedule - DS. (The DS is for Door Schedule).

    The type of parameter is Text.

    This will replace the current Family and Type column.

    Move the field so it's after the Thickness field.

    Click OK to close the dialog box.

Parameter Properties for Type Field

12. Select the header text row and click on the Font tool in the appearance tab.

    To select the text, click and hold on the Type Mark text and drag across to the Fire Rating text,

    Set the Header Text to 9/64" and check the Bold checkbox.

    Set the Door Schedule text to 1/4" and Bold.

Font Tool

Edit Font Dialog Box

13. Click in the thickness cell for Door A.

    Click on the Format Unit tool in the Parameters panel.

    Set the parameters settings as shown.

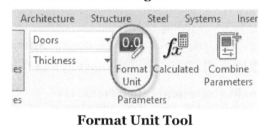

Format Unit Tool

Format Units Settings

14. Change the thickness of the Curtain Wall-Store Front-Dbl: Store Front Double Door door to 1/4".

    As you fill out the field you will see an alert box indicating that the entry will be applied to all elements of the same type.

    All the other fields are based on the door properties and will be correct.

Revit	×
This change will be applied to all elements of type Curtain Wall-Store Front-Dbl: Store Front Double Door.	
	OK Cancel

Alert Box

15. Stretch the Family and Type field so that the entire field is visible.

16. Rename the Name on Schedule – DS field, TYPE.

    Refer to the example at the end of the for the column entries.

17. Fill in the blank boxes for the Fire Rating column.

    The 1 HR field for Door D will already have a choice available.

18. Hide the Family and Type column.

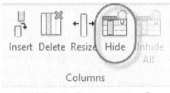

Hide Columns Tool

19. Change the text in the header boxes to all caps and match the words in the example.

20. When finished, the Door Schedule will look like this...

<DOOR SCHEDULE>						
A	B	C	D	E	F	G
MARK	QTY.	TYPE	WIDTH	HEIGHT	THICK.	FIRE RATING
A	1	STOREFRONT DBL DOOR	5' - 9 1/2"	6' - 10 3/4"	1/4"	NONE
B	12	FLUSH	3' - 0"	6' - 8"	2"	20 MIN.
C	3	FLUSH	3' - 0"	7' - 0"	2"	20 MIN.
D	2	SINGLE PANEL	2' - 10"	6' - 8"	2"	1 HR
E	2	FLUSH w/MEN'S SIGNAGE	3' - 0"	6' - 8"	2"	20 MIN.
F	2	FLUSH w/WOMEN'S SIGNAGE	3' - 0"	6' - 8"	2"	20 MIN.

Door Schedule View

21. This is the end of Part 1. Save your file as CL4-1.

CL4-2   Creating the Window Schedule

1. Open the CL4-1 file, save the file as CL4-2.

2. Delete the existing Window Schedule.

3. Create the new schedule.

    In the New Schedule dialog box add the following fields:

    Type Mark
    Count
    Family and Type
    Width
    Height

    Create a new field called, Name on Schedule – WS. The parameter type is Text.

4. Sort by Type Mark.

5. Uncheck the Itemize every instance checkbox.

6. Align all the fields by Center.

7. Set the Outline to Wide Lines and uncheck the "Blank row before data" checkbox.

8. Close the dialog box and modify the title and header text.

9. Set the text sizes to the same setting as the Door Schedule.

10. Fill in the Name on Schedule – WS column as shown.

11. Hide the Family and Type column.

12. Change the header text as shown.

13. The Window Schedule should now look like this...

\<WINDOW SCHEDULE\>				
A	B	C	D	E
MARK	QTY.	TYPE	WIDTH	HEIGHT
1	4	FIXED	3' - 0"	4' - 0"
2	2	FIXED	3' - 0"	6' - 0"
3	8	FIXED	4' - 0"	6' - 0"
4	6	FIXED	4' - 0"	3' - 0"
5	10	FIXED	1' - 4"	6' - 0"

Window Schedule View

14. This is the end of Part 2. Save your file as CL4-2.

CL4-3   Adding the First and Second Floor Room Tags

Adding the First Floor Room Tags

In this tutorial, you will create rooms and room tags. Room tags are necessary to label the rooms of a structure. A room tag shows the name of the room, room number, and the square footage. In a later tutorial you will create a Room Finish Schedule which will reference these rooms and tags.

1. Open the CL4-2 file, save the file as CL4-3.

2. Open the 1st Floor plan view.

    Before you can add the tags you will need to create the rooms.

    Note: The dimensions, grids, tags, callout bubbles, and cutting plane lines have been turned off for clarity in this tutorial part. You will leave these elements turned on.

3. Click on the Room tool in the Architecture tab, Room & Area panel.

    If you select the Tag on Placement toggle, the tags will be placed at the same time.

Room Tool

4. You may also choose the Place Rooms Automatically tool to place all the rooms at the same time.

    Or, you can also click in the rooms individually to place the tags one at a time.

    Use the Room Tag With Area tag before adding the rooms.

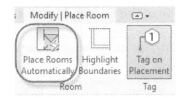

Place Rooms Automatically Tool

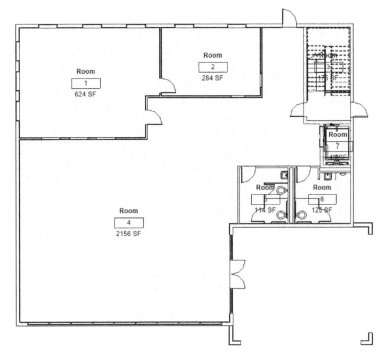

First Floor Room Tags Placed

5. If you used the automatic option, you will need to remove the small room tag and room for the small areas between the restrooms and next to the Men's Restroom.

   Note: You will see a Warning box when the tags and the rooms are removed.

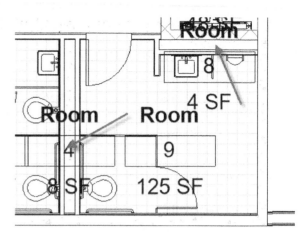

Rooms to be Removed

6. After adding the tags for the restrooms, elevator shaft, and stairwell you will need to select the leader box in the options bar.

   Select the tag and check the Leader checkbox in the Options bar.

   Also, click on the Edit Type button below the Type Selector then change the Leader Arrowhead to Filled Dot 1/16".

   Grab the room label by the Move Icon when moving the tags.

Move Icon

7. After the tags have been added, edit the room labels and room numbers as shown in the example below.

8. Refer the diagram for reference.

   The dimensions and schedule symbols have been hidden for clarity.

   Note: Your square footages may be slightly different.

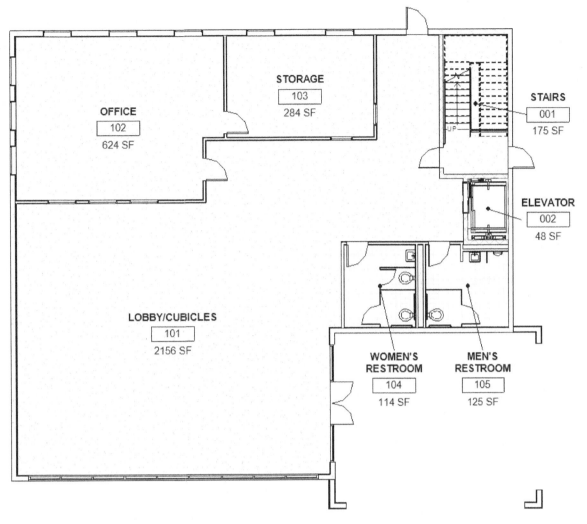

First Floor Room Tags

<u>Adding the Second Floor Room Tags</u>

1.   Open the 2nd Floor view.

2.   Before placing the rooms, you will need to place room separation lines to divide the cubicle area and the hallways.

     Click on the Room Separator tool in the Architecture tab, Room and Area panel. The room separation lines will be placed at the south hallway entrances.

Room Separator Tool

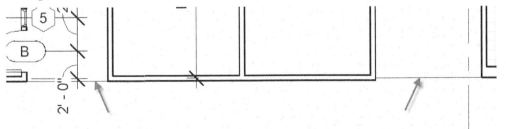

Room Separator Lines

3. Before placing the tags for the Stairwell and Elevator areas, you will need to modify the rooms on the first floor.

    Open the 1st Floor view.

4. Select the room area for the Stairwell.

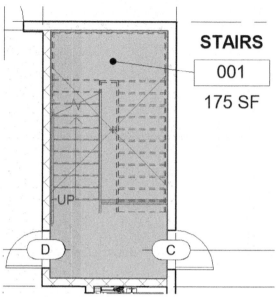

Room Area Selected

5. In the Properties dialog box, set the upper limit of the room to 2ND FLOOR.

    Repeat these settings for the Elevator room.

Upper Limit Set to 2nd Floor

6. Open the 2nd Floor view.

7. Tag the Stairs and Elevator rooms.

    You will not create new rooms for these spaces on the second floor.

    They will have the same name and number as the first floor rooms.

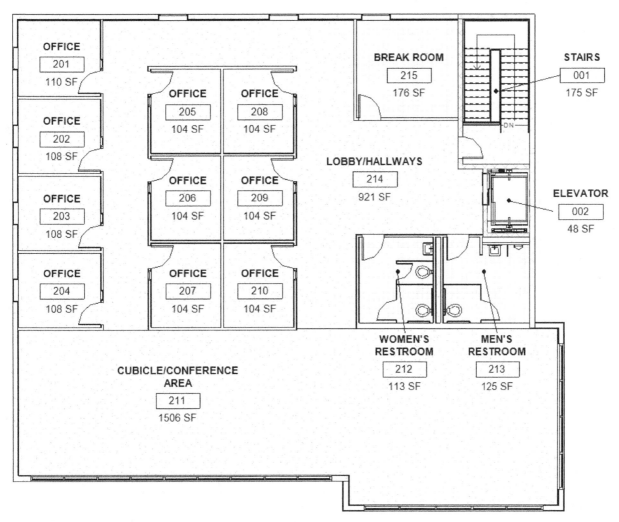

Second Floor Room Tags

8. Hide the room separator lines between the hallways and the cubicle area.

9. Create the remaining rooms and tag them as shown in the example.

10. This is the end of Part 3. Save your file as CL4-3.

CL4-4   Creating the Room Finish Schedule

1. Open the CL4-3 file, save the file as CL4-4.

2. Click on the Room Schedule in the Project Browser. You will use the existing schedule for your room finish schedule.

   In the Schedule Properties dialog box, add the Area field and remove the Comments field.

3. Delete the Ceiling Height field and use the Add Parameter tool to add it in again. Use Text as the type of parameter. The name of the new field is "Ceiling Height – RS".

4. Click the OK button to see the schedule.

   Set up the schedule the same way as the Door and Window Schedules.

5. If you cannot see the rooms, you might need to change the Phase from Project completion to New Construction.

   This is done in the Properties dialog box.

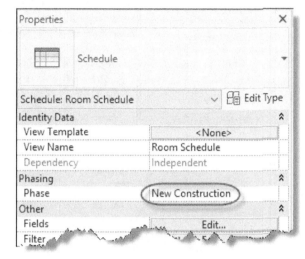

Phasing Set to New Construction

6. Open the Schedule Properties dialog box.

   Click on the Sorting/Grouping tab.

7. Set the Sort by: setting to Number.

8. Check the Grand totals: checkbox at the bottom of the Sorting/Grouping tab.

   Select the Title and totals pull-down.

   Change the Custom grand total title to all caps.

Sorting/Grouping Settings

9. Check the Calculate totals checkbox for the Area field in the Formatting tab.

Schedule Properties

10. If you have any rooms that show as not placed, delete them.

			`<Room Schedule>`		
A	B	C	D	E	F
Number	Name	Floor Finish	Ceiling Height	Wall Finish	Area
106	STORAGE				285 SF
102	OFFICE				633 SF
109	WOMEN'S REST.				113 SF
4	Room				Not Placed
101	LOBBY/CUBICL				2148 SF
001	STAIRS				175 SF
002	ELEVATOR				48 SF
8	Room				Not Placed
110	MEN'S RESTRO				123 SF
201	OFFICE				112 SF

Rooms to be Deleted

11. To center the header row vertically select the entire row and select the Align Vertical tool in the Appearance panel.

Align Vertical Tool

12. Group the Floor, Base, Ceiling, and Wall Finish columns together using the Group tool in the Title & Headers panel.

Group Tool

13. Some of the fields will be blank.

    You will need to fill-in the Floor Finish, Base Finish, Wall Finish, Ceiling Finish, and Ceiling Height fields. You will be adding the actual ceilings in Tutorial 5.

    This will also fill in the Properties dialog box for each room.

14. Change the font size for the title to 1/4" and the header row to 9/64".

15. The schedule will look like this when finished...

\<ROOM FINISH SCHEDULE\>

A	B	C	D	E	F	G	H
		FINISH				CEILING HEIGHT	AREA
NUMBER	ROOM NAME	FLOOR	BASE	WALL	CEILING		
001	STAIRS	CONCRETE	N/A	CONCRETE	5/8" GYP BD	10'-0"	175 SF
002	ELEVATOR	N/A	N/A	CONCRETE	N/A	N/A	48 SF
101	LOBBY/CUBICLES	CARPET	VINYL	5/8" GYP BD	2'x4' ACT	10'-0"	2156 SF
102	OFFICE	CARPET	VINYL	5/8" GYP BD	2'x2' ACT	10'-0"	624 SF
103	STORAGE	CARPET	VINYL	5/8" GYP BD	5/8" GYP BD	10'-0"	284 SF
104	WOMEN'S RESTROOM	8" TILE	4" TILE	5/8" GYP BD	5/8" GYP BD	9'-0"	113 SF
105	MEN'S RESTROOM	8" TILE	4" TILE	5/8" GYP BD	5/8" GYP BD	9'-0"	125 SF
201	OFFICE	CARPET	VINYL	5/8" GYP BD	2'x4' ACT	9'-0"	110 SF
202	OFFICE	CARPET	VINYL	5/8" GYP BD	2'x4' ACT	9'-0"	108 SF
203	OFFICE	CARPET	VINYL	5/8" GYP BD	2'x4' ACT	9'-0"	108 SF
204	OFFICE	CARPET	VINYL	5/8" GYP BD	2'x4' ACT	9'-0"	108 SF
205	OFFICE	CARPET	VINYL	5/8" GYP BD	2'x4' ACT	9'-0"	104 SF
206	OFFICE	CARPET	VINYL	5/8" GYP BD	2'x4' ACT	9'-0"	104 SF
207	OFFICE	CARPET	VINYL	5/8" GYP BD	2'x4' ACT	9'-0"	104 SF
208	OFFICE	CARPET	VINYL	5/8" GYP BD	2'x4' ACT	9'-0"	104 SF
209	OFFICE	CARPET	VINYL	5/8" GYP BD	2'x4' ACT	9'-0"	104 SF
210	OFFICE	CARPET	VINYL	5/8" GYP BD	2'x4' ACT	9'-0"	104 SF
211	CUBICLE/CONFERENCE AREA	CARPET	VINYL	5/8" GYP BD	2'x4' ACT	9'-0"	1506 SF
212	WOMEN'S RESTROOM	8" TILE	4" TILE	5/8" GYP BD	5/8" GYP BD	9'-0"	113 SF
213	MEN'S RESTROOM	8" TILE	4" TILE	5/8" GYP BD	5/8" GYP BD	9'-0"	125 SF
214	LOBBY/HALLWAYS	CARPET	VINYL	5/8" GYP BD	2'x4' ACT	10'-0"	921 SF
215	BREAK ROOM	12" TILE	VINYL	5/8" GYP BD	5/8" GYP BD	9'-0"	176 SF
GRAND TOTAL							7422 SF

Room Finish Schedule View

16. This is the end of Part 4. Save your file as CL4-4.

CL4-5   Creating the Color Room Legends

The next item in this Tutorial is to create a room legend. The room legend is used to color code the various rooms in a structure and to provide a key or legend with the drawing. This process involves creating a duplicate of the floor plan view and modifying it.

1. Open the CL4-4 file, save the file as CL4-5.

2. Open the 1st Floor Plan view.

3. Right click on the name of the view in the Project Browser.

4. Select Duplicate View and then Duplicate.

    This will create a copy of the view without dimensions or other annotation elements.

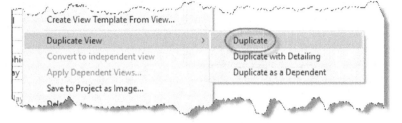

Duplicate Option

5. A new view called 1ST FLOOR Copy 1 appears in the project browser.

6. Set the scale of the view to 3/32" = 1'-0" scale.

7. Right click on the new view and rename it 1st FLOOR – Color Legend.

8. Hide the Grid Lines, Section Mark, Interior Elevation Marks, and the Exterior Elevation Marks.

9. Click on the Tag All tool in the Annotate tab, Tag panel.

10. Select the Room Tags category and the Room Tag.

11. Click the OK button to tag all the rooms.

12. Adjust the tag locations and drag the restroom, stairs, and elevator tags outside the rooms.

    Update the tag type to have filled dots at the end of the leader lines.

    You will need to check the leader checkbox for these tags.

13. At this point your drawing will look like this...

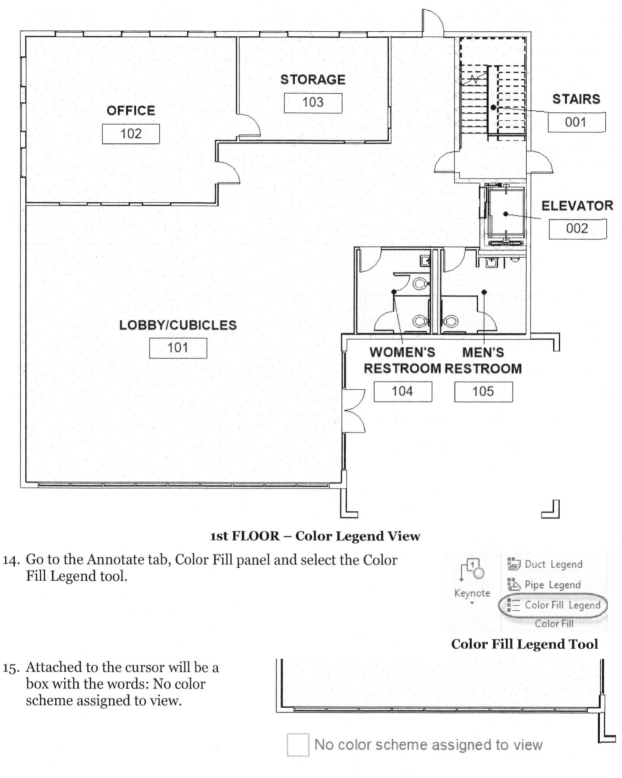

1st FLOOR – Color Legend View

14. Go to the Annotate tab, Color Fill panel and select the Color Fill Legend tool.

Color Fill Legend Tool

15. Attached to the cursor will be a box with the words: No color scheme assigned to view.

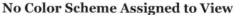

No Color Scheme Assigned to View

16. This is the legend. Place it at the bottom left corner of the view.

17. The Choose Space Type and Color Scheme dialog box opens.

    Change the Space Type: setting to Rooms and the Color Scheme: setting to Name.

Choose Space Type and Color Scheme Dialog Box

18. Press the OK button.

19. The rooms will now have colors assigned to them.

    Click on the Room Legend and then the Edit Type button to change the font for the Room Legend text.

    Set the Text font size to 1/8"

    In the Title Text parameter group check the Bold and Underline checkboxes.

Title Text Checkboxes Checked

20. After the view is placed click on the room legend and drag the handle at the bottom of the legend to create two columns.

Also narrow the column widths by dragging the arrows at the tops of the columns.

Room Legend

■ ELEVATOR		■ STAIRS	
■ LOBBY/CUBICLES		■ STORAGE	
■ MEN'S RESTROOM		■ WOMEN'S RESTROOM	
■ OFFICE			

Room Legend Handle

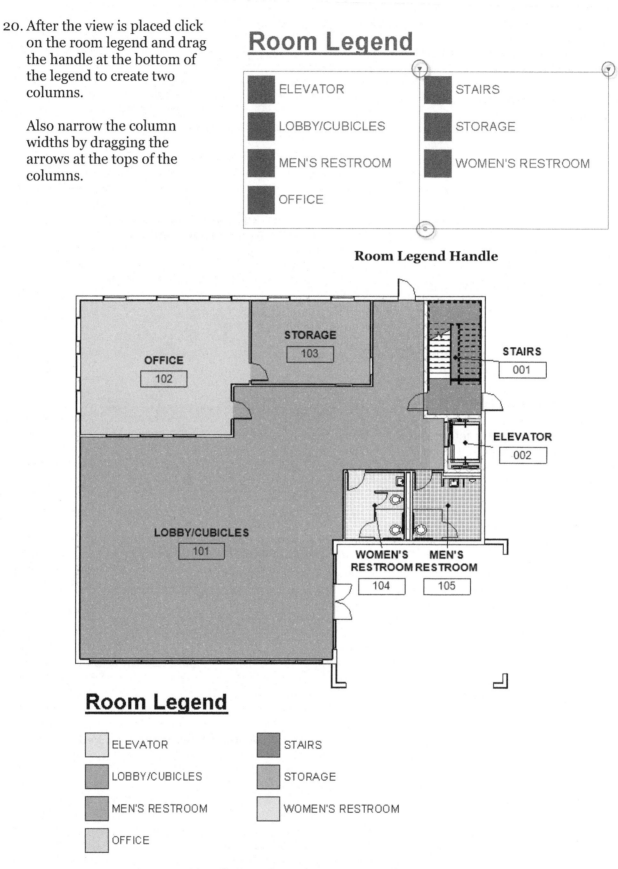

Room Legend

■ ELEVATOR		■ STAIRS	
■ LOBBY/CUBICLES		■ STORAGE	
■ MEN'S RESTROOM		■ WOMEN'S RESTROOM	
■ OFFICE			

First Floor Color Room View and Legend

21. Repeat the process for the 2nd Floor view. Use the same settings.

22. To speed up the process of placing the room tags select the tags in the original second floor view, copy then to the clipboard, then paste them to the second floor color legend view.

    To select all the tags at once, right click on one of the room tags and choose the Select all instances, Visible in View option. You will also need to change the copied tags to the type without square footage.

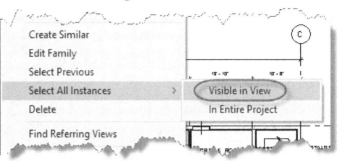

Visible in View Option

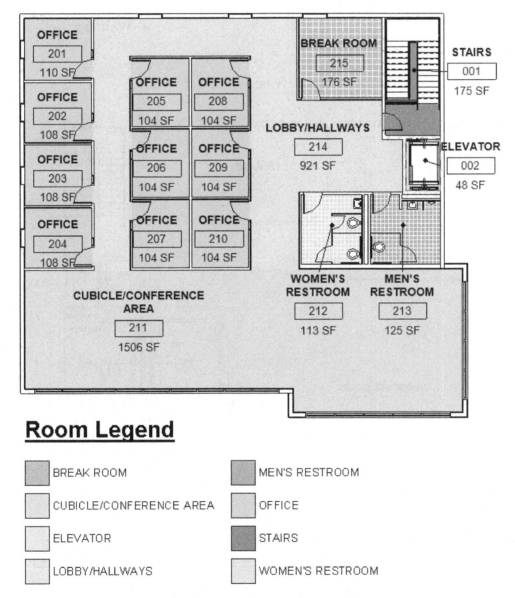

Room Legend

Second Floor Color Room View and Legend

23. This is the end of Part 5. Save your file as CL4-5.

CL4-6   Creating the Wall Schedule

The next item in this Tutorial is to create a Wall Schedule. The purpose of the wall schedule is to show the different types of walls in the project by use of tags similar to a door or window schedule.

1.   Open the CL4-5 file, save the file as CL4-6.

2.   Open the 1st Floor view.

3.   Click on the Annotate, Tag by Category tool.

4.   Click on the east exterior wall. A diamond shaped tag will appear.

     Later you will fill out the tag with a number.
     .

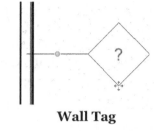

Wall Tag

5.   Tag the remaining walls as shown...

     The dimensions, door, and window tags have been hidden for clarity.

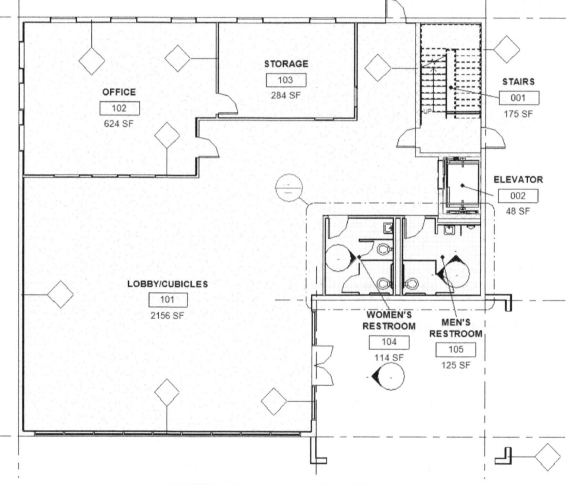

Wall Tag Locations – First Floor

6. The tags are too large.

   Select the tags and change the type to 1/4".

   Use the Filter tool to select the Wall Tags at the same time.

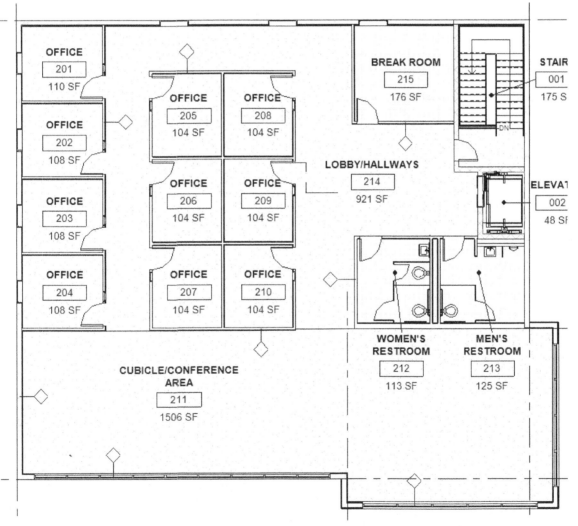

Wall Tag Changed to 1/4"

7. After changing the size, you may need to move the tags closer to the walls.

8. Open the first floor restroom view and tag the outside walls and wet walls.

9. Open the 2nd Floor Plan view and tag the walls as shown.

Wall Tag Locations – Second Floor

10. The next step is to create the Wall Schedule and fill in the tag symbols. You will use uppercase letters for the tags.

    Click on the Schedules tool in the View, Create panel. Select the Walls category.

New Wall Schedule

11. Add the fields Type Mark, Family and Type.

    Turn off Itemize every instance.

    Set the Sort by: to Family and Type

Sorting/Grouping Properties

12. Fill in the numbers in the Type Mark column in the schedule. There will be an alert box stating that the change will apply to all elements of type.

    Not all numbers will appear on the drawings. The ones that do not will be tagged later.

    There will be 11 different wall types.

<Wall Schedule>	
A	**B**
Type Mark	Family and Type
1	Basic Wall: Exterior - 9 1/2" Partition
2	Basic Wall: Exterior - Concrete
3	Basic Wall: Exterior - Concrete on Mtl. Stud
4	Basic Wall: Exterior - Stucco on Mtl. Stud
5	Basic Wall: Exterior - Stucco on Mtl. Stud w/Gyp Bd Interior
6	Basic Wall: Foundation - 1'-8" Wide
7	Basic Wall: Generic - 8" Masonry
8	Basic Wall: Interior - 4 1/4" Wet Wall
9	Basic Wall: Interior - 4 7/8" Partition (1-hr)
10	Basic Wall: Interior - 5 1/2" Partition (1-hr)
11	Curtain Wall: Curtain Wall

Numbers Filled

13. Create a new text field called Name on Schedule. This will be used for the uppercase version of the Family and Type column.

When creating the new column, choose the Type option next to the Name field.

Fill in the column.

Note: To speed up the process you may decide to export the schedule as a text file and change the text in another program such as Microsoft Word.

Parameter Properties   ✕

Parameter Type
◉ Project parameter
   (Can appear in schedules but not in tags)

◯ Shared parameter
   (Can be shared by multiple projects and families, exported to ODBC, and appear in schedules and tags)

Select...   Export...

Parameter Data
Name:
Name on Schedule   ◉ Type
Discipline: ◯ Instance
Common
Type of Parameter: Values are aligned per group type
Text
                                         Values can vary by group instance
Group parameter under:
Text

Type Option Selected

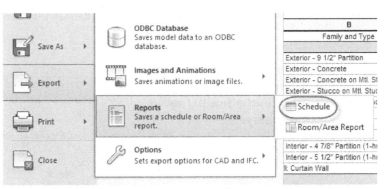

Export, Reports, Schedule Tool

14. Change the size of the fonts to match the Door, Window, and Room Finish Schedules.

Remove the Basic Wall: and Curtain Wall: notation in front of the name of the wall type.

<WALL SCHEDULE>

A	B
MARK	WALL TYPE
1	EXTERIOR - 9 1/2 PARTITION
2	EXTERIOR - CONCRETE
3	EXTERIOR - CONCRETE ON MTL. STUD
4	EXTERIOR - STUCCO ON MTL. STUD
5	EXTERIOR - STUCCO ON MTL. STUD W/GYP BD INTERIOR
6	FOUNDATION - 1'-8" WIDE
7	GENERIC - 8 MASONRY
8	INTERIOR - 4 1/4" WET WALL
9	INTERIOR - 4 7/8" PARTITION (1-HR)
10	INTERIOR - 5 1/2" PARTITION (1-HR)
11	CURTAIN WALL

Completed Wall Schedule

15. This is the end of Part 6. Save your file as CL4-6.

CL4-7   Creating the Path of Travel Schedules

The last item in this Tutorial is to create a Path of Travel Schedule. The schedule and associated graphics are used to show the maximum travel distance and times to exit the building. Path of travel to the exit is one of the building code requirements to verify that the building is safe for the occupants.

1.   Open the CL4-6 file, save the file as CL4-7.

2.   Open the 1st Floor view.

     Duplicate the view without detailing. Hide the grids, elevation markers, section marks, and interior elevation marks. Add the room labels.

     Name the view, 1ST FLOOR – Path of Travel. The scale of the view is 3/32"=1'-0".

You will create a path of travel from each room to the nearest exit and then to the discharge area. There are two exits and two exit discharges. One will be located at the front exit and the other is to the rear of the building. The size of the egress court or area is based on the number of occupants of the building and is 5 square feet per person.

3.   Click on the Path of Travel tool located in the Analyze tab, Route Analysis panel.

     You can also view the obstacles by clicking the Reveal Obstacles tool. The obstacles will show as orange in color.

Path of Travel Tool

4.   Begin with the path of travel from the first floor office to the south exit discharge.

     Repeat for the north exit discharge.

     Estimate the size of the exit discharge areas.

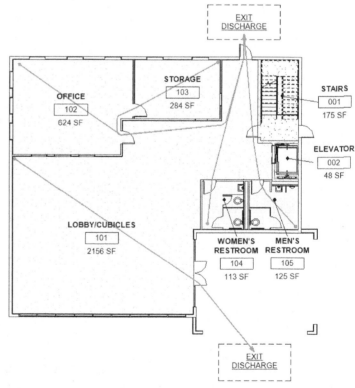

First Floor Path of Travel

5. After creating the two paths, click on the path line and
    determine the distance and time of travel.

    This is based on a speed of 3 mph.

    The To Room and From Room is also shown.

    Note: The speed cannot be changed.

Properties	×
R	

<Path of Travel Lines> (1) ∨		Edit Type
Graphics		☆
Line Style	<Path of Travel Lines>	
Detail Line	✓	
Dimensions		☆
Length	74' 5 123/256"	
Time	16.922 s	
Speed	3.000 mph	
Identity Data		☆
Mark		
Level	1ST FLOOR	
View Name	1ST FLOOR - Path of Travel	
From Room	LOBBY/CUBICLES 101	
To Room		

**Properties for Path of Travel from
Office to South Discharge Area**

6. Add path of travel lines for the other rooms.

    Only include the shortest path from the furthest point to the nearest exit discharge.

7. If you attempt to calculate
    path of travel for the
    elevator, you will receive
    this alert.

Path of Travel – No path found	×

Unable to find a route between the points.

This may be due to the following:

- The Path of Travel only calculates routes inside the crop region.
- The Path of Travel does not calculate ramps or stairs.
- The clearance between obstacles is less than 8" or 20 cm.
- The Path of Travel cannot start or end on an obstacle.
- There is an obstacle blocking the analysis zone.

→ Check Route Analysis Settings
    Specify additional categories as obstacles to ignore, or adjust the analysis zone.

→ Cancel
    Exit the dialog and continue placing points.

How is the path of travel determined?

Path of Travel – No Path Found Alert Box

8. You can change the Route Analysis
    Settings by clicking on the Check Route
    Analysis Settings button.

    This will allow you to change the
    elements that are considered obstacles.

    By default only Doors are removed from
    the list.

Route Analysis Settings Dialog Box

9. Create a new view for the second floor and add paths of travel from the rooms as shown.

Note: Since Revit will not allow a path of travel to go to another floor, end the path of travel at the stairs. This is a valid distance for fire/life safety calculations since the distance from the occupied portion of the building to the exit access is also included as a required maximum egress distance.

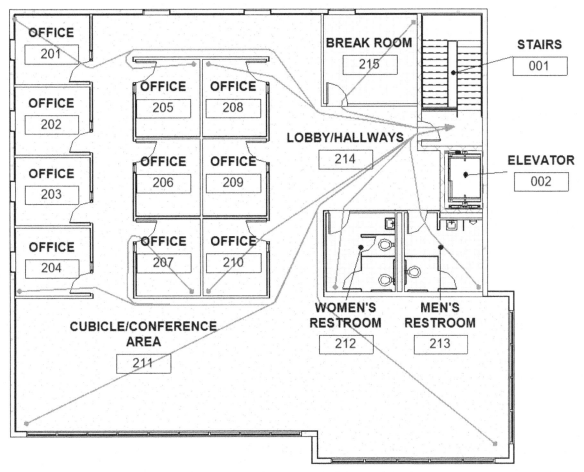

Second Floor Path of Travel

Tagging the Paths of Travel and Creating the Path of Travel Schedule

Now that you have added the paths of travel, you will now tag them. There is a tag family included with the software, but you will need to modify it.

1. Open the 1ST FLOOR – Path of Travel view.

2. Click on the Tag by Category tool and click on one of the paths of travel.

   You will receive an alert box the says that there is no tag loaded.

No Tag Loaded   ✕

There is no tag loaded for <Path of Travel Lines>. Do you want to load one now?

Yes   No

No Tag Loaded Alert Box

3. Click Yes to load the tag.

   The tag is in the Annotations folder under
   the English-Imperial folder.

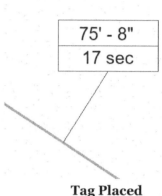

Path of Travel Family File

4. Click on the path of travel and place the tag.

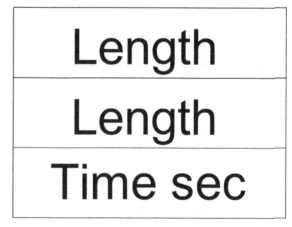

Tag Placed

5. The current tag shows the distance and the time of travel. You will modify the tag to show the
   tag number.

   Select the tag, right-click and select Edit Family.

6. Save the tag family as Path Of Travel w-Number Tag.rfa

   Note: This family is also in the Annotation folder in the
   Commercial Families (2021) folder on the website.

7. In the family file, copy the Length label and
   the top line above the two labels.

   Extend to right and left lines up to the
   corners.

Tag Modified

8. Click on the upper Length label and click the Edit…
    button next to the Label parameter in the Properties
    dialog box.

Edit… Button

9. In the Edit label dialog, change the label
    parameter to Mark.

Mark Parameter Label

10. Save the family in a folder on your
    storage drive and click the Load into
    Project and Close tool

Load into Project and Close Tool

11. Reopen the 1ST FLOOR – Path of Travel view and change the tag to the new version.

    You will add the tag number later when you create the Path of Travel Schedule.

12. Tag the remaining paths of travel on the first and second floors

13. Create a new schedule called Path of
    Travel.

    This is located under the Lines Category.

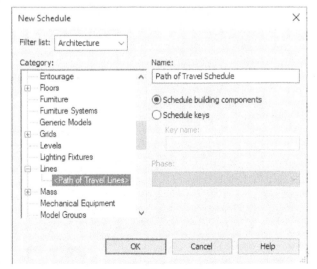

New Path of Travel Schedule

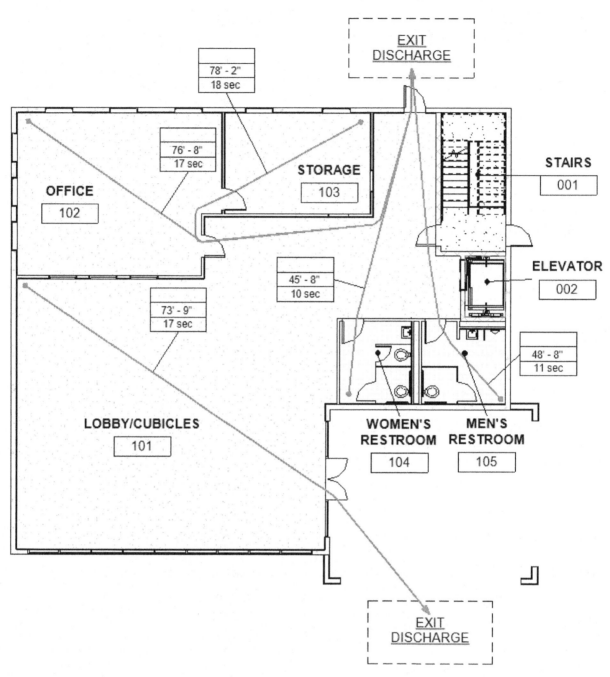

First Floor Path of Travel Tag Locations

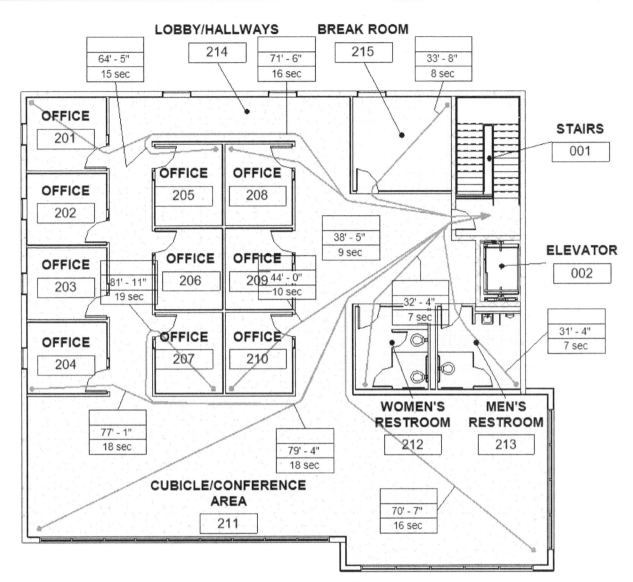

Second Floor Path of Travel Tag Locations

14. Add the fields Mark, Length, Time, and Level.

15. In the Filter tab, set the Filter by to Level then equals and use 1ST FLOOR and the filter parameter.

    The reason for this is so that only the First Floor tags will show up in the schedule. You will create a schedule for the Second Floor later.

Filter Settings

16. Sort the schedule by Mark.

17. Format the schedule the same as the other schedules.

18. Click on the letter above the column.

    Click on the Format Unit tool and change the rounding to the nearest 1".

Format Unit Tool

Format Dialog Box

19. Fill in the Mark column and name the schedule PATH OF TRAVEL SCHED. (1ST FLR.).

    Hide the Level column.

<PATH OF TRAVEL		
A	B	C
MARK	LENGTH	TIME
1	76' - 8"	17.4 s
2	78' - 2"	17.8 s
3	45' - 8"	10.4 s
4	73' - 9"	16.8 s
5	48' - 8"	11.1 s

Path of Travel Schedule (First Floor)

20. Duplicate the schedule.

21. Rename the schedule PATH OF TRAVEL SCHED. (2ND FLR.)

22. Change the filter setting to 2ND FLOOR.

This will remove the lines for the First Floor and only show the second floor.

Fill in the Mark column. The numbers will continue from the First Floor schedule.

Later you will place these schedules with their respective plan views on their sheets.

A	B	C
MARK	LENGTH	TIME
7	38' - 5"	8.7 s
8	44' - 0"	10.0 s
9	81' - 11"	18.6 s
10	64' - 5"	14.6 s
11	77' - 1"	17.5 s
12	71' - 6"	16.2 s
13	33' - 8"	7.6 s
14	31' - 4"	7.1 s
15	32' - 4"	7.4 s
16	70' - 7"	16.0 s
17	79' - 4"	18.0 s

Path of Travel Schedule (Second Floor)

23. This is the end of Part 7 and Tutorial 4. Save your file as CL4-7.

Tutorial 5   Creating the Site Elements, Reflected Ceiling Plans, and Furniture Plans

Part 1	Creating the Topography and Property Lines
Part 2	Creating the Concrete Walkway and Roof Symbols
Part 3	Creating the Reflected Ceiling Plans and Setting Up the Lighting Layout
Part 4	Creating the First and Second Floor Furniture Plans and Break Room Cabinetry
Part 5	Adding the Baseboards in the First and Second Floors

Note: All screenshots are from the Autodesk® Revit® software.

Starting the Tutorial

1. Open the drawing file from Tutorial 4 named CL4-7.

2. Save the file as CL5-1.

CL5-1   Creating the Topography and Property Lines

In this tutorial you will create topography and add property lines for the project. Unlike an actual site, this topography will be perfectly flat. Usually a slight incline/decline is included for water runoff.

1. Open the Site Plan view.

2. Set the scale of the view to 1/16" = 1'-0".

3. If the grids are on, turn them off.

4. Go to the Topo surface tool in the Massing and Site tab, Model Site panel. ...

Topo surface Tool

5. The Place Point tool is automatically selected.

   Before placing your points, set the elevation to -0'-6".

Elevation Set to -0'-6"

6. Place four points around the perimeter of the building as shown. (They do not need to be in the same location.)

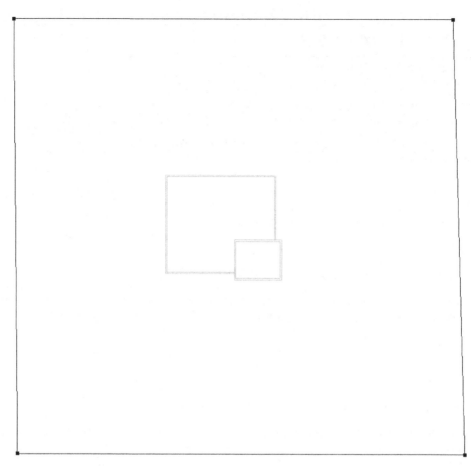

Perimeter of Topography

7. Click the green check to complete the process.

8. Click on the edge of the topography.

9. In the Properties dialog box, change the material to Asphalt, Pavement, Dark Grey.

    You will need to load the material from the Autodesk Materials folder.

Creating the Building Pad for the Elevator Shaft

You will need to create a depression in the topography for the elevator pit.

1. In the Site Plan view, set the cut plane of the view to 4'-0".

2. Click on the Building Pad tool in the Massing & Site tab, Model Site panel.

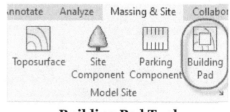

Building Pad Tool

3. Draw a shape for the pad around the inside edge of the elevator shaft walls.

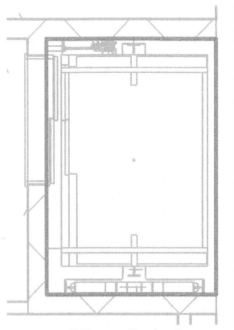

Building Pad Boundary

4. In the Height Offset From Level parameter, set the height to -5'-0".

**Height Offset From Level
Parameter Setting**

5. Edit the pad properties.

    Change the thickness to 4". Click the Green Check to place the pad.

    There is no need to set the material, the pad will intersect the floor slab that was added in Tutorial One.

6. Change the cut plane back to 200'-0".

Add the Property Lines

1. Continuing in the Site Plan view, click on the Property Line tool in the Massing & Site tab, Modify Site panel.

2. You are asked what method you will use to create the property lines. Use the "Create by entering distances and bearings" method.

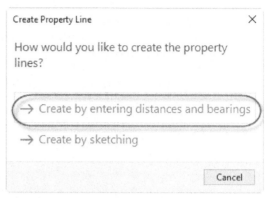

"Create by entering distances and bearings" Method

3. Use the Property Lines example to add your lines.

   You may type only the numbers. Leave spaces between the numbers for the degrees, minutes, and seconds.

   After entering the first three lines, click the Add Line to Close button for the last line.

   Press the OK button to complete the lines.

   Note: The N/S and E/W fields set the quadrant that the line will be located in.

Property Lines

Deed Data

	Distance	N/S	Bearing	E/W	Type	Radius	L/R
1	151' 8 1/4"	N	2° 05' 08"	W	Line	0' 0"	R
2	161' 6"	S	90° 00' 00"	E	Line	0' 0"	R
3	161' 4 1/8"	S	5° 30' 12"	E	Line	0' 0"	R
4	171' 8 9/32"	N	86° 59' 27"	W	Line	0' 0"	R

Add Line to Close   Insert   Up

From last to first point: Delete   Down

Closed

OK   Cancel   Help

Property Lines Dialog Box

4. The cursor will be attached to the lower left corner of the property lines.

    Snap the corner to the Base Point at the lower left corner of the site.

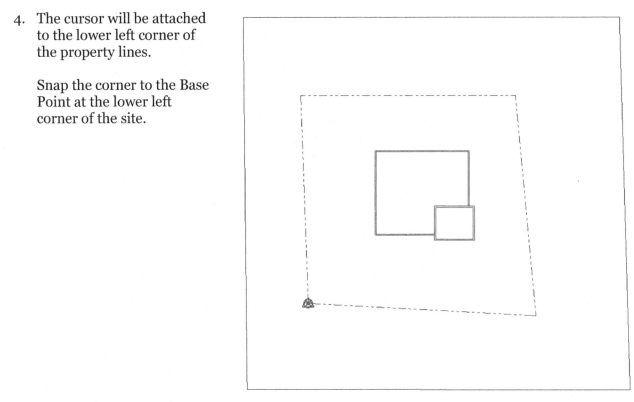

Property Lines Placed

5. Next you will tag the property lines.

    Click on the Tag by Category tool in the Annotate tab, Tag panel.

    Turn off the Leader checkbox in the options bar.

Modify | Tag |⌖. Horizontal ∨ | Tags... ☐ Leader Attached End   ⊢⊣ 1/2"

Leader Checkbox Unchecked

6. Click on the Property lines to tag the lines.

    The Bearing and Distance will be shown. Place the tags at the midpoint of the lines.

S 90° 00' 00" E
161.50'

Property Line Tag

7.   Open the Visibility/Graphic Overrides dialog box and set the Property Lineweight to 7.

Setting the Lineweight to 7

8.   This is the end of Part 1. Save your file as CL5-1.

CL5-2   Creating the Concrete Walkway and Roof Symbols

1. Open the CL5-1 file, save the file as CL5-2.

Next you will create a concrete walkway for the building. This is separate from the concrete floor of the building and will be placed around the outside edge of the structure.

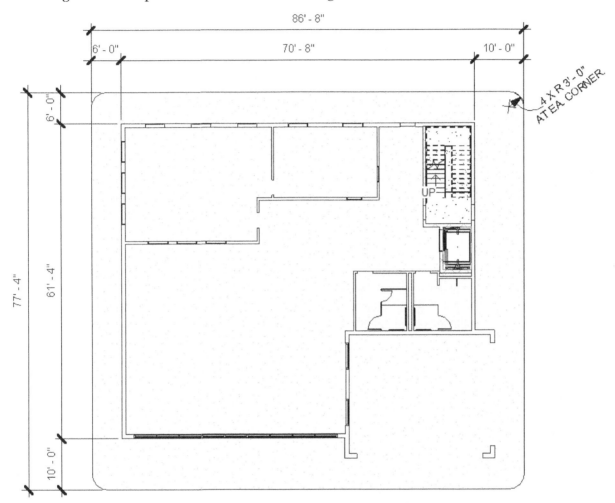

Concrete Walkway Dimensions

2. Open the Site Plan view.

3. Set the cut plane for the view to 4'-0"

4. Click on the Floor tool.

5.   Begin with the 4" Concrete Slab floor type.

  a.   Create a floor slab type called: Exterior Sidewalk - 6" Slab on 2" Sand.
  b.   Set the slab properties to 6" thick concrete with a 2" layer of sand.
  c.   Duplicate the Concrete, Cast-in-Place material and create a new concrete   material called "Site – Concrete".
  d.   Set the surface pattern to Sand.

Edit Assembly   ✕

Family: Floor
Type: Exterior Sidewalk - 6" Slab on 2" Sand
Total thickness: 0' 8" (Default)
Resistance (R): 1.6884 (h·ft²·°F)/BTU
Thermal Mass: 14.2598 BTU/°F

Layers

	Function	Material	Thickness	Wraps	Structural Material	
1	Core Boundar	Layers Above Wrap	0' 0"			
2	Structure [1]	Site - Concrete	0' 6"		☑	[
3	Core Boundar	Layers Below Wrap	0' 0"			
4	Substrate [2]	Sand	0' 2"			[

<   >

Insert   Delete   Up   Down

OK   Cancel   Help

<< Preview

Exterior Sidewalk Settings

6.   Add the floor slab using the dimensions shown in the example.

     You will also create an opening that matches the exterior shape of the building.

     You may use dimensions to help place the magenta lines in the correct locations.

7.   Set the level of the slab to 1ST FLOOR.

8.   Click the green check. The layout dimensions will turn off.

Adding the Sidewalk Control Joints, Roof Drains, and Roof Slope Lines

Next you will add lines on the sidewalk to indicate the curb around the edge of the walkway slab and the control joints on the sidewalk. Control joints are used to control the cracking within a concrete slab.

1. Using the Model Line tool, draw a square the same dimensions as the walkway slab off to the side of the building. Use the <Thin Lines> linestyle.

    Note: Model lines are lines that will show up in all views. They behave the same as other 3D elements.

2. Use the Array tool to make copies of the vertical lines.

    Make a total of 14 copies horizontally and 13 copies vertically.

3. Round the corners at a 3'-0" radius.

4. Draw a model line around the outside edge of the building. Copy the lines to the square.

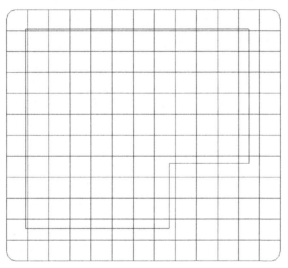

Model Lines for Edge of Building Added

5. Use the Trim/Extend Multiple Lines tool to trim out the lines within the building outline.

    It will help to split the portion of the lines that are inside the building outline.

6. Trim the lines that are inside of the curb edge.

7. Select all the lines and place them into a group. Name the group Sidewalk Control Joints.

    This will make it easier to modify these lines later if needed.

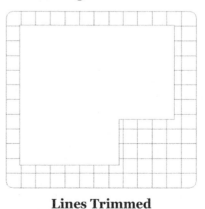

Lines Trimmed

8. Copy all the lines to the top of the sidewalk slab.

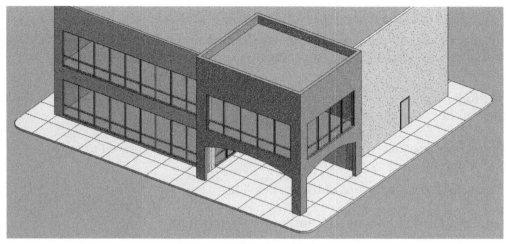

Lines Added to Slab

9. Set the cut plane of the view back to 200'-0".

10. Add the note and the dimensions for the walkway.

11. To add the symbols for the roof, use the Detail Line tool in the Annotate tab, Detail panel.

    Use Thin Lines for the line style.

12. Place the lines and circles as shown. Use 8" radius for the 10 circles.

13. Place the Roof Drain note as shown.

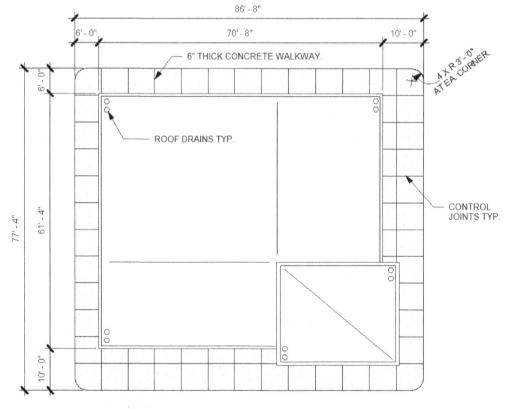

Roof Notes, Control Joints, and Dimensions

14. This is the end of Part 2. Save your file as CL5-2.

CL5-3   Creating the Reflected Ceiling Plans and Setting Up the Lighting Layout

Creating the First Floor Reflected Ceiling Plan

1. Open the CL5-2 file, save the file as CL5-3.

2. Open the 1st Floor ceiling plan view.

3. Turn off the Section Line, View Bubbles, Elevation Markers, and Reference Planes.

    Do not hide the reference planes category, only the individual lines.

    Turn on any missing Grid Bubbles.

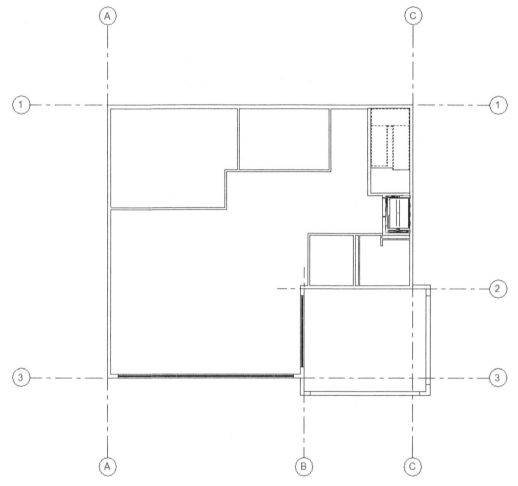

First Floor Reflected Ceiling Plan View

4. Click on the Ceiling tool located in the Architecture tab, Build panel.

Ceiling Tool

5. Select the Compound Ceiling 2' x 4' ACT Ceiling.

    Verify that the level is set to 1ST FLOOR and the Height Offset From Level to 10'-0".

Ceiling Type and Height Selected

6. Click inside the Lobby/Cubicle area. The boundary will highlight in red and the ceiling panels will appear after clicking.

    Note: If the boundary overlaps the restroom walls, set the height of the walls to the 1ST FLOOR CLG. level and the top offset to 2'-0".

Highlighted Boundary

7. Click the Component tool in the Architecture, Build panel.

    Select the Troffer Light – Lens 2'x4'(4 Lamp) -277V.

8. Place the lamps as shown on the example.

    Align the edges of the lamps with the ceiling tiles.

    You will also need to shift the ceiling grid. The lamps will move with the grid.

9. Place the six diffusers as shown.

    Use the Square Supply Diffuser - Mask 24" x 24" component.
    (This family is available in the custom family folder on the website.)

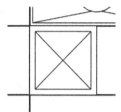

**Square Supply
Diffuser 24" x 24"**

10. Place the two returns as shown.

    Use the Square Return Register 24" x 24" - Mask component.
    (This family is available in the custom family folder on the website.)

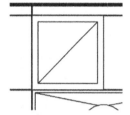

**Square Return
Register 24" x 24"**

Lobby/Cubicle Lights, Diffusers, and Registers Placed

11. Start a new ceiling. Select the Compound Ceiling 2' x 2' ACT Ceiling.

12. Click inside the Office Area.

13. Place the lights, diffusers, and return as shown.

    Use the Troffer Light – Lens 2'x2' (4 Lamp) -277V component for the lights.

    Use the same diffuser and return as before.

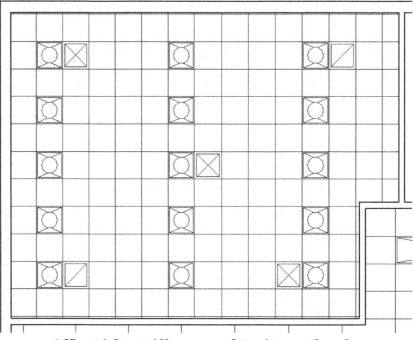

Office Lights, Diffusers, and Registers Placed

14. Start a new ceiling.

    Select the 5/8" GWB on Mtl. Stud ceiling type.

15. Click inside the Storage Area.

16. Place the lights and diffusers as shown.

    a. Use the Downlight – Recessed Can 8"
       Incandescent – 277V for the lights.
    b. Equally space the lights as shown.
    c. Use the equality constraint as shown.
    d. Use the same diffuser and return as before.
    e. Hide the dimensions after locating the lights.

    Note: Use reference planes and the align tool to
    locate the lights. Dimension to the reference planes to
    accurately locate the lights.

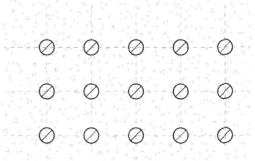

Lights Aligned to Reference Planes

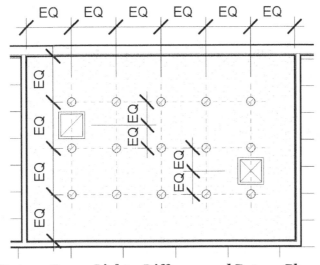

Storage Room Lights, Diffuser, and Return Placed

17. Zoom in on the Restroom area.

18. Select the Ceiling tool. Using the same ceiling type as the Storage Area, click inside the Women's Restroom Area.

    Set the height of the ceiling for the restrooms to 9'-0".

19. Place the lights and diffusers as shown.

20. Use the Downlight – Recessed Can 8" Incandescent – 277V for the lights.

21. Use the Square Supply Diffuser - Mask 12"x12" for the diffuser and the Square Return Register - Mask 12" x 12" for the return.

22. Repeat the process for the Men's Restroom.

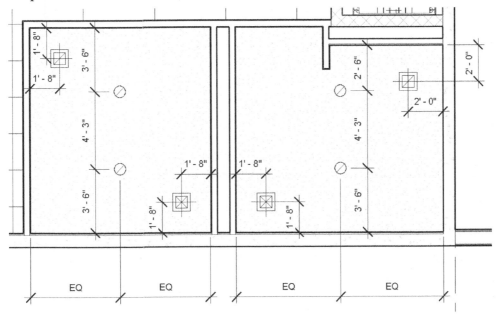

Restroom Lights, Diffusers, and Returns with Dimensions

23. When the view is completed verify the height of the cut plane is 7'-6".

    If you can still see the windows in the office area, you may need to set the head height of the windows to 7'-0".

24. Check the corners of the building.

    If the corners are not joined correctly, click on the Wall Join tool and set the join type to Miter.

25. Hide the Reference Planes and dimensions.

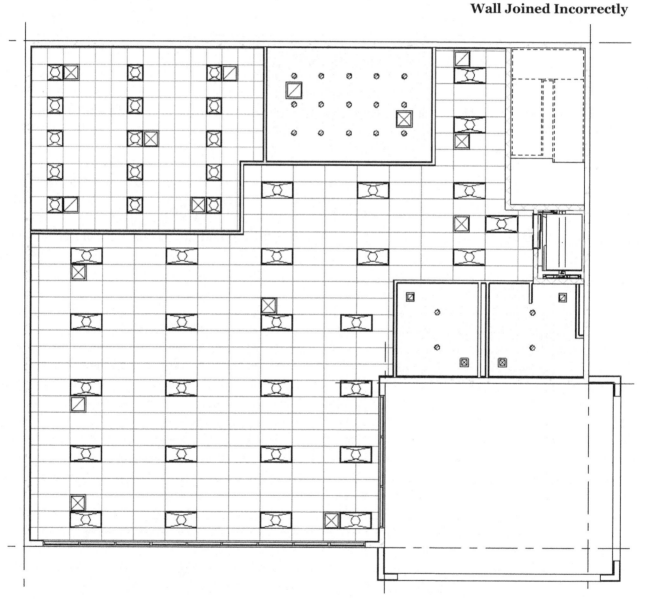

Wall Joined Incorrectly

Completed First Floor Reflected Ceiling Plan

Creating the Second Floor Reflected Ceiling Plan

1. Open the 2nd Floor Ceiling Plan view.

    Hide the elevation markers, reference planes, and property lines.

    Note: You may not have a 2nd Floor Celling view. Use the Plan Views tool in the View tab, Create panel to create the view. Pick the Reflected Ceiling Plan view type.

Plan Views Tool

New RCP   ✕

Type

Ceiling Plan   ∨   Edit Type...

Select one or more levels for which you want to create new views.

```
1ST FLOOR CLG.
2ND FLOOR
2ND FLOOR CLG.
T.O. FOOTER
T.O. ROOF
T.O. SHFT. FTR.
T.O. TOWER
T.O. WALL
```

☑ Do not duplicate existing views

OK   Cancel

2nd Floor View Selected

2. Add two walls to separate the Lobby/Hallway Area and the Cubicle/Conference Area.

    a. Add the two walls at the south end of the hallways.
    b. Use the settings as shown.
    c. These walls will separate the change in ceiling height between the hallways and cubicle area.

Properties   ✕

Basic Wall
Interior - 4 7/8" Partition (1-hr)

New Walls   ∨   Edit Type

Constraints	
Location Line	Wall Centerline
Base Constraint	2ND FLOOR
Base Offset	9' 0"
Base is Attached	
Base Extension Distance	0' 0"
Top Constraint	Up to level: 2ND FLOOR C...
Unconnected Height	2' 0"
Top Offset	1' 0"
Top is Attached	
Top Extension Dist...	.0"

Wall Settings

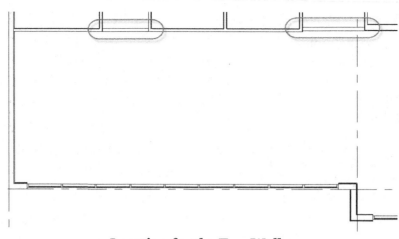

Location for the Two Walls

3. Add the ceilings for the rooms.

   a. Use the 2'x4' ceiling type for all rooms/areas except the break room, restrooms, and stairs.
   b. Use the 5/8" GWB on Mtl. Stud for these rooms.
   c. Set the ceiling height at 10'-0" for the Cubicle/Conference Area. Use 9'-0" for all other rooms and spaces.

   Note: You do not need to create the partial section at this time.

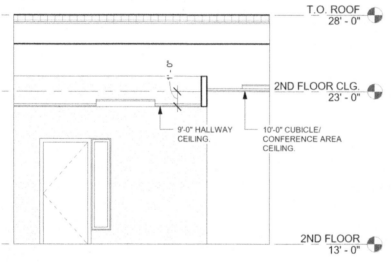

Partial Section View

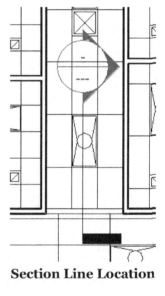

Section Line Location

4. To see the tiles for the Cubicle/Conference Area you will need change the view range.

   Use these settings for the View Range dialog box.

2nd Floor RCP View Range Settings

5. When adding the hallway ceiling divide the area into three areas. The horizontal hallway will need to have the tiles facing a different direction than the vertical hallways.

   Use the Sketch Ceiling option to do this.

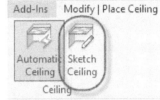

Sketch Ceiling Option

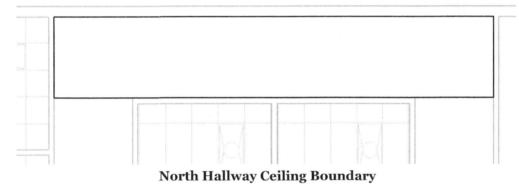

North Hallway Ceiling Boundary

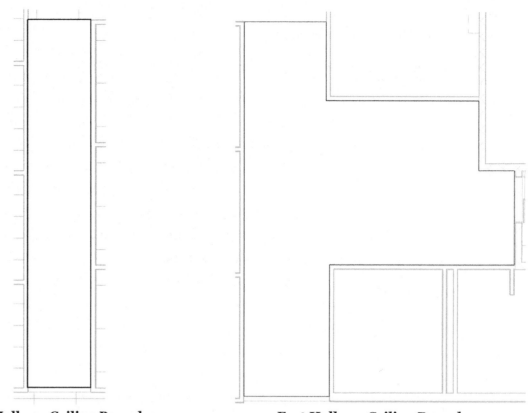

West Hallway Ceiling Boundary   **East Hallway Ceiling Boundary**

6. Add the lights for the rooms as shown. Use the same lights as in the first floor.

    You may wish to use reference planes to aid in locating the lights. Your dimensions for the center of the lights may be different. The second floor restroom lights may be copied from the first floor restrooms.

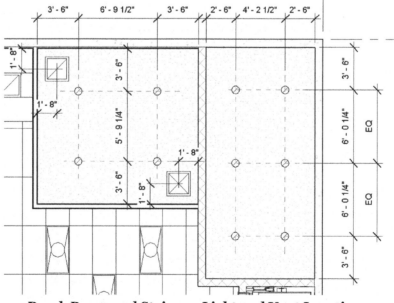

Break Room and Stairway Light and Vent Locations

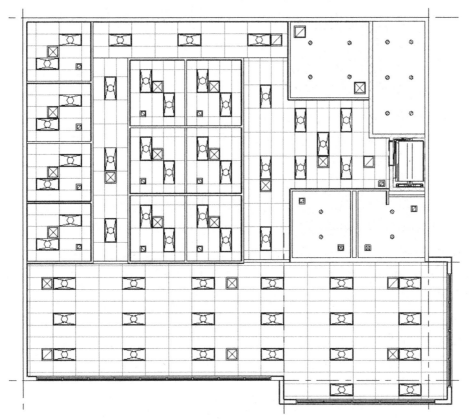

Completed Second Floor Reflected Ceiling Plan

7. This is the end of Part 3. Save your file as CL5-3.

CL5-4   Creating the First and Second Floor Furniture Plans and Break Room Cabinetry

Creating the First Floor Furniture View

1. Open the CL5-3 file, save the file as CL5-4.

2. Open the 1st Floor view.

3. Hide the concrete walkway, model lines, property lines, and reference planes that were created in the previous tutorials.

4. Right click on the view name in the project browser and click Duplicate View, Duplicate.

5. Rename the new view as 1ST FLOOR – Furniture Plan.

6. Hide the grid lines, elevation markers, section marks, and view bubbles.

7. Set the view scale for the view to 3/32" = 1'-0".

8. Turn on the Crop Window and locate the edges outside the edge of the view. Hide the crop window when finished.

9. Return to the 1st Floor view, select all the room tags, copy to the clipboard.

10. Re-open the 1st Floor furniture plan view.

11. Paste the room tags into the view.

    Change the tag type to not show the area of the room.

12. Adjust the location of the tags as shown.

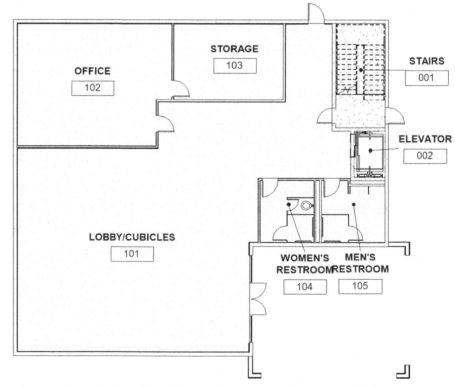

First Floor Furniture Plan View with Room Labels

13. Use the chart to select the first floor furniture:

Some furniture will already be included with the template file.

Room	Furniture	Location
Office	Furniture_System-Storage-Cabinet-2_Vertical_File (36" x 18 Lat.)	Furniture System, Storage Folder
	Desk - Modified (72" x 36")	Custom Families from Website
	Chair-Executive	Furniture, Seating Folder
	Work Station Cubicle (96" x 96")	Custom Families from Website
	Computer_Keyboard_129	Custom Families from Website
	Dell_Monitor_11282	Custom Families from Website
	Cheiftec_ATX_Tower_2930	Custom Families from Website
Lobby/ Cubicles	Work Station Cubicle (96" x 96")	Custom Families from Website
	Work Station Cubicle (Receptionist) (96" x 96")	Custom Families from Website
	Chair-Executive	Furniture, Seating Folder
	Computer_Keyboard_129	Custom Families from Website
	Dell_Monitor_11282	Custom Families from Website
Elevator	Cheiftec_ATX_Tower_2930	Custom Families from Website
Stairs	None	N/A
Storage	None	N/A
	Shelving 132" x 12" x 84"	Create size.
	Shelving 108" x 12" x 84"	Create size.
	Shelving 96" x 12" x 84"	Furniture, Storage Folder
Restrooms	Shelving 84" x 12" x 84"	Create size.
	No Furniture, only Fixtures	N/A

First Floor Furniture

Notes:

- This is the recommended amount of furniture
- You may add additional chairs and office equipment if you wish.
- Insert the furniture in the location based on the drawing shown.
- Add the notes for the cabinets and cubicles.
- When placing the computer, keyboard, and monitor set the offset to 2'-5 3/4" to place the components on the top surface of desk.
- After creating one workstation with the chair and computer, you may wish to group and copy them to the other locations.

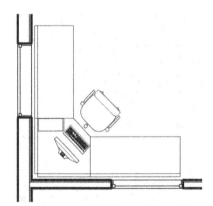

Typical Layout for Workstation

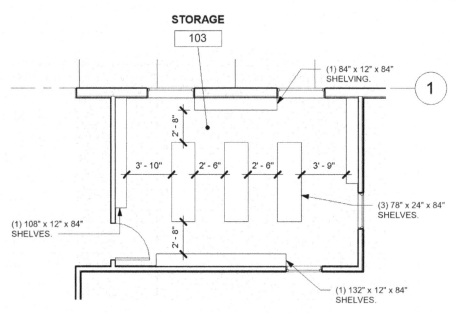

Storage Room Shelving Dimensions

14. When finished, your first floor furniture plan should look like this...

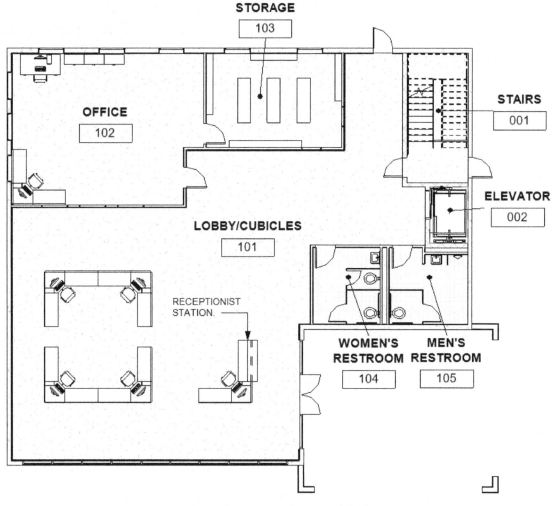

First Floor Furniture Added

Creating the Second Floor Break Room Cabinetry

1. Create the 2nd Floor furniture plan view.

2. Copy the room tags but do not include the ones for the offices.

3. Zoom in to the Break Room.

4. Load the following cabinetry, counter top and fixture into the file.

Lower Cabinets	Location
Base Cabinet-Double Door & 2 Drawer 22" and 48"	Casework, Base Cabinets
Base Cabinet-Double Door Sink Unit 48"	Casework, Base Cabinets
Base Cabinet-Corner Unit-Angled 36"	Casework, Base Cabinets
Sink Kitchen-Double 42" x 21"	Plumbing, Architectural, Fixtures, Sinks
Counter Top-L Shaped w Sink Hole 2 24" Depth	Casework, Counter Tops

Upper Cabinets & Equipment	Location
Upper Cabinet-Double Door-Wall 30"	Casework, Wall Cabinets
Upper Cabinet-Corner Unit-Wall 12"	Casework, Wall Cabinets
Copier-Floor	Custom Families from Website

Break Room Cabinet Families

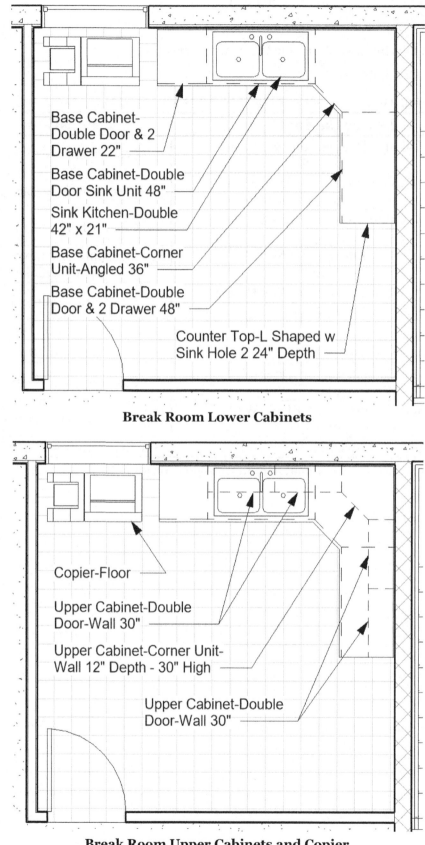

Break Room Lower Cabinets

Base Cabinet-Double Door & 2 Drawer 22"

Base Cabinet-Double Door Sink Unit 48"

Sink Kitchen-Double 42" x 21"

Base Cabinet-Corner Unit-Angled 36"

Base Cabinet-Double Door & 2 Drawer 48"

Counter Top-L Shaped w Sink Hole 2 24" Depth

Copier-Floor

Upper Cabinet-Double Door-Wall 30"

Upper Cabinet-Corner Unit-Wall 12" Depth - 30" High

Upper Cabinet-Double Door-Wall 30"

Break Room Upper Cabinets and Copier

5. You will need to duplicate the Base Cabinet-Double Door & 2 Drawer family and create a type that is 22" wide.

6. You will need to duplicate the Upper Cabinet-Corner Unit family and create a type that is 30" high.

7. Use these settings for the counter top.

Properties		✕
Counter Top-L Shaped w Sink Hole 2 24" Depth		
Casework (1)	∨	⊞ Edit Type
Constraints		⮝ ∧
Level	2ND FLOOR	
Host	Floor : Steel Bar Joist 14" -...	
Offset	0' 0"	
Moves With Nearby Ele...	☐	
Dimensions		⮝
Length - Leg 1	8' 10"	
Length - Leg 2	7' 0"	
Sink Location	3' 5"	
Sink Location To Wall	0' 6"	
Sink Opening Depth	1' 3"	
Sink Opening Width	3' 3"	
Identity Data		⮝
Image		
Comments		∨
Properties help		Apply

Counter Top Settings

Creating the Second Floor Furniture View

1. Use the chart for the second floor furniture:

    Note: Some furniture was loaded when setting up the 1st Floor Furniture Plan view.

Room	Furniture	Location
Offices	Desk - Modified (72" x 36")	Custom Families from Website
	Chair-Executive	Furniture, Seating
	Cabinet-File 4 Drawer (15" x 18")	Furniture, Storage
	RPC Notebook Computer	Entourage
	Chair-Desk	Include with Template File
Cubicles/ Conference Area	Work Station Cubicle (96" x 96")	Custom Families from Website
	Chair-Executive	Furniture, Seating Folder
	Computer_Keyboard_129	Custom Families from Website
	Dell_Monitor_11282	Custom Families from Website
	Chieftec_ATX_Tower_2930	Custom Families from Website
	Copier-Floor	Custom Families from Website
	Chair-Task	Furniture, Seating
	COALESSE_E-TABLE_-_Faceted_10039_8771 10' x 60" x 29" (3 Utility Box)	Custom Families from Website
Break Room	Table-Dining Round w/Chairs 36" Diameter	Furniture, Tables
	Copier-Floor	Custom Families from Website
Elevator	None	
Stairs	None	
Storage	None	
Restrooms	No Furniture, only Fixtures	

Second Floor Furniture

2. When placing the RPC Notebook Computer, set the offset to 2'-6" to place the component on the top surface of the desk.

3. After adding the furniture for one of the offices, group the elements together and copy to the other offices.

4. Create one interior elevation view of the break room showing the north wall.

    Set the scale to 1/4" – 1'-0"

5. Open the interior elevation view and set the height of the wall cabinets to 7'-3" high.

6. Set the head height of the 48" x 36" fixed window to 7'-0" (if needed).

    Note: You will need to set the cut plane for the 2nd Floor plan views to 5'-6" to see this window.

7. Name the interior elevation view: BREAK ROOM - NORTH.

8. Open the Object Styles dialog box in the Manage tab, Settings panel.

In the Casework category, set the elevation swing line setting to 1/8"

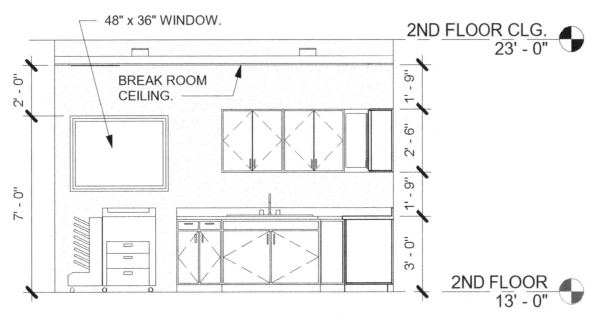

Elevation Swing Settings

Break Room – North Interior Elevation View

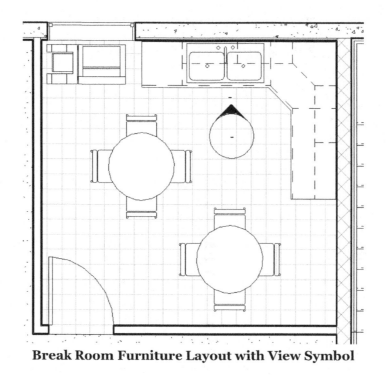

Break Room Furniture Layout with View Symbol

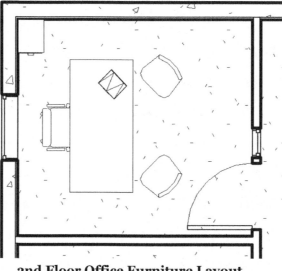

2nd Floor Office Furniture Layout

9. When finished, your second floor furniture plan should look like this...

Turn off the interior elevation view symbol in the furniture plan view.

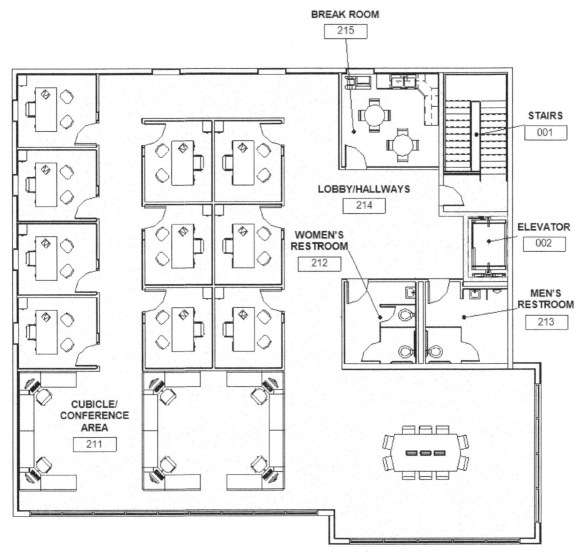

Second Floor Furniture Added

Updating the Path of Travel Views

Before finishing the tutorial, you will update the path of travel for both floors. Since the furniture is considered an obstacle, the path of travel will be diverted around these elements.

1. Open the 1ST FLOOR – Path of Travel view.

2. Select each of the paths of travel and click on the Update tool in the contextual tab. The path will update to go around the furniture.

    Note: If the path begins too close or on top of an obstacle, the start point will need to be moved.

Update Tool

3. Update the Path of Travel Schedules if needed. You may need to retag the paths that were removed and redrawn.

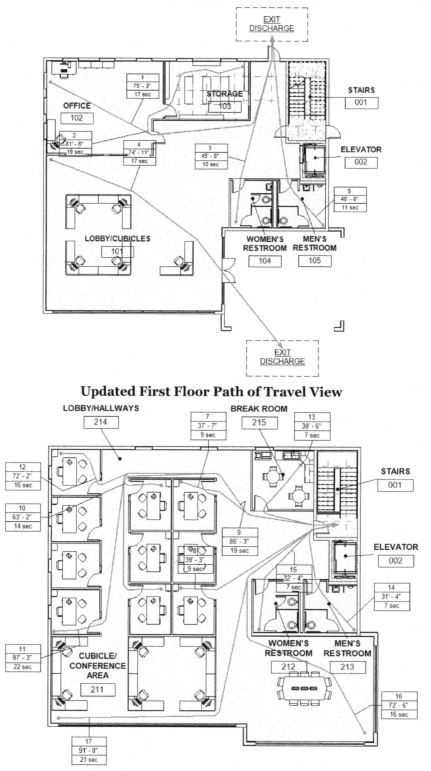

Updated First Floor Path of Travel View

Updated Second Floor Path of Travel View

4. This is the end of Part 4. Save your file as CL5-4.

CL5-5   Adding the Baseboards in the First and Second Floors

1. Open the CL5-4 file, save the file as CL5-5.

2. Open the 1st Floor view.

3. Hide the furniture and reference planes.

4. Duplicate the view without detailing and name the view 1ST FLOOR – Baseboards

   This view will only be used to add the baseboards and will not be part of the portfolio.

5. Create an interior elevation on the west side of the Lobby/Cubicle Area.

6. Open the elevation view and hide the furniture.

7. Click on the arrow beneath the Wall tool and choose the Wall: Sweep tool.

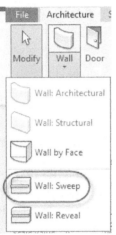

Wall Sweep Tool

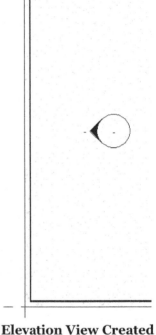

Elevation View Created

8. In the Properties dialog box choose the Wall Sweep, Wall Sweep – Trim.

   Click the Edit Type button to open the Type Properties dialog box.

9. Choose the Base-Vinyl:4 profile.

Type Properties for the Baseboard

10. Click on the <By Category> text and open the Material Browser.

11. Search for and then choose the PVC, Flexible material.

12. Load it into your drawing file and change the color to anything you wish.

Material Browser - PVC, Flexible

PVC   ✕

Project Materials: All ▼ ▾   ≣ ▾

Search results for "PVC"

Name

PVC, Flexible - Baseboard

Vapor Retarder

Baseboard Material

13. Click a point on the vertical wall.

    The baseboard is attached to the cursor.

    Place the baseboard at the bottom edge and end the command. You will see the baseboard appear.

14. Open the 1st Floor – Baseboard view and click on the baseboard that you added.

    Click on the Add/Remove Walls tool and then click the walls the you will to add the baseboards to. It will only add baseboard on one side. If you wish to add the baseboard to the other side of the wall, you will need to create another interior elevation view and select the vertical wall.

15. Add the baseboards to as many walls as you wish. This is a time-consuming process so you may wish to add the baseboards to walls that are in views that you will be rendering later in the book.

    Also, only leave the baseboards on in this view, interior elevation views, and in the 3D views that you will create later. Turn off the baseboards in the plan views so that the walls do not appear thicker than they are.

16. This is the end of Part 4 and Tutorial 5. Save your file as CL5-5.

Tutorial 6   Adding the Roof Cap, Setting Up the Design Options, and Creating the Wall Sections

Part 1	Adding the Roof Cap and Changing the Wall Material
Part 2	Creating the Tower Wall and Tower Roof Design Option Sets
Part 3	Creating the Tower Roof Design Options
Part 4	Setting Up the Design Option Views
Part 5	Creating and Annotating the Wall Sections and Detail

Note: All screenshots are from the Autodesk® Revit® software.

Starting the Tutorial

1. Open the last file from Tutorial Five, CL5-5.

2. Save the file as CL6-1.

In this tutorial you will add the roof cap to the main building and tower walls. You will also set up two different design options of the project. One will show two different roof styles for the tower and the other will show two entry openings for the tower walls. You will then set up four different of views that show the different design options.

CL6-1   Adding the Roof Cap and Changing the Wall Material

To finish up the look of the building you will add coping (parapet cover cap) around the top edge of the exterior and tower walls. You will also change the appearance of the tower wall material.

1. Open the 3D view of the project.

    Change the display style to Hidden Line. This will allow you to see the path of the sweep clearly.

2. Select the top portion of one of the tower walls and click the Edit Profile tool.

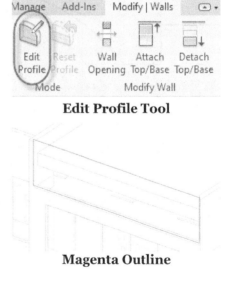

Edit Profile Tool

3. The outline will turn magenta.

    Modify the top of the wall with some additional shapes.

Magenta Outline

4. This is the completed modified parapet.

    Increase the height of the two rear walls an
    additional 2'-0".

Modified Parapet Design

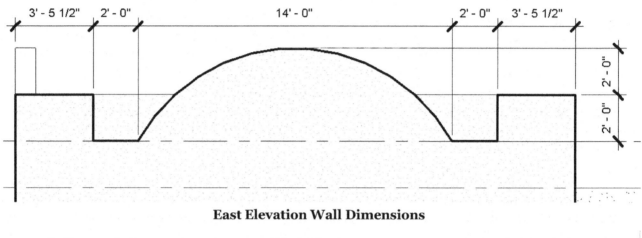

3' - 5 1/2"   2' - 0"   14' - 0"   2' - 0"   3' - 5 1/2"

2' - 0"

2' - 0"

East Elevation Wall Dimensions

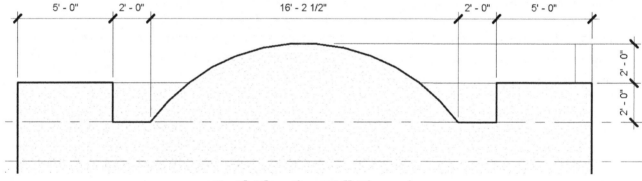

5' - 0"   2' - 0"   16' - 2 1/2"   2' - 0"   5' - 0"

2' - 0"

2' - 0"

South Elevation Wall Dimensions

5. To begin the sweep, first open the 3d view.

6. Zoom in on the top of the tower.

7. Click on the Component - Model-In-Place tool in the
    Architecture tab, Build panel.

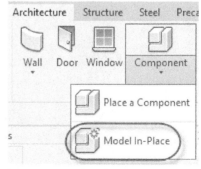

Component, Model-In-Place Tool

8. In the Family Category and Parameters dialog, choose Generic Models for the Family Category.

   Name the category Coping 1.

9. Select the Sweep tool in the Form panel.

10. Click on the Pick Path tool.

    Pick the outside corners of the parapet. There will be one path around the entire tower.

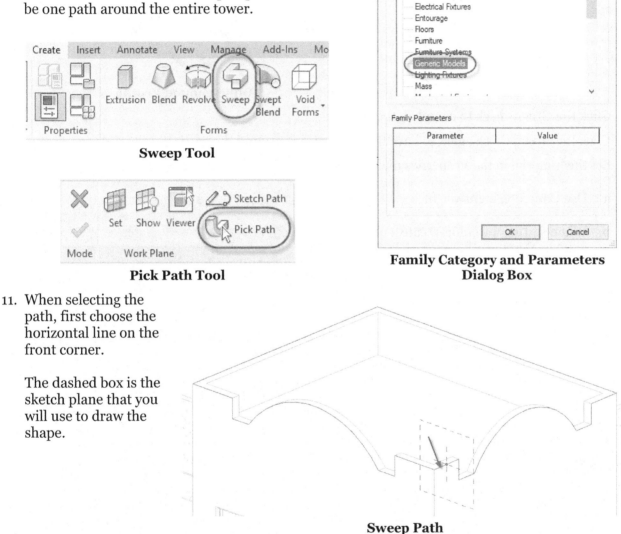

Sweep Tool

Pick Path Tool

Family Category and Parameters Dialog Box

11. When selecting the path, first choose the horizontal line on the front corner.

    The dashed box is the sketch plane that you will use to draw the shape.

Sweep Path

12. Click the Green check to accept the path and starting the sketch.

13. Rotate to the front view using the 3D cube.

14. Click the Edit Profile button to sketch the shape for the profile.

Edit Profile Button

15. You may choose to draw the profile
    as shown or draw your own version.

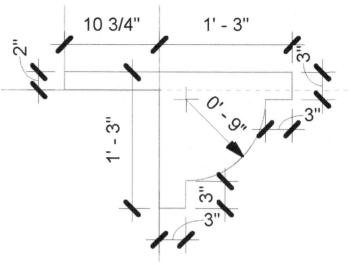

Dimensioned Profile

16. Click the Green check to complete the profile.

17. Click the Green check again to have the profile track around the path.

18. Set the material in the Properties dialog box.

    a. Use Concrete, Lightweight.

    b. When setting the color, create a new
    asset so that the other materials don't
    change as well.

    c. Click the Green check one last time to
    finish the model.

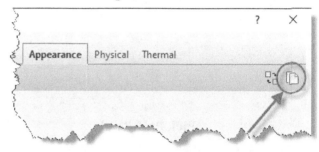

Duplicates This Asset Button

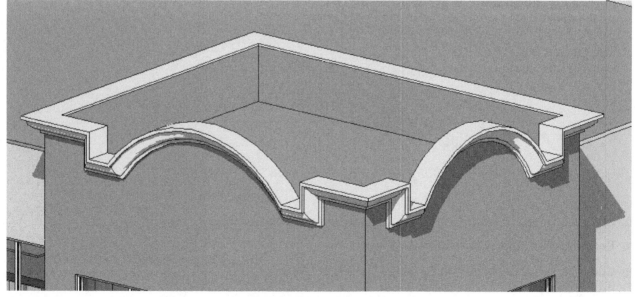

Finished Roof Coping

Adding the Coping for the Exterior Walls

1. Repeat the process for the coping on top of the exterior walls.

    Name the family: Coping 2.

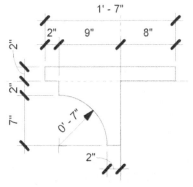

Sketch Path for Exterior Walls

2. The sketch path does not need to be a closed loop.

3. Draw the same shape or use a different one for the profile.

    Refer to the drawing for the wall coping.

Profile Dimensions

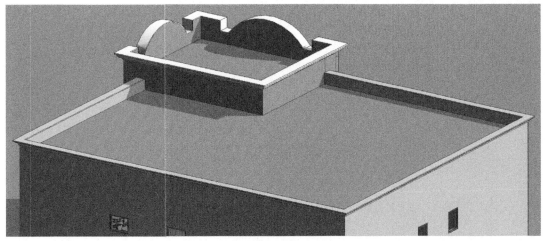

Coping Placed

Changing the Material of the Tower Walls

Next you will update the material of the tower walls. These walls were set to a stucco material back in Tutorial 1. Now you will change the color of the material.

1. Open the Material Browser dialog box.

2. Search for the Stucco material.

3. Duplicate the material and call it Stucco – Tower Walls. Duplicate the asset.

4. In the dialog box click on the Appearance tab.

5. Scroll down to the Tint area and click the checkbox.

6. Click the arrow next to Tint and match the Tint Color as shown.

Tint Color Setting

7. Click on the Graphics tab and change the Shading color bar to match the example.

    This will change the material of the wall when the view is shaded.

Use Render Appearance Checkbox

8. Edit the wall types for the tower walls and change the stucco material to the Stucco – Tower Walls material.

9. Click the OK button to close the dialog box and apply the changes.

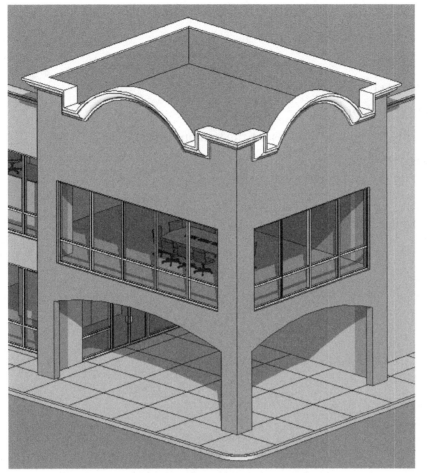

Tower Wall Material Changed

10. This is the end of Part 1. Save your file as CL6-1.

CL6-2   Creating the Tower Wall and Tower Roof Design Option Sets

1.   Open the CL6-1 file, save the file as CL6-2.

2.   Open the default 3D view.

3.   Zoom in on the tower walls.

<u>Setting up the Tower Wall Options</u>

At this point you will set up place holders for the two option sets.

1.   Open the Design Options dialog box by clicking on the tool at the bottom of the screen.

Design Options Tool

2.   The Design Options dialog box opens.

Design Options Dialog Box

3.   Click on the New button under the Option Set. Click again to make a second option set.

4.   Name the two option sets, Tower Walls and Tower Roofs

5.   With the Tower Walls option set selected, click the New button under the Option area.

6.   Rename the options: 1 – Arched Opening and 2 – Rectangular Opening.

7.   Select the Tower Roof option; click the New button under the Option area.

8.   Rename the options: 1 – Flat Roof and 2 – Hip Roof.

9. When finished your Design options dialog box should look like this...

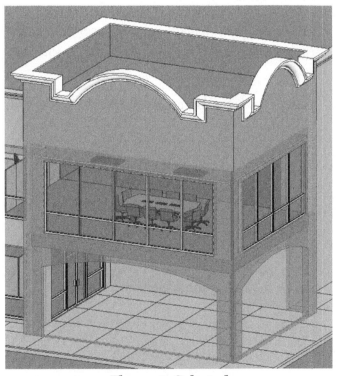

Design Options Added

10. Select the following walls:

The four bottom portions of the tower walls, and the bottom four short side walls.

To avoid a possible error message you should also pick the two curtain wall windows.

When you are finished selecting the elements you will have 10 elements selected.

Check for this at the bottom right of the screen next to the filter symbol.

Number of Elements Selected

Elements Selected

11. Click the Add to Set tool at the bottom of the screen next to the Design Options tool.

Add to Set Tool

12. The Add to Design Option Set dialog box opens.

    Select the Tower Wall option. Click the OK to close the box and add the elements to the two options.

    Note:
    What just happened is the 10 elements that were selected were removed from the Main Model. These two sets of the elements were added back into the model, one for each of the Tower Wall Design Options. This way you will be able to change the second set of elements without affecting the first set.

Add to Design Option Set Dialog Box

13. You may get a warning box that states that the elements highlighted in orange are joined but do not intersect.

    Click the Unjoin Elements button to unjoin the walls and clear the box.

14. Once the elements have been added to the design options you will not be able to select any of the elements.

    To access these elements you will need to activate one of the design options for the Tower Wall.

15. Click on the Active Design drop-down at the bottom of the screen.

    Select the second option on the Tower Wall option.

Active Design Option Drop-Down

16. The rest of the model is grayed out and you will be able to pick the design option elements.

    Note:
    Since the Primary Option (#1) will not change, you will not be modifying those elements.

Tower Wall – Option #2 Elements

Modifying the Openings for the South and East Tower walls.

1. Confirm that you are still in the Design Option #2 for the Tower Walls.

    Click on the bottom portion of the south tower wall.

2. Rotate the view to the Front orientation.

    Click the Edit Profile tool.

3. Rotate the view to the Front orientation.

    Draw a new profile line starting at the top midpoint of the arc.

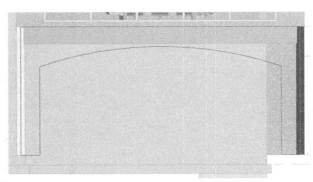

New Profile Line

4. Delete the arc and trim/extend the horizontal line to the two inside vertical lines.

Profile of Rectangular Opening Created

5. Click the Green Check to complete the modification.

6. Repeat the process for the east tower wall.

7. Your model should look like
    this when finished...

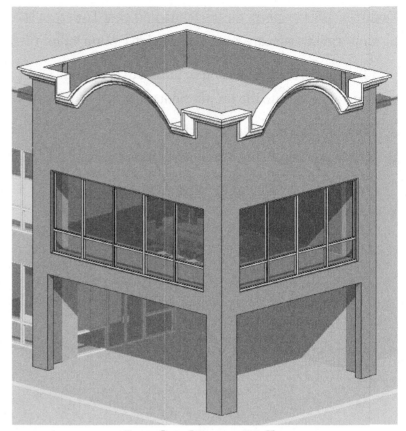

**Completed Tower Wall –
Option #2 – Rectangular Opening**

8. Change the Design Option to Main Model. The Option #2 elements will turn off.

    Later you will set up a 3D view that will show this option.

9. This is the end of Part 2. Save your file as CL6-2.

CL6-3   Creating the Tower Roof Design Options

You have already created the Design Option for the Tower Roof. Now you will add elements to create a Hip roof structure for the second option.

1.   Open the CL6-2 file, save the file as CL6-3.

2.   If needed, open the 3D view.

3.   Confirm that you are in the Main Model.

4.   Select the Flat Roof and the Roof Coping on the tower walls.

5.   Cut the elements to the clipboard.

6.   Switch to the Tower Roofs Option 1 – Flat Roof.

7.   Paste the two elements.

Use the Aligned to Same Place option.

Aligned to Same Place Option

8.   This will add the elements to the design option.

The reason for this is so these elements will not appear in the second roof design option.

This is all you will need to do for the first roof design option.

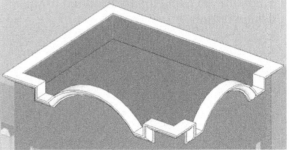

Elements Added to the Design Option

9.   Switch to the Main Model.

10. Select the six portions of the top of the tower wall.

11. Click on the Add to Set tool and add the elements to both Tower Roof options.

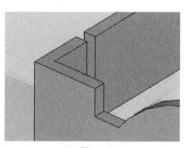

Add to Design Option Set Dialog Box

12. Switch to the Tower Roofs Option 2 – Hip Roof.

13. Paste the elements aligned to the same place.

14. There may be gaps on the tower walls at the top right and the lower left corners of the tower.

    To fix this, drag the end of the wall to that it overlaps with the other wall. Ignore the error message.

    Then use the Join tool to join them together.

Wall Gaps

15. There are no elements to be added to this design option.

    Also, the flat roof and the roof cap are not visible.

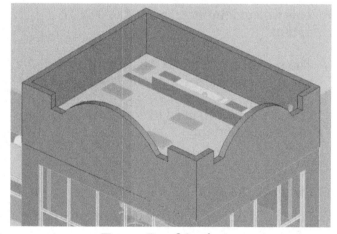

Tower Roof Option 2

16. Select the south tower wall and reset the profile. Do the same with the east tower wall.

    Lower the tops of the other four walls 2'-0" so that the tops of all the walls are at the same level.

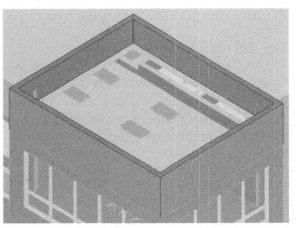

Tower Walls Modified

17. Open the T.O. Tower view.

    Set the view range so that the View Depth is set to Level Below (T.O. Wall). This will make the walls visible in this view.

View Depth set to Level Below (T.O. Wall)

18. Click on the Roof by Footprint tool.

    Set the Base Offset From Level setting to 0'-0".

    You will use the Basic Roof Generic – 12" roof style.

    Use a 2'-0" overhang.

    After placing and extending the lines together, pick the lines and set the roof slope to 4:12.

    Click the Green check to complete the roof.

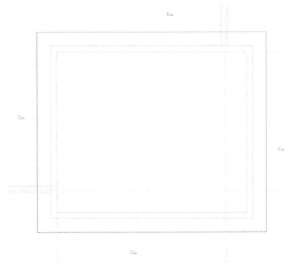

Roof Footprint Sketch

19. Return to the 3D View to view the roof.

    The roof will appear green in color.

    Click on the roof and edit the roof type.

20. Change the roof material to Metal Deck in the Edit Assembly dialog box.

    The surface of the roof will now be gray.

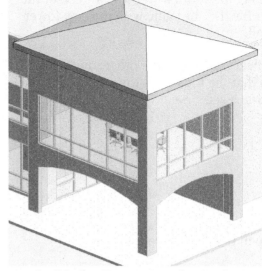

Roof Added to Tower Roof – Option #2

21. Create a sweep that covers the space under the overhang.

    Refer to the drawing for the shape of the profile.

    Use the bottom edge of the roof for the path of the sweep.

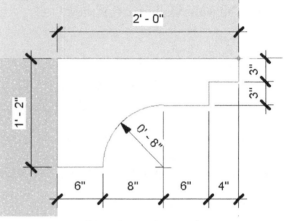

Roof Coping Dimensions

22. Choose a color for the Roof Coping. Create a unique material and asset.

23. This completes second Tower Roof design option.

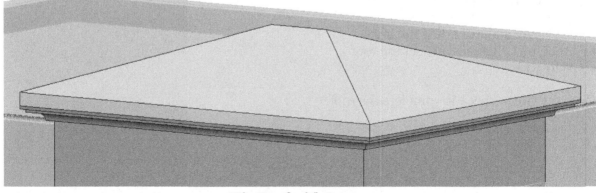

Hip Roof with Sweep

24. Return to the Main Model. The roof will revert to the flat roof.

25. This is the end of Part 3. Save your file as CL6-3.

CL6-4   Setting Up the Design Option Views

Next you will set up the four views that show the different design option combinations. Since there are a total of four options, you will need four views.

1. Open the CL6-3 file, save the file as CL6-4.

2. In the 3D view, right click on the view in the project browser and select Duplicate View, Duplicate.

3. The new view opens. Hide the topography.

4. Rotate the view so that you can clearly see the tower walls and roof.

5. Before duplicating the view again, reset the home position of the view.

6. Hover over the ViewCube so that the Home icon appears.

Home Icon

7. Right click on the icon.

8. Select: Set Current View as Home

9. This will place this view rotation in memory so that you will be able to return to it if you need to rotate the view.

Set Current View as Home

10. Click the Show Crop Region tool at the bottom of the view.

    Adjust the crop region around the edge of the building,

    Hide the crop region when finished.

1/8" = 1'-0"

Hide/Show Crop Region

11. Click on the Set Settings... option on the Sun Path tool.

Sun Settings... Option

12. Set the Ground Plane at Level: setting to the T.O. FOOTER level.

    This will move the shadows to a higher level and will appear correct.

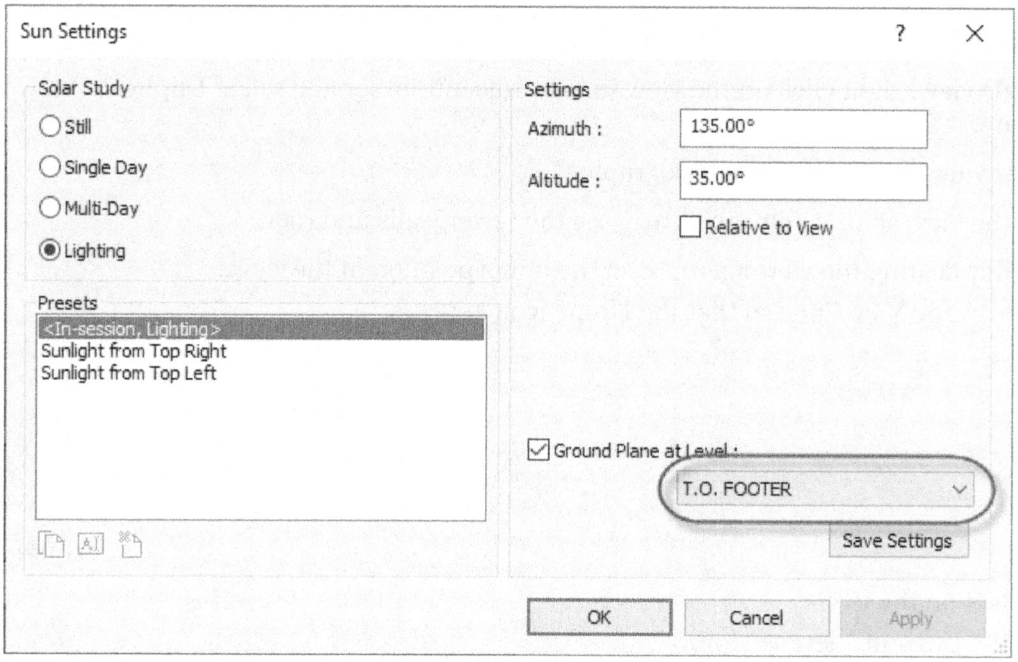

Sun Setting Dialog Box

13. Rename the view: Design Option – Wall 1, Roof 1

14. Repeat the process to create three more views.

    Refer to the Project Browser screenshot for the names.

    Update the shadows to the T.O. Footer level for these views.

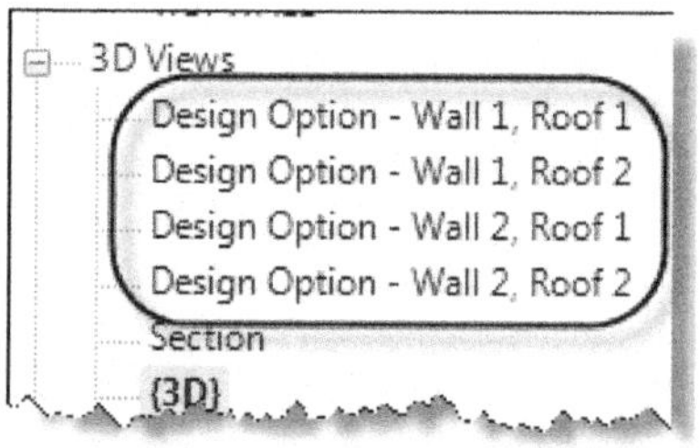

View Names for Design Options

15. Open the Visibility/Graphics Overrides dialog box by typing "VV" on the keyboard.

16. In the dialog box, click on the Design Options tab.

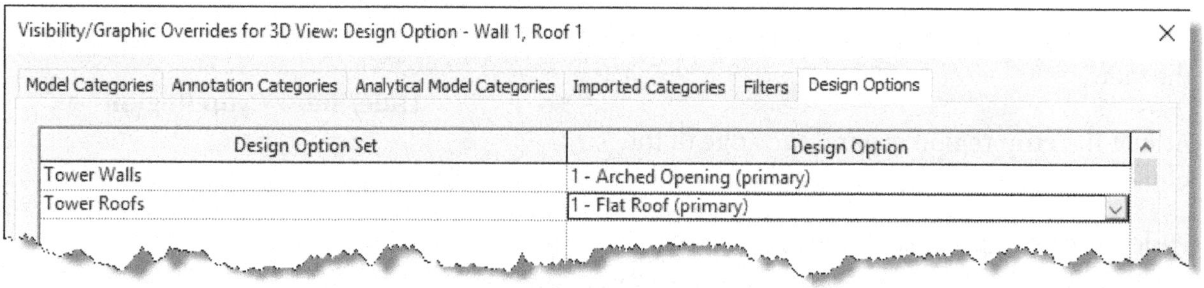

Design Options Tab

17. Refer to the table for the setup.

View Name	Design Option	
	Tower Wall Option	Tower Roof Option
Design Option – Wall 1, Roof 1	1 – Arched Opening (Primary)	1 – Flat Roof (Primary)
Design Option – Wall 1, Roof 2	1 – Arched Opening (Primary)	2 – Hip Roof
Design Option – Wall 2, Roof 1	2 – Rectangular Opening	1 – Flat Roof (Primary)
Design Option – Wall 2, Roof 2	2 – Rectangular Opening	2 – Hip Roof

Design Option Settings for Views

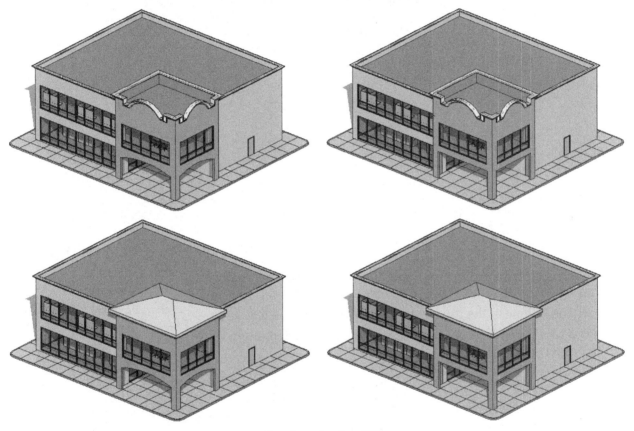

Four Design Option Views

18. After you have set up the views you may notice that there are lines between the different tower walls.

To remove them use the Linework tool to change the seam lines to invisible. Open each of the design option views and change the design option. As you cycle through each one, change the seam line for each wall corner to invisible.

19. Later you will set up a sheet in the Portfolio that will show these four views.

20. This is the end of Part 4. Save your file as CL6-4.

CL6-5   Creating and Annotating the Wall Sections and Detail

In this part you will create and annotate the elevator shaft wall section, exterior wall section, and the exterior footing detail. Wall sections and details are used to show the materials and methods of construction for portions of the structure such as the connections between the floor slab and the exterior wall.

Creating the Elevator Shaft Section

1. Open the CL6-4 file, save the file as CL6-5.

2. Open the Longitudinal Section view created earlier.

    Name the view LONGITUDINAL SECTION if the view has not been named.

    Select and hide the reference planes and the furniture.

3. Zoom in on the right side of the building.

4. Click on the Callout tool in the View tab, Create panel.

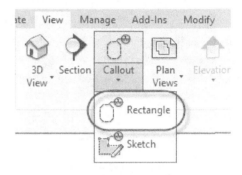

Callout Tool, Rectangle Option

5. Draw a rectangular callout area surrounding the elevator shaft from the top of the roof to below the footer.

6. Move the bubble to the top right or left, away from the text.

7. As you add the section, set the section type to Wall Section in the Properties dialog box.

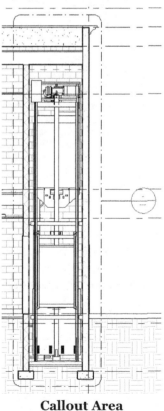

Callout Area

8. The wall section view will be named: LONGITUDINAL SECTION – Callout 1.

   Rename the view: ELEVATOR SHAFT SECTION

9. Open the wall section view.

10. Select and right click on the elevator family in the view.

    Select Override Graphics in View, By Element...

    Check the Halftone checkbox to grayscale the elevator and equipment.

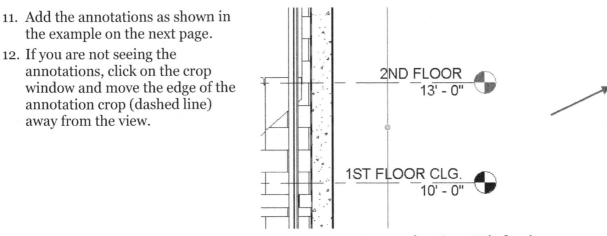

Halftone Checkbox

11. Add the annotations as shown in the example on the next page.

12. If you are not seeing the annotations, click on the crop window and move the edge of the annotation crop (dashed line) away from the view.

Annotation Crop Window`

13. Select the block walls, stairs, and handrail, beyond the cut plane of the view.

    Hide the elements.

14. Hide the reference planes.

15. When adding the notes and
dimensions:

   a. Use 3/32" inch text for the
       notes.

   b. Set the scale of the view to
       3/8"=1'-0".

   c. Draw the Cant Strip using the
       Detail Line tool set to
       Medium Lines.

   d. Use the Detail Component
       tool in Annotate tab, Detail
       panel, Component tool to add
       the Break Line.

   e. Copy the Break Line up the
       side of the view. Stretch the
       line ends until they join.
       Continue the copies until you
       have four break lines.

   f. Line up the notes vertically
       when placing the text.

   Note: Set the cut pattern for the
   Earth material to light gray.

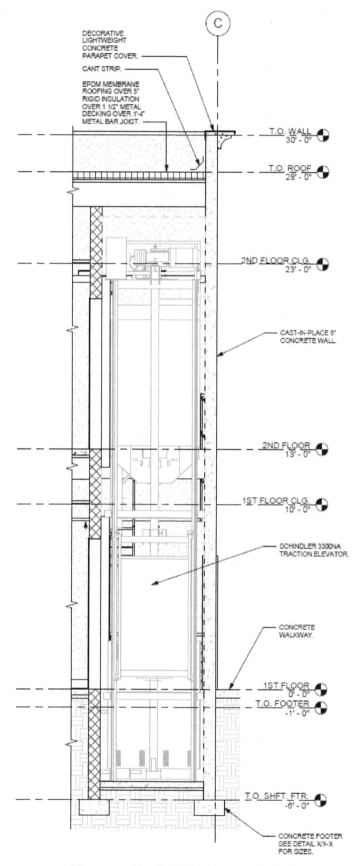

Elevator Shaft Section Annotation

Adding the Footer Around the Edge of the Sidewalk

1. Before creating the next wall section, you will add a curb and gutter around the outside edge of the sidewalk.

2. Load the following family from the Custom Families folder: Sidewalk Edge.rfa.

   This contains a profile that consists of a curb and gutter.

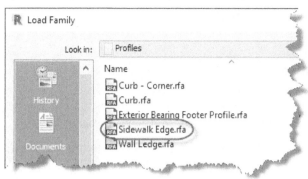

Sidewalk Edge.rfa File

3. Open the 3D view of the structure. Hide the topography.

4. Click on the Slab Edge tool in the Architecture tab.

5. Click the Edit Type button and duplicate the Slab Edge type.

   Name the type: Sidewalk Curb edge.

Floor: Slab Edge Tool

6. Click in the Value box next to the Profile parameter and choose the Sidewalk Edge: Ledge profile.

   Set the material to Concrete, Cast-in-Place.

Type Properties for Slab Edge

7. Click on the top corner of the sidewalk slab and continue around the edge of the slab.

    If the slab edge is reversed, select it and click the flip arrow.

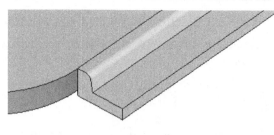

Slab Edge Placed

Creating the Exterior Wall Section

1. Open the Longitudinal Section view.

2. Create a new callout view on the left side of the section view as shown.

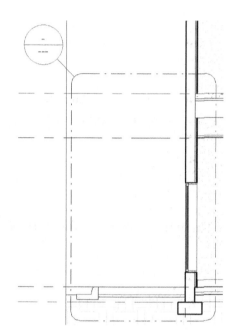

Exterior Wall Section Callout

3. Open the view and name the view: EXTERIOR WALL SECTION.

4. Hide the furniture and the cubicle.

5. If needed, join the geometry between the second floor and the exterior wall.

6. Add baseboards to the first and second floors if desired.

7. Annotate the view as shown.

   Note: To get a consistent sized break line, you may copy the break line symbol for the previous wall section view.

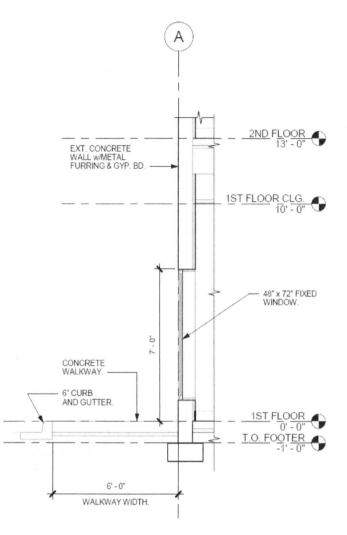

Exterior Wall Section Annotation

Creating the Exterior Footing Detail

1. Open the Elevator Shaft Section view.

2. Use the Callout tool to create a detail view of the footer.

   Place it in the Detail View category in the project browser.

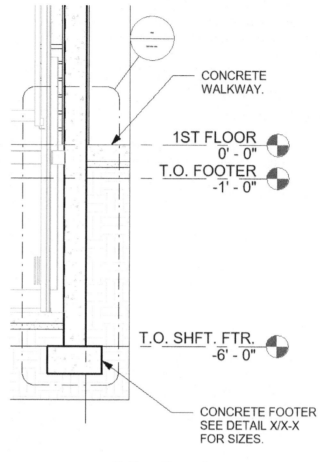

CONCRETE
WALKWAY.

1ST FLOOR
0' - 0"

T.O. FOOTER
-1' - 0"

T.O. SHFT. FTR.
-6' - 0"

CONCRETE FOOTER
SEE DETAIL X/X-X
FOR SIZES.

Callout Boundary

3. Name the new detail: EXTERIOR FOOTING DETAIL.

4. Open the view. The scale will be set to 3/4" = 1'-0"

5. Create a new dimension style for the detail.

   Click on the Aligned Dimension tool

6. Click on the Edit Type button.

7. Click on the Duplicate button.

8. Create a new linear dimension style based on the Linear - 3/32" Arial style.

9. Name the new style:
   Linear - 3/32" Arial (Inches Only).

   Note: This style is to be used for the dimensions that are less than 1'-0".

Duplicate... Button

10. Scroll down to the Units Format Parameter and click the button to the right.

Read Convention	Up, then Left
Text Font	Arial
Text Background	Opaque
Units Format	1' - 5 11/32" (Default)
Alternate Units	None
Alternate Units Format	1235 [mm]
Alternate Units Prefix	
Alternate Units Suffix	

Units Format Parameter

11. Uncheck the "Use project settings" checkbox.

Format   ×

☐ Use project settings

Units: Fractional inches   ∨

Rounding: Rounding increment:

To the nearest 1/4"   ∨

Unit symbol:

☐ Suppress trailing 0's

☐ Suppress 0 feet

☐ Show + for positive values

☐ Use digit grouping

☐ Suppress spaces

OK   Cancel

Format Settings for New Dimension Style

12. Set the Tick Mark to Diagonal 3/32" and the Tick Mark Line Weight to 7.

Do this for both Linear 3/32" Arial styles.

Note: This may have been done in a previous tutorial.

Show Leader When Text Moves	Away From Origin
Tick Mark	Diagonal 3/32"
Line Weight	1
Tick Mark Line Weight	7
Dimension Line Extension	3/32"
Flipped Dimension Line Extension	3/32"
Witness Line Control	Gap to Element

Tick Mark Type and Lineweight Settings

13. Annotate the detail as shown.

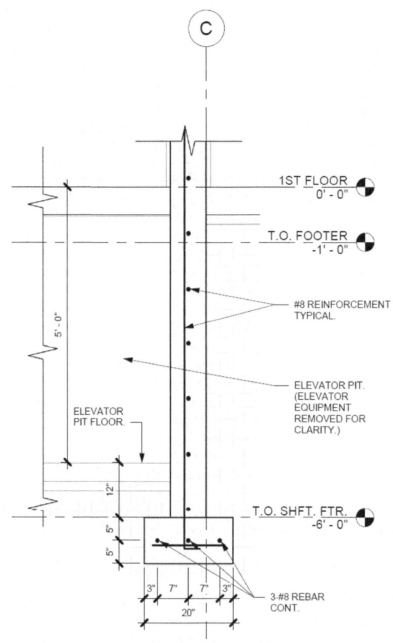

Annotated Exterior Footing Detail

14. When placing the rebar ends, use the Filled Region tool.

Space the bars in the wall 12".

Set the region Solid Black.

Use the Circle option in the Draw panel to draw the shape.

The radius is 1/2". (The actual size of the rebar is 1/2" diameter, the size is exaggerated for clarity.)

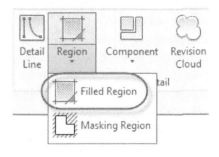

Filled Region Tool

15. When placing the lines for the rebar, use the Detail Line tool, Wide Lines style.

    Estimate the location based off the drawing.

16. To mask out a portion of the earth patterning:

    Click on the Masking Region tool in the Annotate tab, Detail panel.

    Set the linestyle of the boundary to Invisible Lines. This way the boundary will not show.

    Draw a rectangular shape for the portion of the patterning that you wish to mask out.

    Click the Green Check to finish.

Masking Region Tool

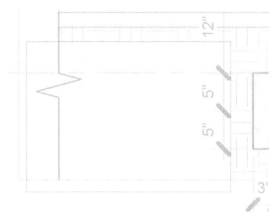

Masking Region Boundary

17. Click on the Materials tool in the Manage tab.

    Find the Earth material and change the cut pattern to light gray.

    Note: This may have been done earlier.

Earth Surface Pattern Changed to Light Gray

18. When locating the rebar ends in the footer you may need to use reference planes to locate the centers of the bar ends.

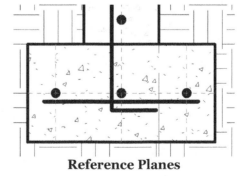

Reference Planes

19. This is the end of Part 5 and Tutorial 6. Save your file as CL6-5.

Tutorial 7   Adding Additional Site Elements and Creating the Renderings

Part 1	Applying Materials to the Walls and Walkway
Part 2	Adding Additional Elements to the Project
Part 3	Setting Up the Camera Views
Part 4	Setting up the Sky Background
Part 5	Rendering the Views

Note: All screenshots are from the Autodesk® Revit® software.

CL7-1   Applying Materials to the Walls and Walkway

The following procedures will help you set up the exterior view of the structure. These procedures will cover materials, backgrounds, and additional site elements.

You will setup the materials for the exterior surface of the walls, walkways, and parking lot. Use these settings to set the correct materials.

1. Open the drawing file from Tutorial 6 named CL6-5. Save the file as CL7-1.

2. Open the Material Browser dialog box.

3. Right click on the "Concrete, Cast-in-Place" material and duplicate it. Name the new material Concrete, C.I.P – Formwork Holes (2' Spacing).

Material Browser Setting for Exterior Wall Material

4. Click on the Appearance tab.

5. In the Assets area under tabs, click on the two white papers to the right.

    This will duplicate the asset.

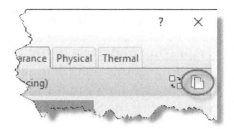

Duplicates this asset. Button

6. Click the arrow next to the Information area to open the category.

    Rename the asset "Formwork Holes (2' Spacing)".

7. Click on the filename in the area beneath the image.

    Change the image file to: Concrete.Cast-In-Place.Formwork.Holes.jpg.

8. Click on the image sample to open the Texture Editor dialog box.

9. Change the scale setting to 16'-0" for the Width and 8'-0" for the Height.

    You will need to unlock the width/height lock.

    This will space the holes 2'-0" in both directions.

    Click the Done button to close the box.

10. Click OK in the Material Browser to save the settings and close the box.

Texture Editor Dialog Box

11. Update the two exterior wall types to use this material for the surface.

    You will change the "Exterior – Concrete on Mtl. Stud" and the "Exterior – Concrete" wall types.

12. Repeat the process to create the Concrete Walkway material.

    Begin with the Site – Concrete material you originally created for the walkway.

    Use these settings:
      Asset Name: Concrete Walkway
      Image File: Concrete.Cast-In-Place.Flat.Polished.Grey
      Scale: 16'-0" Width, 16'-0" Height

    Also change the material for the curb and gutter to this material.

13. To check if the materials will appear correctly, open a 3D view and render the view.

    Click on the Render tool at the bottom of the tools in the View Control Bar.

Render Tool

14. When the Render dialog box opens, match the setting to this example:

    Quality – Medium
    Lighting – Exterior: Sun Only
    Style – Sky: Few Clouds

    The rendering will take a few minutes.

    When the rendering has finished, click the Save to Project... button to save the file with the project.

    Note: Rendering will be covered in more detail in a later tutorial.

Render Dialog Box

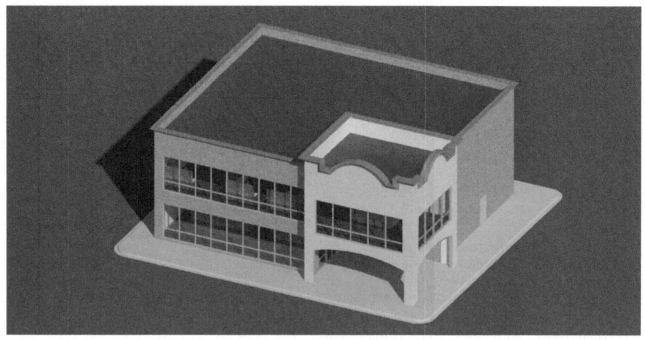

View is Rendered

15. This is the end of Part 1. Save your file as CL7-1.

CL7-2   Adding Additional Elements to the Project

To add realism to your project you may choose to add additional site elements to your project. To add people, cars, and parking stalls follow this procedure.

1. Open the CL7-1 file, save the file as CL7-2.

2. Click on the Component tool in the Architecture tab, Build panel.

3. Click on the Load Family tool and load the following families:

    All of the families are in the Entourage folder.

    RPC Male
    RPC Female
    RPC Beetle
    Van

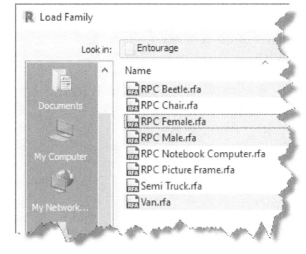

Entourage Families

4. Open the 1st Floor view.

    Hide the Furniture category.

5. Place two people near the front entrance as shown.

    The arrow on the family indicates the direction the person is facing.

    After placing, hide the category.

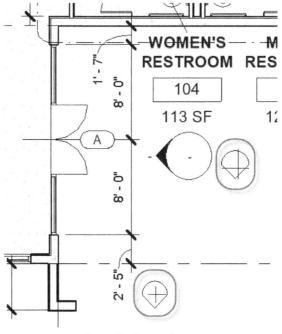

People Locations

6. Open the Site Plan view.

7. Click on the Parking Component tool in the Massing & Site tab, Model Site panel.

Parking Component Tool

8. Place a parking stall at the top right corner of the concrete walkway as shown.

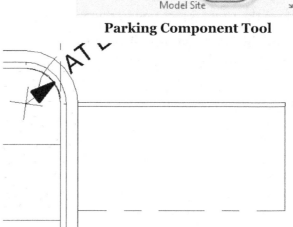

First Parking Stall Placement

9. After placing the first stall, click on the stall and then the Pick New Host tool.

    Click on the surface of the concrete walkway.

Pick New Host Tool

10. Set the offset to -0'-6" in the Properties dialog box.

Offset Set to -0'-6"

11. Click on the stall and then select the Array tool.

Set the Number: setting to 9 and the Move To: to 2nd.

12. Click the second point 9'-0" in a downward direction.

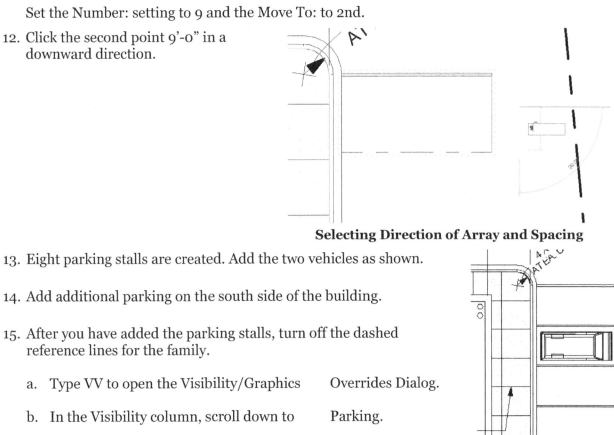

Selecting Direction of Array and Spacing

13. Eight parking stalls are created. Add the two vehicles as shown.

14. Add additional parking on the south side of the building.

15. After you have added the parking stalls, turn off the dashed reference lines for the family.

a. Type VV to open the Visibility/Graphics   Overrides Dialog.

b. In the Visibility column, scroll down to   Parking.

c. Uncheck the box next to the Parking Layout and Reference Line subcategory.

Note:
This will need to be done in each separate view that you wish to change.

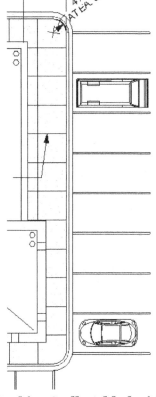

Parking Stalls Added with Vehicles

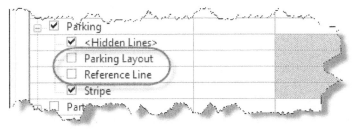

Parking Layout and Reference Line Subcategories

Adding the Window Shading (Eyebrows)

Next, you will add window shading (also known as eyebrows) above the windows and doors. After that, you will add two block walls on the north and west side of the building.

1. Open the North Elevation view.

   Hide the Reference Planes.

2. If the exterior walls are showing the gypsum-plaster pattern as black, change it to light gray.

3. If some of the windows appear to be too low or too high, click on the window and verify that the head height is set to 7'-0" in the Properties dialog box.

4. Go to the Component Model In-place tool.

5. Pick Generic Models for the Family Category.

6. Name the family, Eyebrow 1.

7. The view will turn gray. Set the work plane to the wall facing you.

   You may need to mouse over the edge and press the Tab key until the wall highlights.

8. Pick the Extrusion tool in the Forms panel.

Extrusion Tool

9. Draw the shape above the door at the left side of the view as shown in the diagram.

10. After drawing the shape, dimension and lock the 8" and 4" sizes.

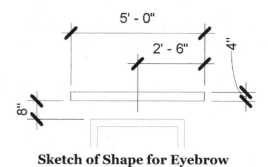

Sketch of Shape for Eyebrow

11. Set the Extrusion End distance to 1'-6".

12. Set the material to Concrete – Cast-in-Place.

Extrusion End Distance

13. Click the green check to complete the component.

    Click the green check one more time to finish the model.

3D View of Eyebrow

14. Open the North Elevation view.

15. Click on the eyebrow.

16. Click the Edit-in-Place tool. Click on the edge of the eyebrow and then the Edit Extrusion tool.

17. Select the shape and copy it over each of the windows.

    You do not need to include the dimensions.

18. Click the Green Check twice to complete the process.

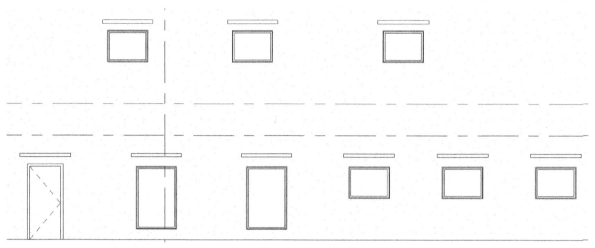

Eyebrows Copied

19. Open the West Elevation view.

20. Repeat the process for the windows. Name the family Eyebrows 2.

    Use the same size and location for the eyebrows used for the second floor windows.

    Refer to the diagram for the first floor windows.

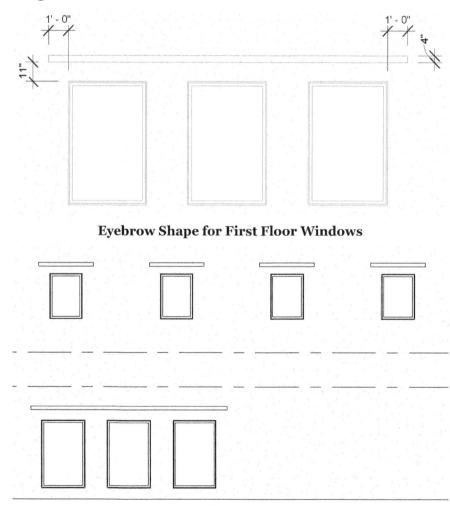

Eyebrow Shape for First Floor Windows

West Elevation Eyebrows

21. Open the South Elevation view.

22. Draw the shape as shown in the diagram.

Note that the thickness is now 6". Name the eyebrow family, Curtain Wall Eyebrows.

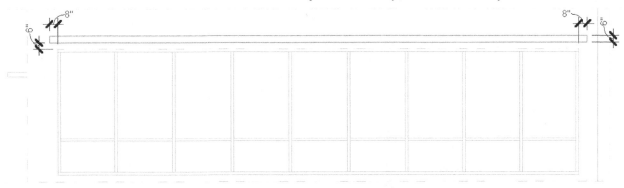

Curtain Wall Eyebrow

23. Set the extrusion distance to 3'-0".

24. Copy the shape to the other curtain wall.

25. Click the green check to complete the component.

Completing the Exterior Wall Section

1. Open the wall section view called: EXTERIOR WALL SECTION.

2. Now that the eyebrows have been added to the project, you may now add the dimensions for the location of the structure.

    A completed view is shown for reference.

3. You will need to add a separation line between the curb and gutter and the concrete walkway.

    To do this you will need to create a new linetype.

4. Click on the Manage tab, Additional Settings, and Line Styles.

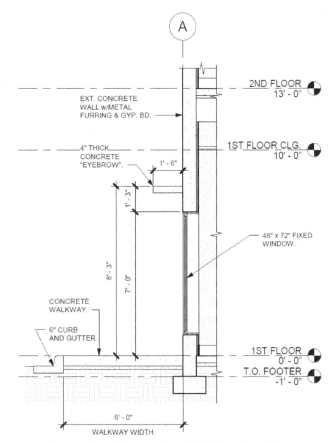

Completed Exterior Wall Section View

5. The Line Styles dialog box opens.

    Click on the "+" next to the Lines category

Category	Line Weight Projection	Line Color	Line Pattern
\<Demolished\>	1	Black	Demolished 3/16"
\<Fabric Envelope\>	1	RGB 127-127-127	Dash
\<Fabric Sheets\>	1	RGB 064-064-064	Solid
\<Hidden Lines\>	1	RGB 000-166-000	Dash
\<Hidden\>	1	Black	Hidden 1/8"
\<Insulation Batting Lin...\>	1	Black	Solid
\<Lines\>	1	RGB 000-166-000	Solid
\<Medium Lines\>	3	Black	Solid
\<Overhead\>	1	Black	Overhead 1/16"
\<Path of Travel Lines\>	5	RGB 000-166-000	Solid
\<Room Separation\>	1	Black	Solid
\<Sketch\>	3	RGB 225-000-255	Solid
\<Space Separation\>	1	Black	
\<Thin Lines\>	1	Black	Solid
\<Wide Lines\>	5	Black	Solid
Lineweight 2	2	Black	Solid

Select All   Select None   Invert

Modify Subcategories

New   Delete   Rename

OK   Cancel   Apply   Help

Line Styles Dialog Box

6. Create a new linestyle called Lineweight 2.

    Set the lineweight to 2.

7. Draw a line between the curb and the walkway.

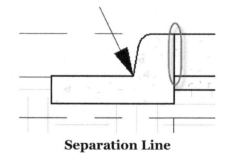

Separation Line

Adding the Block Walls

1. Open the Site Plan view.

2. Add two walls. Use these settings:

   Wall Type: Generic – 8" Masonry
   Base Constraint: 1ST FLOOR
   Base Offset: -0'-6"
   Top Constraint: Unconnected
   Unconnected Height: 6'-0"

3. Place the two walls along the west and north property lines.

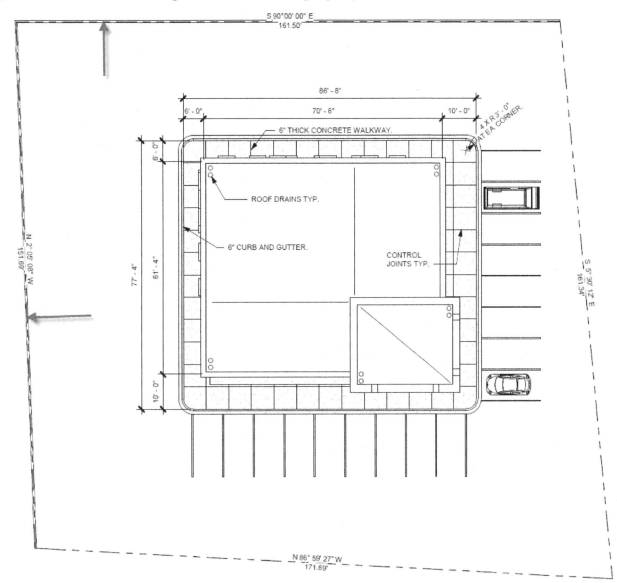

Masonry Walls Placed

Adding the Bollard Lights, Remaining People, 3D Address Text, and Exterior Wall Lights

1. Open the Site Plan view.

2. Load the Bollard Light family.

    The family is in the Lighting, Architectural, External folder.

3. Locate the six lights as shown.

    Add the note when finished.

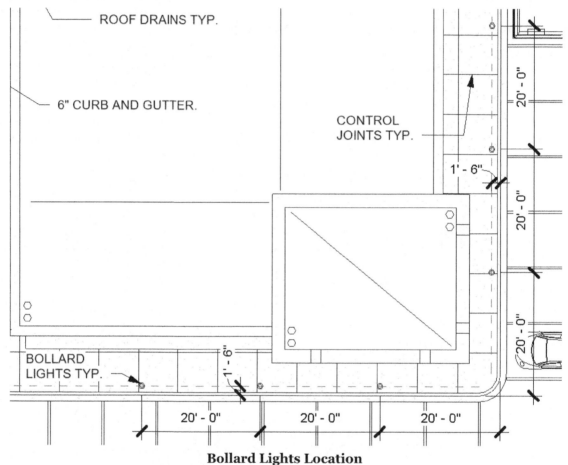

Bollard Lights Location

4. Add the three additional people on the sidewalk and near one of the cars.

5. Open the South Elevation view.

6. Zoom in to the upper right corner of the building.

7. Click on the Model Text tool in the Architecture tab, Model panel.

Set the work plane to the face of the tower wall.

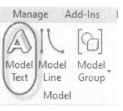

Model Text Tool

   a. Set height of the text to 36".
   b. You will need to create a new type.
   c. The font is Arial.
   d. The depth is 6"
   e. The Material is: Metal –Aluminum, Brushed.
   f. Position the text 4'-6" down and 3'-0" from the edge of the wall.

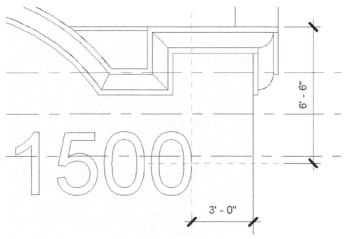

Model Text Placed

8. Place the text on the east wall in the same relative location.

9. Continue with the East Elevation view open.

Load the family: Wall Pack Light – Exterior. The family is in the Lighting, Architectural, External folder.

Note: If you receive an error message when placing the light, use the Wall Pack Light located in the Commercial Families folder.

10. Position the lights as shown. You may use a reference plane for the vertical location.

The dimensions are for reference only, delete/hide them when finished.

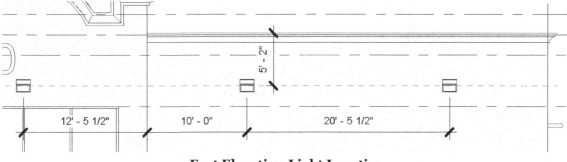

East Elevation Light Location

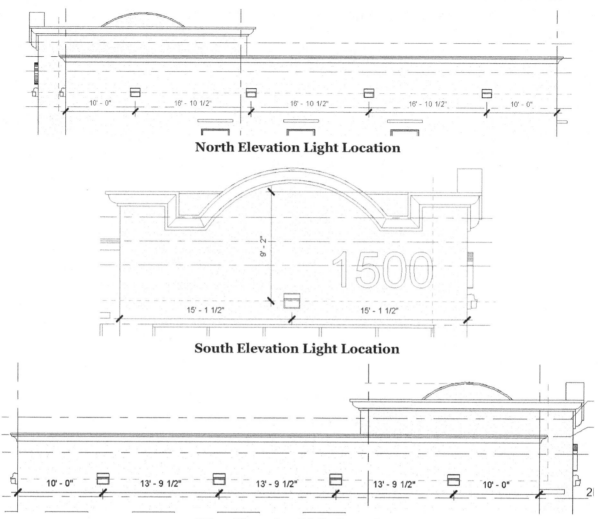

North Elevation Light Location

10' - 0"   16' - 10 1/2"   16' - 10 1/2"   16' - 10 1/2"   10' - 0"

9' - 2"

15' - 1 1/2"   15' - 1 1/2"

South Elevation Light Location

10' - 0"   13' - 9 1/2"   13' - 9 1/2"   13' - 9 1/2"   10' - 0"

West Elevation Light Location

11. This completes the building elements.

Exterior View

12. This is the end of Part 2. Save your file as CL7-2.

CL7-3   Setting Up the Camera Views

Setting Up the Exterior Camera View

1. Open the CL7-2 file, save the file as CL7-3.

2. Open the Site Plan view.

3. Start by creating a camera view for the exterior view.

4. Click on the 3D View tool in the View tab, Create panel.

   Select the Camera tool.

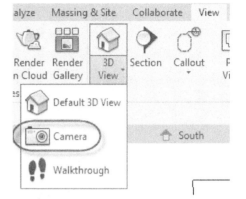

Camera Tool

5. Click a point for the camera and drag through the area.

Camera Location for Exterior View

6. A new 3D view opens of the exterior of the structure.

Initial Camera View of Exterior View

7. Adjust the shape of the crop window and the rotation of the view.

8. Turn on the shadow toggle and adjust the sun angle.

9. For this view the azimuth is set to 110° and the altitude is set to 45°. The Relative to View checkbox is unchecked.

Exterior View with Shadows

10. Name the view: Exterior View – Southeast Day

<u>Setting Up the Interior Camera Views</u>

1. Open the 1st Floor Plan – Furniture view.

2. Turn off any extra elements that are not needed for the view.

3. Add some people to the areas that you will be using for the camera views. You may need to turn on the category temporarily to see the people.

4. Zoom in on the Lobby/Cubicles area.

    Create a camera view for the First Floor Cubicle Area.

5. Click a point for the camera and
    drag through the area.

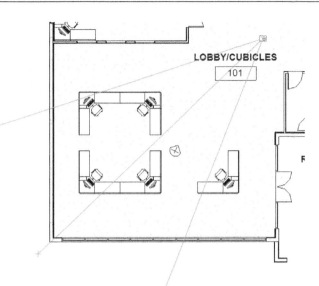

Camera Location

6. Adjust the window to
    match the example shown.

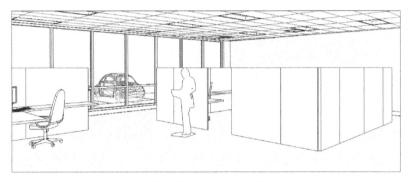

Cubicle Camera View

7. Name the view: First Floor Cubicles

8. Open the 2nd Floor view.

    Add a person to the conference room area.

9. Zoom in on the conference area.

    Create a camera view for the Conference Area.

10. Click a point for the camera and drag through
    the area.

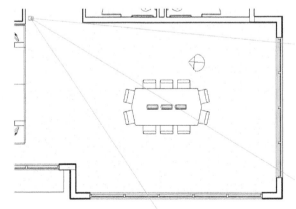

Camera Location

11. Adjust the window to match the
    example shown.

Conference Camera View

12. Name the view: Conference Area

13. Zoom in on the second floor cubicle area.

    Create a camera view for the Second Floor Cubicle and Hallway Area.

14. Click a point for the camera and drag through the
    area.

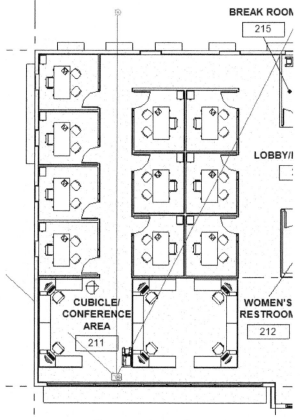

Camera Location

15. Adjust the window to match the example shown.

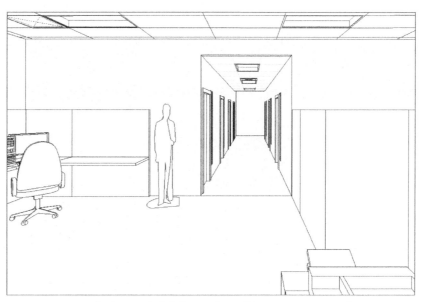

Second Floor Cubicle and Hallway Camera View

16. Name the view: Second Floor Cubicle and Hallway Area.

Setting Up the Section Camera View

1. For the section view, you will need to create a 3d section view. Duplicate the (3D) view.
2. Name the view: Section View
3. In the Properties dialog box, click the Section Box checkbox.
4. Drag the one of the Control Arrows into the building.
5. In the Rendering dialog box, set the background color to White.

   You may wish to rotate the view to drag the other arrows closer to the edge of the building.

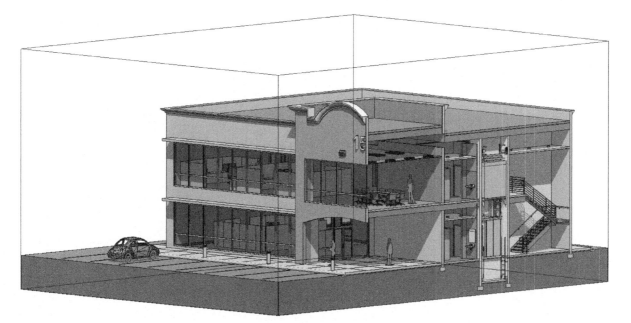

3D Section View

Setting Up the Exterior Night Camera View

1. Open the 3d View, Exterior View – Southeast Day.

2. Duplicate the view.

3. Rename the view: Exterior View – Southeast Night.

   Note: In the next tutorial part you will render the views.

4. These next few steps will have you make the surface of the sign self-illuminating.

   Open the default 3D view.

   Zoom in on the signage at the top corner of the building.

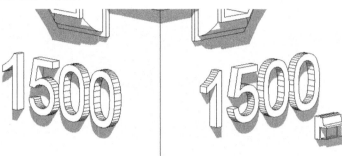

View of Signage

5. Click on Materials tool in the Manage tab, Settings panel.

   Click on the Create New Material option at the bottom left corner of the dialog box.

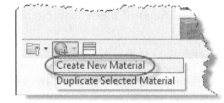

Create New Material

6. Name the new material: Sign Surface.

7. Click on the Appearance tab and then click the Self Illumination checkbox.

   Change the Filter Color to a color of your choice

Image Fade		100
Glossiness		50
Highlights	Non-Metallic	

Reflectivity

Transparency

Cutouts

✓ Self Illumination

     Filter Color   RGB 255 128 64

     Luminance   Dim Glow   10.00

     Color Temperature   Custom   6,500.00

Bump

Tint

               OK   Cancel   Apply

Self Illumination and Filter Color Set

8. Set the Surface Pattern to Solid Fill and Light Gray.

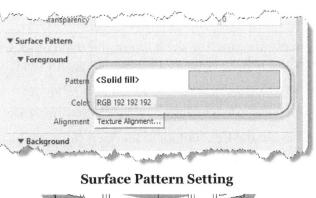

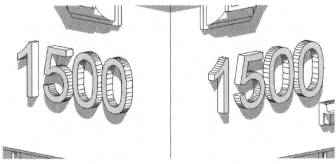

Surface Pattern Setting

9. Use the Paint tool to paint the surface of the sign.

   Select the front surface of each of the numbers in the sign.

Surface of Sign Numbers Painted

10. When you render the view, the numbers will be lighted.

11. This is the end of Part 3. Save your file as CL7-3.

CL7-4   Setting up the Sky Background

You may either use the sky background that comes with the software or use a custom image. This procedure will cover using a custom image for the background of your project.

1. Open the CL7-3 file, save the file as CL7-4.

2. Open the 3D view: Exterior View – Southeast Day.

3. Click on the Render tool in the View tab, Graphics panel.

Render Tool

4. In the Rendering dialog box, make the following changes:

    Quality Setting: Draft
    Lighting Scheme: Exterior: Sun only
    Background Style: Image

5. The Background Image dialog box will open.

Rendering Dialog Box

6. In the Background Image dialog box, click on the Image... button and select the Sky Background.jpg file from the website Families folder.

    Click the Width button to fit the image to the window.

Background Image   ?   X

D:\3 - Instant Revit Files\2 - Commercial Textbook\5 - Commercial Revit 2019 Files\   [Image...]

Scale
- ◯ Original Size
- ◯ Stretch
- ⦿ Width
- ◯ Height

Offset

Width: 0"

Height:

[OK]   [Cancel]

Background Image Dialog Box

7. Adjust the settings so that the background image is positioned correctly depending on the camera position for your project.

8. You must render the view to see the background image.

   It may take a few tries to position the image correctly.

9. To save the rendering to your file, click on the Save to Project... button.

   Save the rendering as: Exterior View – Southeast Day_1

   This will save the rendering to a new view category called: Renderings.

Rendered View

10. This is the end of Part 4. Save your file as CL7-4.

CL7-5   Rendering the Views

In this part, you will create the renderings for six views of the interior and exterior of the building.

There are two methods that you may use to create the renderings. The first method is to render the views using the Revit program and your computer. When using this method, you will use Medium for the quality settings. You may wish to set the quality to Draft when checking the materials and lighting. The rendered views do not need to match exactly with the examples. Use this chart for recommended rendering settings.

View Name	Lighting Scheme
Exterior View – South East Day	Exterior: Sun and Artificial
Exterior View – South East Night	Exterior: Artificial Only
Conference Area	Interior: Sun and Artificial
First Floor Cubicles	Interior: Sun and Artificial
Second Floor Cubicles and Hallway	Interior: Sun and Artificial
Section View East/West	Exterior: Sun and Artificial

Notes:

Rendering times can vary from a few minutes to an hour. To save time, you may use multiple computers (if available) to render the various views.

Rendering times may be shortened by reducing the number of lights that are turned on. This can be adjusted by using the Artificial Lights... button in the Rendering dialog box.

Once the rendering is complete, export the rendering as a separate file to your folder.

The second method is to use the Cloud Rendering website provided by Autodesk. This will allow you to render your project on their website rather than using your own computer. Not only is this method quicker (approx. 30 times faster) but it will not tie up your computer while your file is rendered.

To use this free service, you will need to have Autodesk Student Community account. If you do not have an account and are a current college or high school student, you may visit the Autodesk website to create one. If you are not a current student, you may sign up at the Autodesk Rendering site for a free trial.

Render in Cloud Tool

Once the renderings are complete you may insert the file onto a sheet either by dragging and dropping the rendering from your project browser or by inserting the file from the folder on your drive.

1. Open the 3D view: Exterior View – Southeast Day.

2. Before continuing, you will create a category for the 3D views to be rendered and the Design Option views.

   Click the Edit Type button in the Properties box.

3. Click the Duplicate... button to create a new view category.

   Name the new category, To Be Rendered.

4. Select the other views that you set up earlier and move them to this category.

5. Open one of the Design Options views.

   Create a new category called Design Options.

New 3D View Category

6. Open the Exterior View – Southeast Day view.

   Click on the Render in Cloud tool.

   Sign in to your account if needed.

7. The Render in Cloud dialog box opens.

   Note: If you are using the commercial version of the software, you will have a limited amount of Cloud Credits. The image below is from the student version of the software.

Opening Dialog Box   **Render in Cloud Settings**

8. Set the rendering settings in the dialog box.

   Depending on the Render Quality and Image Size settings, the number of credits will increase.

9. Click the Start Render button in the dialog box.

    The scene data will be downloaded to the Autodesk Rendering site.

    Click on the Continue in Background button to close the dialog box.

10. Click on the Render Gallery tool next to the Render in Cloud tool to open the Autodesk Rendering website and view the progress of the rendering.

11. In the Autodesk Rendering site, click on the project name and then the rendering to see the result.

Rendering Result in Autodesk 360 Site

12. Once the rendering is complete, click on the thumbnail to view a larger view.

    You may also re-render the view, create a panorama, stereo panorama, solar study, change the illuminance and turntable, adjust the exposure, download, and delete the file.

Rendering Tools on Webpage

13. For one of these views, you may create a Panorama. This will create a view that will enable panning around the room.

    For this rendering type it is best to place the camera in the center of the room.

Panorama Rendering Tool

Setting Up the Exterior View Night Rendering

1. Open the 3D view: Exterior View – Southeast Night.

    In the Rendering dialog box, make the following changes:

    Quality Setting: Draft
    Lighting Scheme: Exterior: Artificial only
    Background Style: Sky: No clouds

2. Click the Sun Settings... tool to open the Sun
    Settings dialog box.

Sun Settings... Tool

3. Set the time setting
    in the dialog box as
    shown.

    You may wish to
    choose a different
    location for your
    project.

Sun Settings Dialog Box

4. Render the view.

    If you are satisfied with the results, render the view using the Cloud Rendering service.

    Note: To save cloud credits, you may render the view in draft mode to check the settings.

5. Click on the down arrow at the lower right corner of the
    thumbnail.

    Choose Adjust Exposure to change the brightness of the interior
    lights.

    Adjust Exposure Tool

    An additional rendering will be created with the new settings.

Adjust Exposure Settings on Autodesk Rendering Site

6. Download the image to your local drive.

7. When setting up the rendering settings for the Section View, set the background setting to Color.

    Change the color to White.

Rendering the Remaining Views

1. Before rendering your views using the cloud, you will need to make a small change to the families for the people in your project.

    When using the Cloud Rendering service, the people families may appear doubled.

    Click on the entourage family element in the view and click the Edit Type button in the Properties window.

Doubled Entourage Family

2. In the Type Properties dialog box, click the Edit... button next to the Render Appearance Properties parameter.

Type Properties Dialog Box for RPC Family

3. In the Render Appearance Properties dialog box, uncheck the Cast Reflections checkbox.

You will need to do this on all the Entourage People families that you have used in your project.

Open each of your 3D views and check for other families that need to be changed. Each family only needs to be changed once.

Render Appearance Properties Dialog Box

4. You may render the remaining views
    all at once.

    Click the pull down in the 3D View
    section.

    Select the views that you wish to
    render.

    All of the renderings will use the same
    settings.

Rendering Multiple Views

5. Download the remaining renderings to your local drive.

    You may download the renderings as separate files or all at once. If you have downloaded the
    files all at once, they will be in the form as a zip file and in .png format.

6. This is the end of Part 5 and Tutorial 7. Save your file as CL7-5.

Tutorial 8   Assembling the Construction Documents and Portfolio

Part 1	Sheet A100	TITLE SHEET
Part 2	Sheet A101	SITE PLAN
Part 3	Sheet A102	SCHEDULES & CALLOUT VIEW
Part 4	Sheet A103	FIRST FLOOR PLAN
Part 5	Sheet A104	SECOND FLOOR PLAN
Part 6	Sheet A105	1ST FLOOR REFLECTED CLG. PLAN
Part 7	Sheet A106	2ND FLOOR REFLECTED CLG. PLAN
Part 8	Sheet A107	1ST & 2ND FLR. COLOR LEGENDS
Part 9	Sheet A108	1ST & 2ND FLR. FURN. PLANS
Part 10	Sheet A109	1ST & 2ND FLR. PATHS OF TRAVEL
Part 11	Sheet A201	EAST/NORTH ELEVATIONS
Part 12	Sheet A202	WEST/SOUTH ELEVATIONS
Part 13	Sheet A300	GENERAL NOTES (STRUCTURAL)
Part 14	Sheet A301	SECTIONS & INT. ELEVS.
Part 15	Sheet A302	LONG. & HALLWAY SECTS.
Part 16	Sheet A400	DESIGN OPTIONS
Part 17	Sheet A401	RENDERINGS
Part 18	Assembling the PDF Portfolio	

Note: All screenshots are from the Autodesk® Revit® software.

Starting the Tutorial

1. Open the drawing file from Tutorial 7 named CL7-5.

2. Save the file as CL8-1.

At this point you have finished creating the Model Elements and Renderings for the project. All that remains is to assemble these elements into a set of sheets.

Not all of the views have been created. You will need to create these as well.

Some of the views may not have all the dimensions and other annotations placed. These will be added in this tutorial. If you wish to check a high-resolution version of these files, a copy of the Commercial Portfolio is available on the website.

Note: The examples shown in this tutorial are versions of the sheets as they will look as you progress through the tutorials. As you create each sheet, the bubbles for the section, elevation, and callout views will fill in automatically. A completed version of the portfolio is available on the website.

Before beginning the process of setting up the sheets do the following:

1. Go to the Sheets category of the Project Browser.

    Delete any sheets that may have been created during the tutorials.

2. If you rendered the 3D views in low-resolution, re-render them in a high-resolution. Use the cloud rendering method to do this.

    Note: This may take quite some time, so it is a good idea to begin this process at the beginning of this tutorial.

3. You will load the modified version of the "C" Size Border located in the Custom Families folder on the website. The name of the file is C 18 x 24 Horizontal – Instant Revit!.rfa.

4. You will need to save the file at the end of each part. If this is using up too much space on your flash drive/hard drive, you may skip this step and save the file at the end of this tutorial.

CL8-1   Sheet A100 – TITLE SHEET

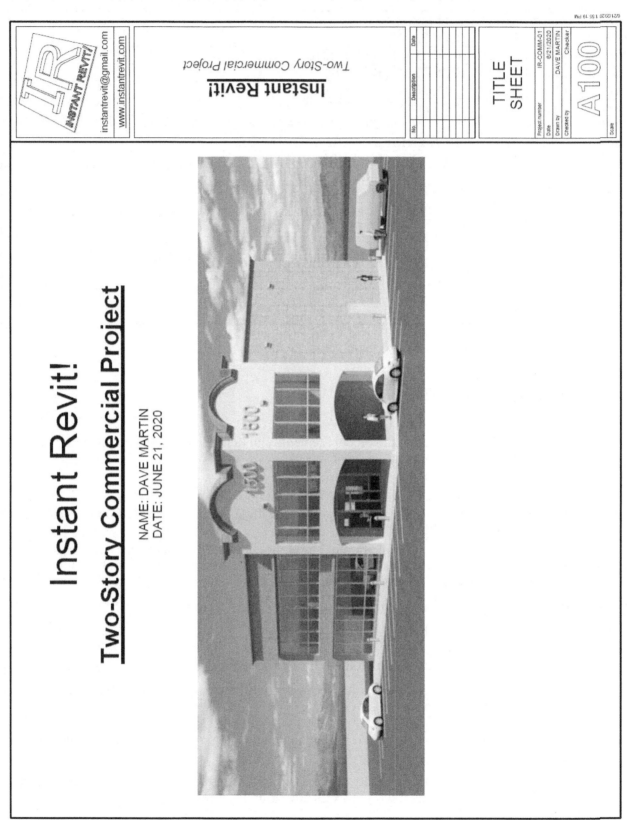

Title Sheet

1. Click on the Sheet tool in the View tab, Sheet Composition panel.

2. Begin by creating the first sheet in the set.

   Click on the Sheet tool in the View tab, Sheet Composition panel.

   Name the sheet A100 – Title Sheet.

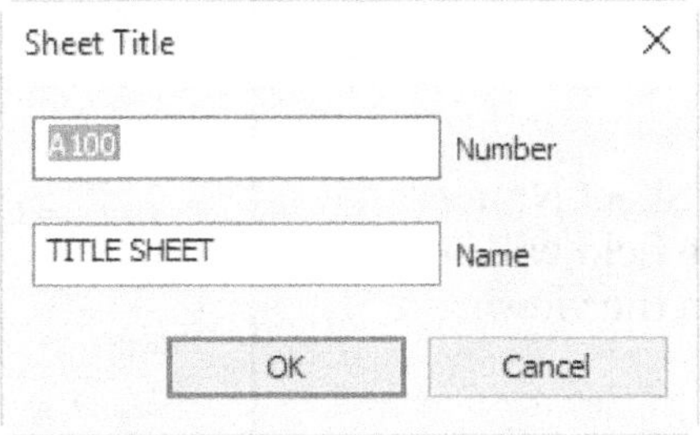

Sheet Title Dialog Box

3. The lineweight setting for the title block elements will need to be adjusted.

   Click on the Object Styles tool in the Manage tab, Settings panel. Click on the Annotation Objects tab and scroll to the Title Blocks category.

4. Expand the category and set the Wide Lines sub-category lineweight to 7.

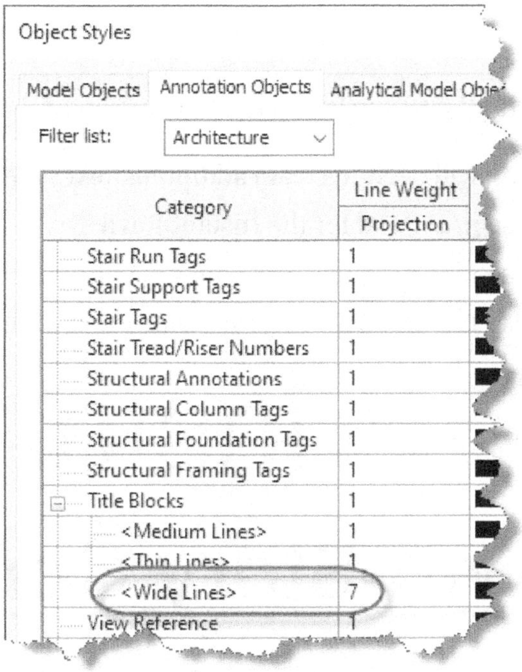

Wide Lines set to 7

5. Zoom in to the lower right corner of the sheet.

    Fill in the following information.

    Project number: IR-COMM-01

    Date: Date you complete the project.

    Drawn by: Your Name

    Note: The Sheet Number and Sheet Name are already filled out. The Scale field will be filled in automatically based on the view scale.

TITLE SHEET

Project number	IR-COMM-01
Date	6/21/2020
Drawn by	DAVE MARTIN
Checked by	Checker

A100

Scale	

6/21/2020 1:07:28 PM

Title Block Filled Out

6. Add the text below to the top portion of the sheet.

    You will need to create additional text types.

7. Use 3/4" Arial for the Instant Revit Text.

8. Use 1/2" Arial for the Commercial Project text.

9. Use 1/4" Arial for the Your Name and Date.

Instant Revit!

Two-Story Commercial Project

NAME: DAVE MARTIN
DATE: SEPTEMBER 15, 2019

Text for Title Sheet

10. At the end of the project you will create a Sheet Index and insert it onto this sheet.

    You will also insert the render of the exterior view of the project.

11. This is the end of Part 1. Save your file as CL8-1.

CL8-2   Sheet A101 – SITE PLAN

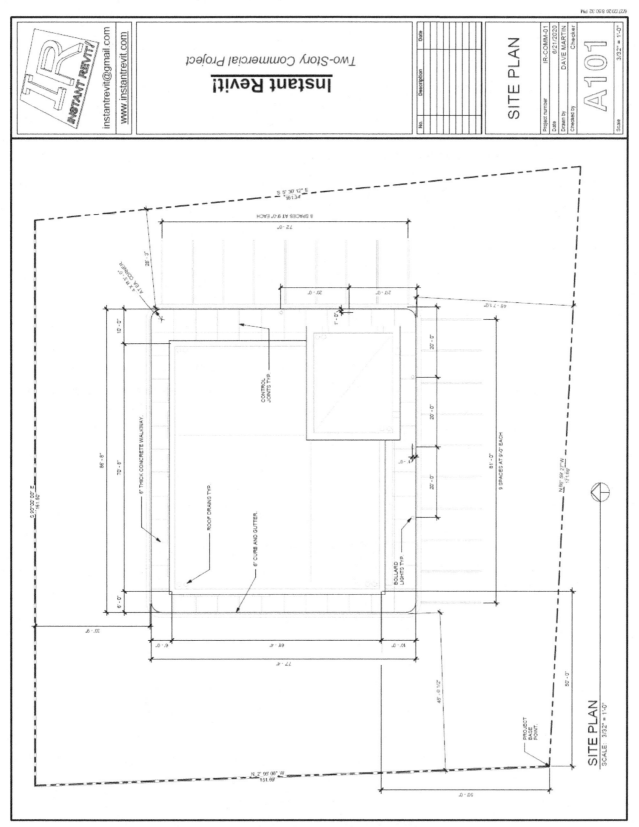

Site Plan Sheet

1. Open the CL8-1 file, save the file as CL8-2.

2. Create a sheet named A101 – SITE PLAN.

3. With the sheet open, drag and drop the Site Plan view from the Floor Plans category onto the sheet.

    a. The scale is of the view is 3/32" = 1'-0".
    b. You may need to crop the view to fit it within the border.
    c. This may be done in the original view or in the sheet view.
    d. To activate the view, double-click on the view in the sheet.
    e. Hide the cars and the people that are visible.
    f. Add and missing dimensions and notes.

4. Locate the dimensions 3/4" (8'-0" radius at scale) for the first dimension line and then offset 1/2" (5'-4" distance at scale) for the second.

    You may wish to add circles at the corners to aid with the spacing.

    Hide the circles after the dimensions are spaced properly.

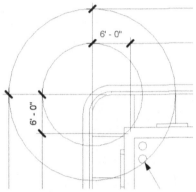

Circles Placed for Dimension Spacing.

5. Add a dimension for both sets of parking spaces.

72' - 0"

8 SPACES AT 9'-0" EACH

Parking Space Dimension

6. Update the name of the view to SITE PLAN in the Title on Sheet field in the Properties window.

    To access this field, select the view on the sheet.

Properties		✕
	Viewport Title w Line	
Viewports (1)		∨ ⊞ Edit Type
Associated Level	1ST FLOOR	
Scope Box	None	
Depth Clipping	No clip	
Identity Data		⊗
View Template	<None>	
View Name	Site Plan	
Dependency	Independent	
Title on Sheet	SITE PLAN	
Sheet Number	A101	
Sheet Name	SITE PLAN	
Referencing Sheet		
Referencing Detail		

View Name Changed to All Caps

7. Add a North Arrow to the sheet.

    Use the Symbol tool in the Annotate
    tab, Symbol panel to do this.

    Note: Add a North Arrow to all plan
    views.

North Arrow Added to Sheet

Modifying the View Title Family

This next section covers the modification of the view title family. You will be changing the text of
the title to 1/4" and remove the number and the circle.

1. In the Families category in the Project Browser, expand
    the Annotation Symbols area.

    Then, right-click on the View Title family and select the
    Edit text.

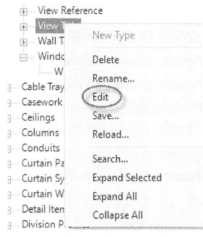

Editing the Family

2. The family file opens. Save the file as View Title – Larger Text.rfa in your drawing folder

3. Click on the View Title text.

    Click on the Edit type button and
    duplicate the family type. Name it:
    Label 1/4".

    Change the Text Size parameter to 1/4".

Family Type Created and Text Size Changed

4. Click on the text and stretch it to make it wider.

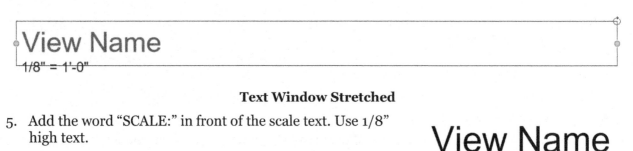

Text Window Stretched

5. Add the word "SCALE:" in front of the scale text. Use 1/8" high text.

    Note: Be careful not to move the original text up or down this will change the relative text location to the line that divides the text labels.

6. Save the family file and then load it into your project.

7. Open your file and zoom in on the view title on the A-1 sheet.

8. Click on the view title and then the Edit Type button in the Properties box.

    Duplicate the Type.
    Name it Title w Line – Plan Views.

    Change the Title parameter to View Title – Larger Text.

    Use this type for the plan views on all future views.

Family Updated

Title w Line Family Type Changed

9. The view title is updated.

View Title Updated

Completing the Sheet

1. The crop window may be left on or turned off. The window will not plot when creating the portfolio.

2. Add in the Project Base Point note at the bottom left corner of the property line boundary.

   Add dimensions from the base point to the lower left corner of the building.

   Note: You do not need to hide the base point or survey point. These elements do not print.

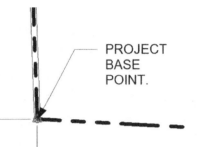

PROJECT
BASE
POINT.

Project Base point

3. Add four dimensions for the set back of the building to the property line.

   The dimensions are perpendicular to the angle of the property lines to the corner of the curb.

4. To make the edges of the concrete walkway stand out, open the Visibility/Graphics Overrides dialog change the Floor lineweight in the Model Categories tab to 5.

Floors Lineweight set to 5

5. You may also wish to increase the lineweight of the edge of the building to Wide Lines.

   Use the Linework tool in the Modify tab, View panel to do this.

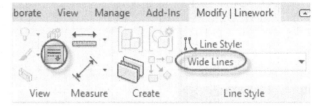

Linework Tool

   You may also draw Detail Lines on top of lines that will not change when using the Linework tool.

6. This is the end of Part 2. Save your file as CL8-2.

CL8-3   Sheet A102 – SCHEDULES & CALLOUT VIEW

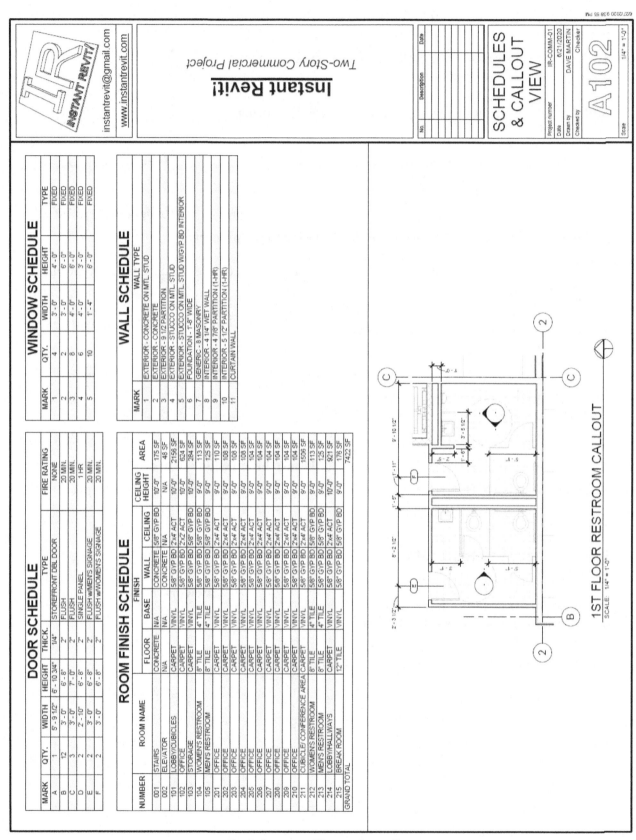

WINDOW SCHEDULE

MARK	QTY.	WIDTH	HEIGHT	TYPE
1	4	3' - 0"	4' - 0"	FIXED
2	2	3' - 0"	6' - 0"	FIXED
3	8	4' - 0"	6' - 0"	FIXED
4	6	1' - 4"	3' - 0"	FIXED
5	10	4' - 0"	6' - 0"	FIXED

WALL SCHEDULE

MARK	WALL TYPE
1	EXTERIOR - CONCRETE ON MTL. STUD
2	EXTERIOR - CONCRETE
3	EXTERIOR - 9 1/2 PARTITION
4	EXTERIOR - STUCCO ON MTL. STUD
5	EXTERIOR - STUCCO ON MTL. STUD W/GYP BD INTERIOR
6	FOUNDATION - 1'-8" WIDE
7	GENERIC - 8 MASONRY
8	INTERIOR - 4 1/4" WET WALL
9	INTERIOR - 4 7/8" PARTITION (1-HR)
10	INTERIOR - 5 1/2" PARTITION (1-HR)
11	CURTAIN WALL

DOOR SCHEDULE

MARK	QTY.	WIDTH	HEIGHT	THICK.	TYPE	FIRE RATING
A	1	5' - 9 1/2"	6' - 10 3/4"	1/4"	STOREFRONT DBL DOOR	NONE
B	12	3'-0"	6' - 8"	2"	FLUSH	20 MIN.
C	3	3'-0"	7' - 0"	2"	FLUSH	20 MIN.
D	2	2' - 10"	6' - 8"	2"	SINGLE PANEL	1-HR
E	2	3' - 0"	6' - 8"	2"	FLUSH w/MEN'S SIGNAGE	20 MIN.
F	2	3' - 0"	6' - 8"	2"	FLUSH w/WOMEN'S SIGNAGE	20 MIN.

ROOM FINISH SCHEDULE

NUMBER	ROOM NAME	FLOOR	BASE	WALL	CEILING	CEILING HEIGHT	AREA
001	STAIRS	CONCRETE	N/A	CONCRETE	5/8" GYP BD	10'-0"	175 SF
002	ELEVATOR	N/A	N/A	CONCRETE	N/A	N/A	48 SF
101	LOBBY/CUBICLES	CARPET	VINYL	5/8" GYP BD	2x4 ACT	10'-0"	2156 SF
102	OFFICE	CARPET	VINYL	5/8" GYP BD	2x2 ACT	10'-0"	624 SF
103	STORAGE	CARPET	VINYL	5/8" GYP BD	5/8" GYP BD	10'-0"	284 SF
104	WOMEN'S RESTROOM	8" TILE	4" TILE	5/8" GYP BD	5/8" GYP BD	9'-0"	113 SF
105	MEN'S RESTROOM	8" TILE	4" TILE	5/8" GYP BD	5/8" GYP BD	9'-0"	125 SF
201	OFFICE	CARPET	VINYL	5/8" GYP BD	2x4 ACT	9'-0"	110 SF
202	OFFICE	CARPET	VINYL	5/8" GYP BD	2x4 ACT	9'-0"	108 SF
203	OFFICE	CARPET	VINYL	5/8" GYP BD	2x4 ACT	9'-0"	108 SF
204	OFFICE	CARPET	VINYL	5/8" GYP BD	2x4 ACT	9'-0"	108 SF
205	OFFICE	CARPET	VINYL	5/8" GYP BD	2x4 ACT	9'-0"	104 SF
206	OFFICE	CARPET	VINYL	5/8" GYP BD	2x4 ACT	9'-0"	104 SF
207	OFFICE	CARPET	VINYL	5/8" GYP BD	2x4 ACT	9'-0"	104 SF
208	OFFICE	CARPET	VINYL	5/8" GYP BD	2x4 ACT	9'-0"	104 SF
209	OFFICE	CARPET	VINYL	5/8" GYP BD	2x4 ACT	9'-0"	104 SF
210	OFFICE	CARPET	VINYL	5/8" GYP BD	2x4 ACT	9'-0"	104 SF
211	CUBICLE/ CONFERENCE AREA	CARPET	VINYL	5/8" GYP BD	2x4 ACT	9'-0"	1506 SF
212	WOMEN'S RESTROOM	8" TILE	4" TILE	5/8" GYP BD	5/8" GYP BD	9'-0"	113 SF
213	MEN'S RESTROOM	8" TILE	4" TILE	5/8" GYP BD	5/8" GYP BD	9'-0"	125 SF
214	LOBBY/HALLWAYS	CARPET	VINYL	5/8" GYP BD	2x4 ACT	10'-0"	921 SF
215	BREAK ROOM	12" TILE	VINYL	5/8" GYP BD	5/8" GYP BD	9'-0"	176 SF
GRAND TOTAL							7422 SF

Title Block:

Instant Revit!
Two-Story Commercial Project
instantrevit@gmail.com
www.instantrevit.com

SCHEDULES & CALLOUT VIEW

Project number	IR-COMM-01
Date	6/21/2020
Drawn by	DAVE MARTIN
Checked by	Checker
Scale	1/4" = 1'-0"

A102

1ST FLOOR RESTROOM CALLOUT
SCALE 1/4" = 1'-0"

Schedules & Callout View Sheet

Inserting the Callout View

1. Open the CL8-2 file, save the file as CL8-3.

2. Create a sheet named A102 – SCHEDULES & CALLOUT VIEW.

3. Open the 1st FLOOR – Callout 1 view.

4. Add the remaining dimensions and the circles for the wheelchair onto the views. The diameter of the circles is 60".

   You may need to adjust some of the features to match the dimensioning.

   The view bubble will fill out when the interior elevations of the restroom are added to the sheets.

5. With the sheet open, drag and drop the callout view of the restrooms from the Floor Plans category onto the bottom of the sheet.

   The scale is 1/4" = 1'-0".

   Set the title on sheet to, 1ST FLOOR RESTROOM CALLOUT.

6. Add a line using the Detail Line tool that divides the sheet into two parts.

Inserting the Schedules

1. With the A102 sheet still open; drag and drop the Door Schedule, Window Schedule, Room Finish Schedule, and Wall Schedule onto the sheet.

2. Re-size the width of the schedule columns to make the lines of the schedules one line high.

DOOR SCHEDULE

MARK	QTY.	WIDTH	HEIGHT	THICK.	TYPE	FIRE RATING
A	1	5' - 9 1/2"	6' - 10 3/4"	1/4"	STOREFRONT DBL DOOR	NONE
B	12	3' - 0"	6' - 8"	2"	FLUSH	20 MIN.
C	3	3' - 0"	7' - 0"	2"	FLUSH	20 MIN.
D	2	2' - 10"	6' - 8"	2"	SINGLE PANEL	1 HR
E	2	3' - 0"	6' - 8"	2"	FLUSH w/MEN'S SIGNAGE	20 MIN.
F	2	3' - 0"	6' - 8"	2"	FLUSH w/WOMEN'S SIGNAGE	20 MIN.

WINDOW SCHEDULE

MARK	QTY.	WIDTH	HEIGHT	TYPE
1	4	3' - 0"	4' - 0"	FIXED
2	2	3' - 0"	6' - 0"	FIXED
3	8	4' - 0"	6' - 0"	FIXED
4	6	4' - 0"	3' - 0"	FIXED
5	10	1' - 4"	6' - 0"	FIXED

WALL SCHEDULE

MARK	WALL TYPE
1	EXTERIOR - CONCRETE ON MTL. STUD
2	EXTERIOR - CONCRETE
3	EXTERIOR - 9 1/2 PARTITION
4	EXTERIOR - STUCCO ON MTL. STUD
5	EXTERIOR - STUCCO ON MTL. STUD W/GYP BD INTERIOR
6	FOUNDATION - 1'-8" WIDE
7	GENERIC - 8 MASONRY
8	INTERIOR - 4 1/4" WET WALL
9	INTERIOR - 4 7/8" PARTITION (1-HR)
10	INTERIOR - 5 1/2" PARTITION (1-HR)
11	CURTAIN WALL

Door, Window, and Wall Schedules

ROOM FINISH SCHEDULE

NUMBER	ROOM NAME	FINISH				CEILING HEIGHT	AREA
		FLOOR	BASE	WALL	CEILING		
001	STAIRS	CONCRETE	N/A	CONCRETE	5/8" GYP BD	10'-0"	175 SF
002	ELEVATOR	N/A	N/A	CONCRETE	N/A	N/A	48 SF
101	LOBBY/CUBICLES	CARPET	VINYL	5/8" GYP BD	2'x4' ACT	10'-0"	2156 SF
102	OFFICE	CARPET	VINYL	5/8" GYP BD	2'x2' ACT	10'-0"	624 SF
103	STORAGE	CARPET	VINYL	5/8" GYP BD	5/8" GYP BD	10'-0"	284 SF
104	WOMEN'S RESTROOM	8" TILE	4" TILE	5/8" GYP BD	5/8" GYP BD	9'-0"	113 SF
105	MEN'S RESTROOM	8" TILE	4" TILE	5/8" GYP BD	5/8" GYP BD	9'-0"	125 SF
201	OFFICE	CARPET	VINYL	5/8" GYP BD	2'x4' ACT	9'-0"	110 SF
202	OFFICE	CARPET	VINYL	5/8" GYP BD	2'x4' ACT	9'-0"	108 SF
203	OFFICE	CARPET	VINYL	5/8" GYP BD	2'x4' ACT	9'-0"	108 SF
204	OFFICE	CARPET	VINYL	5/8" GYP BD	2'x4' ACT	9'-0"	108 SF
205	OFFICE	CARPET	VINYL	5/8" GYP BD	2'x4' ACT	9'-0"	104 SF
206	OFFICE	CARPET	VINYL	5/8" GYP BD	2'x4' ACT	9'-0"	104 SF
207	OFFICE	CARPET	VINYL	5/8" GYP BD	2'x4' ACT	9'-0"	104 SF
208	OFFICE	CARPET	VINYL	5/8" GYP BD	2'x4' ACT	9'-0"	104 SF
209	OFFICE	CARPET	VINYL	5/8" GYP BD	2'x4' ACT	9'-0"	104 SF
210	OFFICE	CARPET	VINYL	5/8" GYP BD	2'x4' ACT	9'-0"	104 SF
211	CUBICLE/ CONFERENCE AREA	CARPET	VINYL	5/8" GYP BD	2'x4' ACT	9'-0"	1506 SF
212	WOMEN'S RESTROOM	8" TILE	4" TILE	5/8" GYP BD	5/8" GYP BD	9'-0"	113 SF
213	MEN'S RESTROOM	8" TILE	4" TILE	5/8" GYP BD	5/8" GYP BD	9'-0"	125 SF
214	LOBBY/HALLWAYS	CARPET	VINYL	5/8" GYP BD	2'x4' ACT	10'-0"	921 SF
215	BREAK ROOM	12" TILE	VINYL	5/8" GYP BD	5/8" GYP BD	9'-0"	176 SF
GRAND TOTAL							7422 SF

Room Finish Schedule

3. This is the end of Part 3. Save your file as CL8-3.

CL8-4   Sheet A103 – FIRST FLOOR PLAN

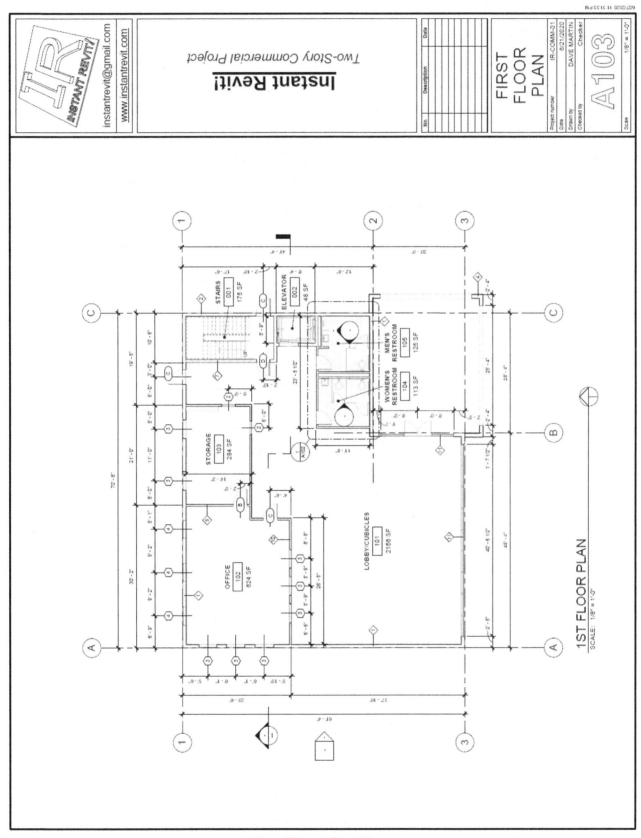

First Floor Plan Sheet

1. Open the CL8-3 file, save the file as CL8-4.

2. Create a sheet named A102 – FIRST FLOOR PLAN.

3. Open the 1ST FLOOR view.

4. Crop the view, add any missing dimensions, and hide any elements that should not be on the sheet.

    If some of the elements are not in the correct location, move them to the location based on the example.

    Note: You may have lost the grid lines when setting up the other views, if this has happened switch to one of the elevation views.

    Right click on the vertical grid line and select Maximize 3D Extents. This will reset the grid line in the plan views.

Maximize 3D Extents

5. If the window and door tags do not mask the extension lines; delete them, drag the extension line to the desired location, and re-tag the door or window.

6. With the sheet open, drag and drop the view from the Floor Plans category onto the sheet.

    The scale is 1/8" = 1'-0".

7. This is the end of Part 4. Save your file as CL8-4.

CL8-5   Sheet A104 – SECOND FLOOR PLAN

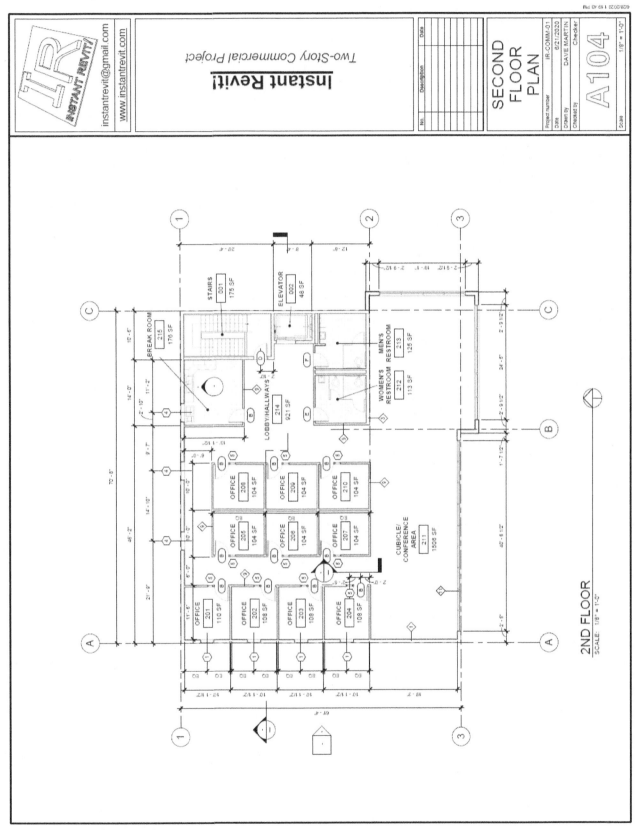

Second Floor Plan Sheet

1. Open the CL8-4 file, save the file as CL8-5.

2. Create a sheet named A104 – SECOND FLOOR PLAN.

3. Open the 2ND FLOOR view.

4. Crop the view, add any missing dimensions, and hide any elements that should not be on the sheet.

5. Drag and drop the view onto your sheet.

    The scale is 1/8" = 1'-0".

6. This is the end of Part 5. Save your file as CL8-5.

CL8-6   Sheet A105 – 1ST FLOOR REFLECTED CLG. PLN.

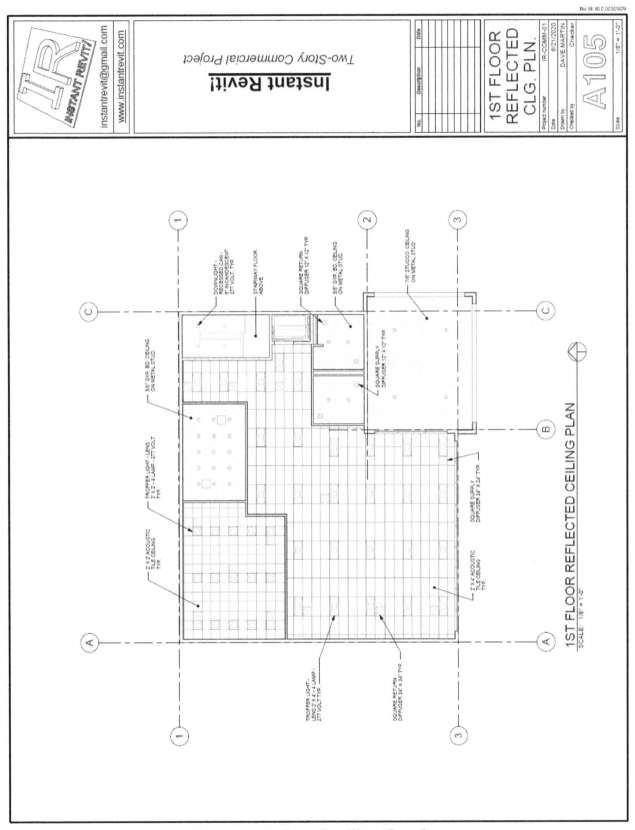

First Floor Reflected Ceiling Plan Sheet

1. Open the CL8-5 file, save the file as CL8-6.

2. Create a sheet named A105 – 1ST FLOOR REFLECTED CLG. PLN.
   (First Floor Reflected Ceiling Plan)

3. Open the 1ST FLOOR view in the Ceiling Plans view category.

4. Crop the view, add any missing dimensions, and hide any elements that should not be on the sheet.

5. Change the ceiling tile material for both ceiling types to light gray.

6. Turn off the eyebrows and the exterior lights.

7. Add the notes for the interior lights, diffusers, registers, and ceiling tiles and materials.

   Use 3/32" inch text for the notes. You will need to create another text style.

   If you have difficulty reading the notes, refer to the portfolio on the website for a better view.

   Note: Later, in Appendix B you will have the option of changing the text notes into keynotes.

8. Add an additional ceiling for the tower wall area, use these materials for the ceiling.

   Name the new ceiling type: 7/8" Stucco/Plaster on Mtl. Stud.

   Place the ceiling around the inside edge of the tower walls at 11'-3" above the first floor.

Edit Assembly				✕
Family:	Compound Ceiling			
Type:	7/8" Stucco/Plaster on Mtl. Stud			
Total thickness:	0' 4 5/8"			
Resistance (R):	21.1605 (h·ft²·°F)/BTU			
Thermal Mass:	1.1744 BTU/°F			

Layers

	Function	Material	Thickness	Wraps
1	Core Boundary	Layers Above Wr	0' 0"	
2	Structure [1]	Metal Stud Laye	0' 3 5/8"	
3	Core Boundary	Layers Below Wr	0' 0"	
4	Substrate [2]	Metal Lath	0' 0 1/8"	
5	Finish 2 [5]	Stucco	0' 0 7/8"	

Tower Walls Ceiling Type

9. Add four lights to the tower wall ceiling. Use the 8" Recessed Can 270 volt light. Layout the lights using reference planes as shown.

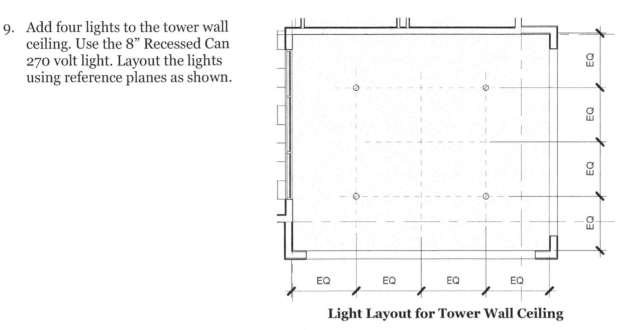

Light Layout for Tower Wall Ceiling

10. Drag and drop the view onto your sheet.

    The scale is 1/8" = 1'-0".

11. Click on the view of the plan in the sheet.

    Fill in the sheet title in the properties for the view.

    Name the sheet, 1ST FLOOR REFLECTED CEILING PLAN

12. This is the end of Part 6. Save your file as CL8-6.

CL8-7   Sheet A106 – 2ND FLOOR REFLECTED CLG. PLN.

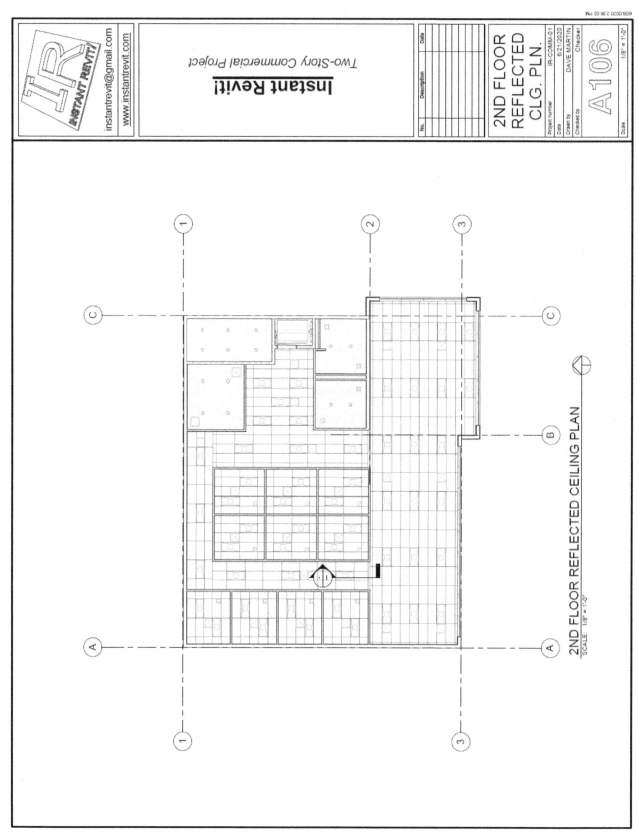

Second Floor Reflected Ceiling Plan Sheet

1. Open the CL8-6 file, save the file as CL8-7.

2. Create a sheet named A106 – 2ND FLOOR REFLECTED CLG. PLN.

3. Open the 2ND FLOOR view in the Ceiling Plans view category.

4. Crop the view and hide any elements that should not be on the sheet.

5. Turn off the eyebrows and the exterior lights.

6. Drag and drop the view onto your sheet.

   The scale is 1/8" = 1'-0".

7. Fill in the sheet title in the properties for the view.

8. This is the end of Part 7. Save your file as CL8-7.

CL8-8   Sheet A107 – 1ST & 2ND FLR. COLOR LEGENDS

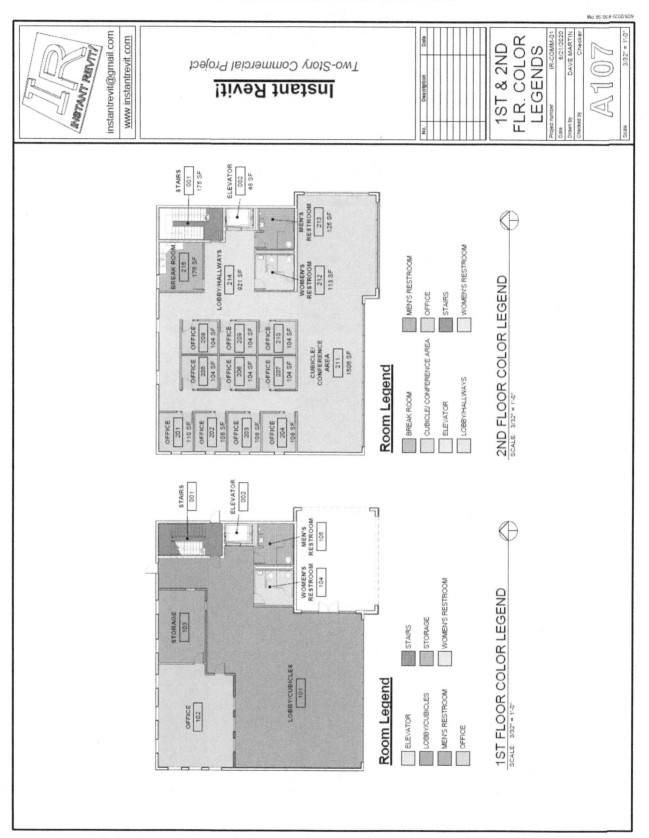

First and Second Floor Color Legends Sheet

1. Open the CL8-7 file, save the file as CL8-8.

2. Create a sheet named A107 – 1ST & 2ND FLR. COLOR LEGENDS

3. Open the 1ST FLOOR – Color Legend view.

Stair Path Tool

   Crop the view and hide any elements that should not be on the sheet.

   Add the stair path symbol.

   The tool is in the Annotate tab, Symbol panel.

4. Open the 2ND FLOOR – Color Legend view.

   Crop the view and hide any elements that should not be on the sheet.

5. Drag and drop the views onto your sheet.

   The scale for each view is 3/32" = 1'-0".

6. Rename the views

7. Align the views so that they are lined up horizontally.

8. The room legends for each view may not be lined up.

   Use the Guide Grid tool to line them up.

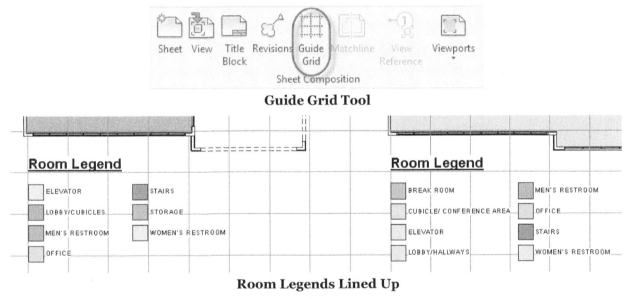

Guide Grid Tool

Room Legends Lined Up

9. You may hide the guide grid after aligning the legends.

10. This is the end of Part 8. Save your file as CL8-8.

CL8-9   Sheet A108 – 1ST & 2ND FLR. FURN. PLANS

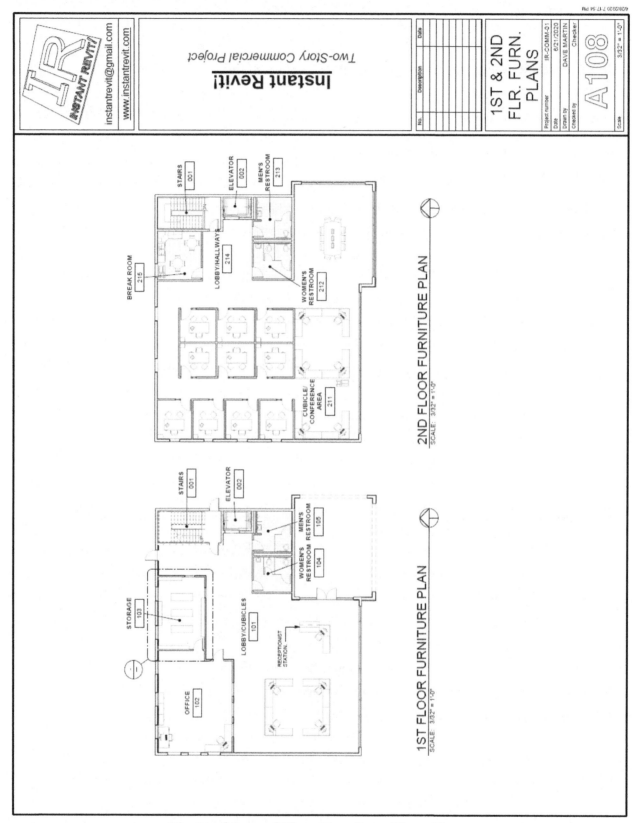

First and Second Floor Furniture Plans Sheet

1. Open the CL8-8 file, save the file as CL8-9.

2. Create a sheet named A108 – 1ST & 2ND FLR. FURN. PLANS
   (First and Second Floor Furniture Plans)

3. Open the 1ST FLOOR – Furniture Plan view.

   Crop the view and hide any elements that should not be on the sheet. Add the stair path symbol.

4. Add the callout for the storage room (103).

   You will place the callout view on another sheet.

5. Label the receptionist station.

6. Open the 2ND FLOOR – Furniture Plan view.

   Crop the view and hide any elements that should not be on the sheet. Add the stair path symbol.

7. Drag and drop the views onto your sheet.

   The scale for each view is 3/32" = 1'-0".

8. Align the views so that they are lined up horizontally.

9. Rename the views.

10. This is the end of Part 9. Save your file as CL8-9.

CL8-10   Sheet A109 – 1ST & 2ND FLR. PATHS OF TRAVEL

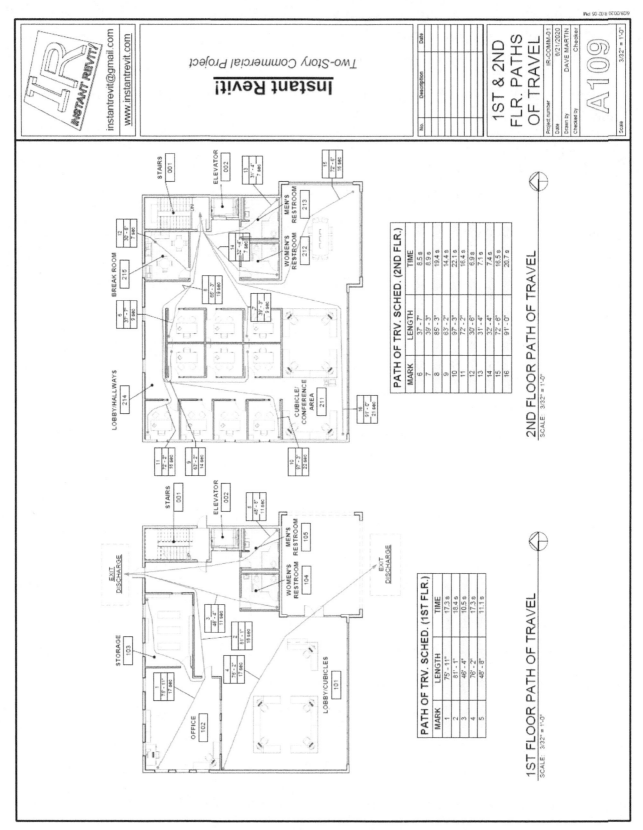

First and Second Floor Paths of Travel Sheet

1. Open the CL8-9 file, save the file as CL8-10.

2. Create a sheet named A109 – 1ST & 2ND FLR. PATHS OF TRAVEL

3. Open the 1ST FLOOR – Path of Travel view.

   Crop the view and hide any elements that should not be on the sheet. Add the stair path symbol.

4. Open the 2ND FLOOR – Path of Travel Plan view.

   Crop the view and hide any elements that should not be on the sheet. Add the stair path symbol.

5. Drag and drop the views onto your sheet.

   The scale for each view is 3/32" = 1'-0".

6. Align the views so that they are lined up horizontally.

7. Rename the views.

8. Open each path of travel schedule and change the size of the title text to 3/16".

9. Drag and drop the Path of Travel Schedule for each floor onto the sheet below the corresponding view.

10. This is the end of Part 10. Save your file as CL8-10.

CL8-11   Sheet A201 – EAST/NORTH ELEVATIONS

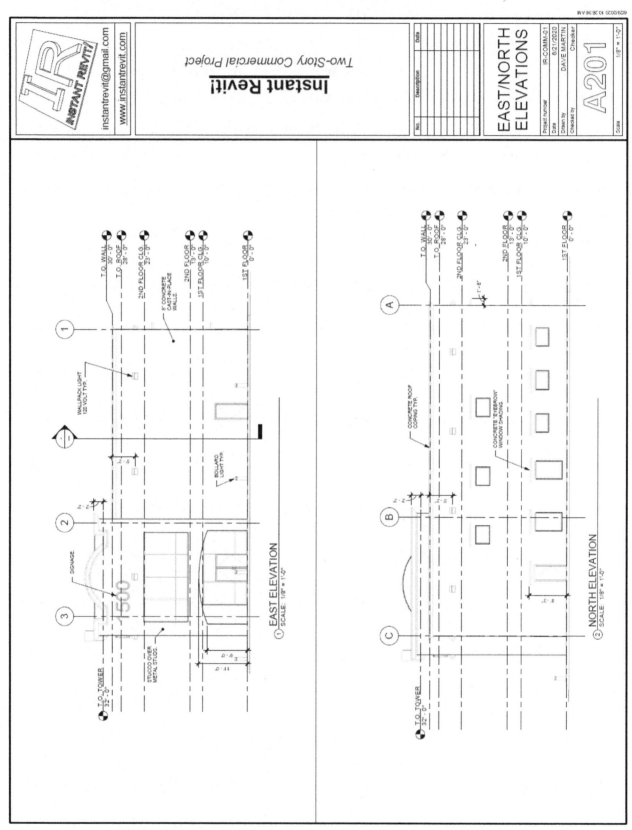

East/North Elevations Sheet

1. Open the CL8-10 file, save the file as CL8-11.

2. Create a sheet named A201 – EAST/NORTH ELEVATIONS

3. Open the East elevation view.

    Turn on the crop window if needed. Crop the view to the bottom of the concrete walkway. The sides of the crop window will be to the edge of the concrete walkway.

4. Hide the block wall in the background, vehicles, people, and parking spaces.

5. Add the additional notes and dimensions. When dimensioning the main entry in the east elevation, you may need to add reference planes at the endpoint of the left edge and the midpoint of the arch.

6. Add a medium line to divide the sheet in half.

7. Increase the wall and floor edges to a line weight of 5.

    Note: This change is specific to the individual view. You will need to do this for each elevation view.

Wall Edge Lineweight Increased

8. Open the North elevation view. Modify the view as needed.

9. Drag and drop the views onto your sheet.

    The scale for each view is 1/8" = 1'-0".

10. Create a new View Title family.

    Change the text size to 3/16" high and add the word SCALE: in front of the scale parameter.
    Name the family, View Title – 3-16 Text.rfa.
    Save the file with your drawing files.

New View Title Family

11. Fill in the sheet title in the properties for the views.

12. This is the end of Part 11. Save your file as CL8-11.

CL8-12   Sheet A202 – WEST/SOUTH ELEVATIONS

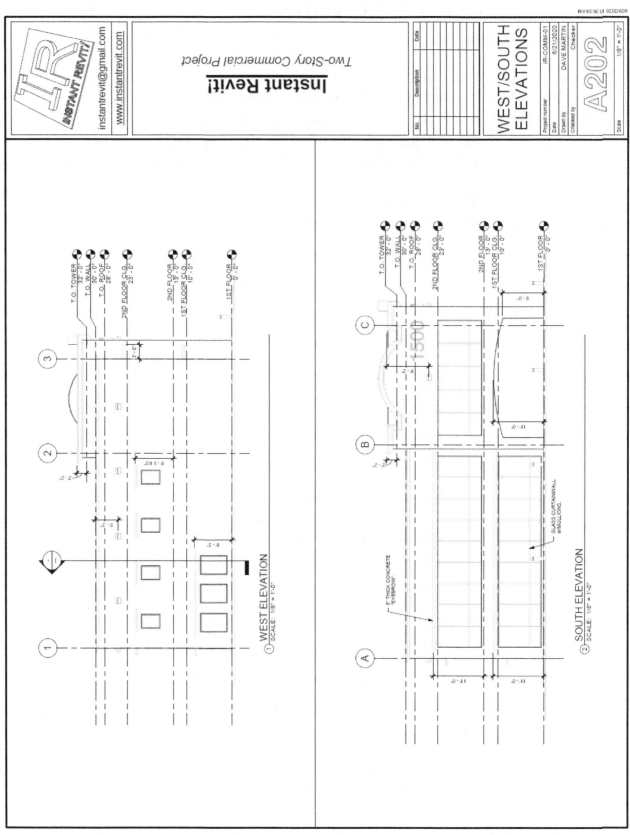

West/South Elevations Sheet

1. Open the CL8-11 file, save the file as CL8-12.

2. Create a sheet named A202 – WEST/SOUTH ELEVATIONS

3. Open the West elevation view. Modify the view as needed.

4. Open the South elevation view. Modify the view as needed.

5. Drag and drop the views onto your sheet.

   The scale for each view is 1/8" = 1'-0".

6. Change the lineweights for the walls and floors in each view.

7. Fill in the sheet information in the properties for the sheet.

8. This is the end of Part 12. Save your file as CL8-12.

CL8-13   Sheet A300 – GENERAL NOTES (STRUCTURAL)

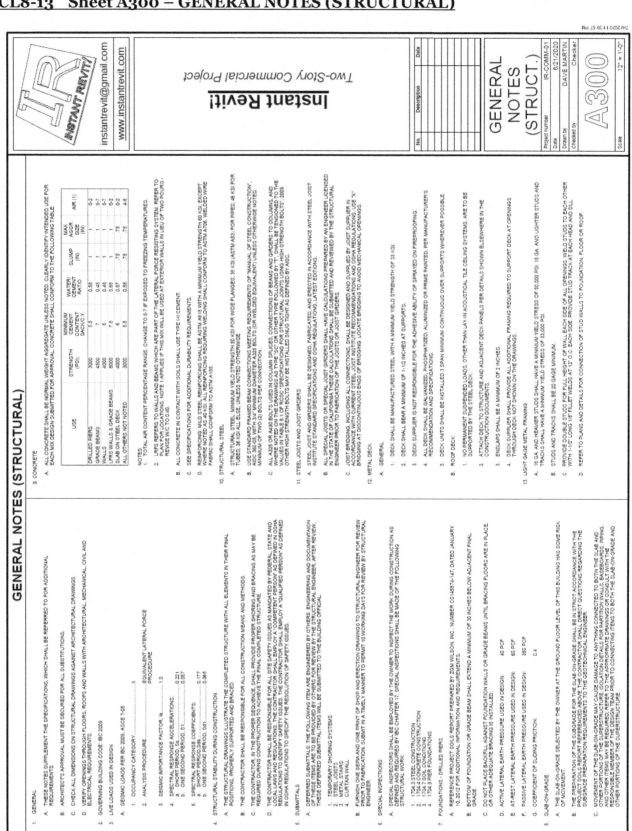

General Notes (Structural) Sheet

1. Open the CL8-12 file, save the file as CL8-13.

2. Create a sheet named A300 – GENERAL NOTES (STRUCT.)

3. In the View tab, click on the Legends dropdown and select the Legend tool.

   This tool will be used to create two text blocks that will be placed on the sheet.

Legend Tool

4. Name the first text block, GENERAL NOTES -1.

   The scale for the notes will be 12" = 1'-0".

New Legend View

5. An .rtf file has been created with the required text. The file is located in the custom families folder. Open the file called GENERAL NOTES.rtf.

   This file may be opened in Microsoft Word or another program.

6. Within this file select the text from Note #1 through Note #8 and copy it to the clipboard.

7. Open the GENERAL NOTES – 1 legend and create a text box using the Text tool.

   Use the Text, 3/32" size and set the alignment to Top Align and Align Left.

8. Select the first line and change it to a numbered note.

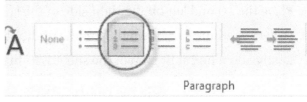

List:Numbers Tool

9. For the next section, select the notes lettered A-D.

   Backspace through the original letters and backspace through the extra letters between each note.

1.	GENERAL
	A. THESE N
	REQUIRE
	B. ARCHITE
	C. CHECK A
	D. VERIFY C
	ELECTRI(
2.	GOVERNING BUI|

Extra Letters Removed

1.	1. GENERAL
	A. A. THESE N(
	B. B. ARCHITE(
	C. C. CHECK A|
	D. D. VERIFY O
2. GOVERNING BUILDIN(	

Letters Added

10. After completing the first page of notes, go back to the top and add a line between each note and sub-section.

    Do this by placing your cursor at the end of the note and then holding the Shift key and pressing the Enter key.

11. When formatting the second section, you will need to create a table for Note #9.

    Refer to the table below for the row and column sizes.

	2 3/16"	1 1/16"	1 1/16"	7/8"	3/4"	3/4"	3/4"
USE	STRENGTH (PSI)	MINIMUM CEMENT CONTENT SACK/C.Y.	WATER/ CEMENT RATIO	SLUMP (IN)	MAX AGGR SIZE (IN)	AIR (1)
DRILLED PIERS	3000	5.5	0.58	1	1	0-2
GRADE BEAMS	4500	7	0.45	1	1	5-7
WALLS	4000	6	0.48	1	1	5-7
LFRS WALLS & GRADE BEAMS	5000	7.5	0.65	1	1	0-2
SLAB ON STEEL DECK	4000	6	0.57	.75	.75	0-2
ALL OTHERS NOT NOTED	3000	5.5	0.58	.75	.75	4-6

(left side dimensions: 3/4", 3/16", 1 1/8")

Table Dimensions

12. After completing the second page of notes open the sheet and drag and drop the first set and place on the left side of the sheet.

13. Place the second left on the right side of the sheet.

14. Draw a medium line down the middle of the sheet and size the notes to fit within the boxes.

15. Lastly add a box at the top of the sheet 1/2" high.

    Using 1/4" bold text, add the words GENERAL NOTES (STRUCTURAL) at the top of the sheet.

GENERAL NOTES (STRUCTURAL)

ED TO FOR ADDITIONAL

9. CONCRETE

    A. ALL CONCRETE SHALL BE NORMAL W
       EACH MIX DESIGN SUBMITTED FOR AF

Title of Sheet

16. This is the end of Part 13. Save your file as CL8-13.

CL8-14   Sheet A301 – SECTIONS & INT. ELEVS.

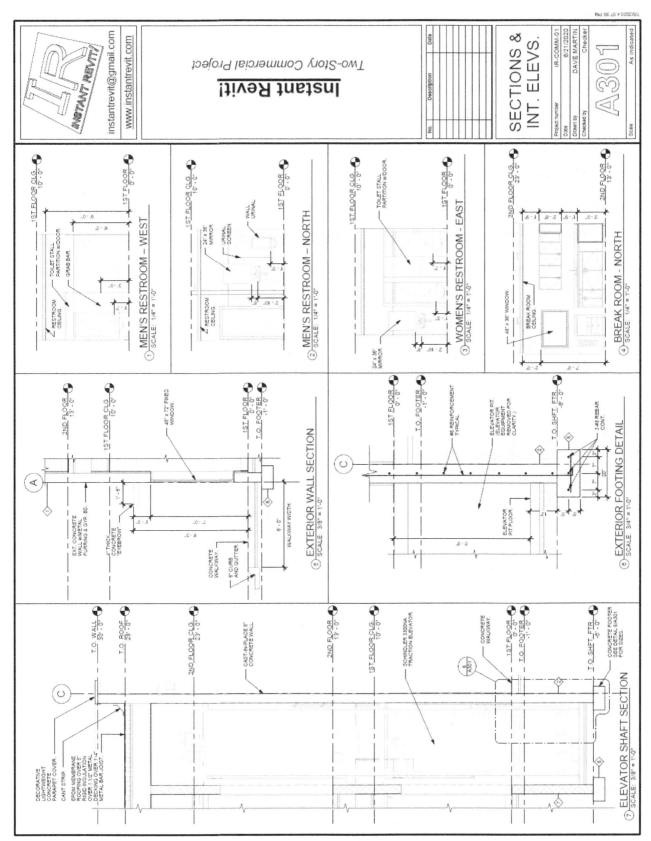

Sections & Interior Elevations Sheet

1. Open the CL8-13 file, save the file as CL8-14.

2. Create a sheet named A301 – SECTIONS & INT. ELEVS.
    (Sections and Interior Elevations)

3. Open the Men's Restroom – West interior elevation view.

    Add the additional notes as shown. Repeat the process for the other three interior elevations to be added to the sheet.

4. Starting from the upper right corner of the sheet, drag and drop the view named:
    Men's Restroom – West from the Elevations (Interior Elevation) view category.

5. Place the view at the upper right corner of the sheet.

    The scale of the view is 1/4" = 1'-0".

6. Working your way down the sheet, add the other three interior elevations.

    These three views are also at 1/4" = 1'-0" scale.

7. Draw detail lines between and on the left side of the views.

    Equally space the horizontal lines.

8. Open the Exterior Wall Section view.

    Add the dimensions and note for the concrete eyebrow and wall tag.

9. Insert the Exterior Wall Section and the Exterior Footing Detail views in the center of the sheet.

    Add the wall tags for the foundation walls.

10. Insert the Elevator Shaft Section view on the left side of the sheet.

    Add the wall tags for the foundation walls.

11. Update the view titles to the 3/8" text version.

12. Change all the cut patterns to light gray.

13. If you didn't insert the views in the order shown, re-number the views as shown.

    Since you cannot have two views with the same number, you may need to place a letter after the number temporarily.

14. Fill in the sheet information in the properties dialog for the views.

15. This is the end of Part 14. Save your file as CL8-14.

CL8-15   Sheet A302 – LONG. & HALLWAY SECTS.

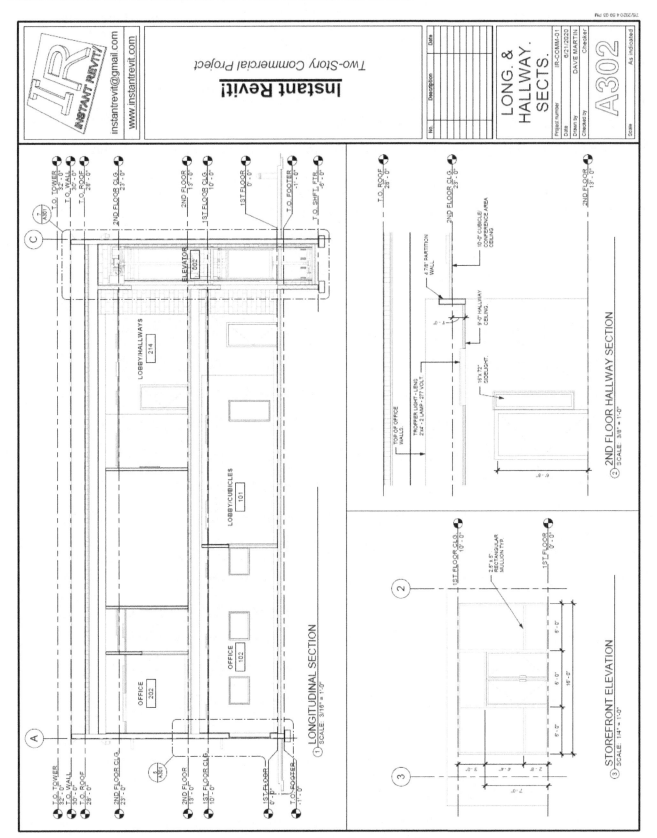

Sections & Interior Elevations Sheet

1. Open the CL8-14 file, save the file as CL8-15.

2. Create a sheet named A302 – LONG. & HALLWAY SECTS. (Longitudinal and Hallway Sections)

3. Open the LONGITUDINAL SECTION view.

   Hide the furniture.

4. Add Room Labels within each room. Use the room label without the area.

5. Add the level markers on the left side of the view.

6. If you see any of the interior walls overlapping with the floor above, click the wall and attach it to the floor.

7. Zoom in to the left side of the sheet. Click on the edge of the Wall Section view bubble.

8. Click on the Edit Crop tool

Edit Crop Tool

9. Adjust the edge of the magenta boundary as shown.

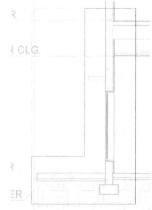

Modified Crop View Boundary

10. Move the view bubble to the new corner.

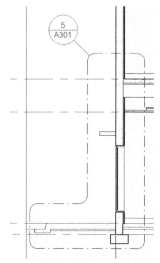

Modified View Bubble

11. Add a masking region at the bottom of the view to mask out the left side of the earth fill pattern. Set the masking region boundary line to the Invisible Lines linestyle.

Masking Region Boundary

12. Create or open the section view for the 2nd floor hallway.

This will show the difference in height between the hallway ceiling and the conference area ceiling.

The scale for the hallway section view is 3/8" = 1'-0".

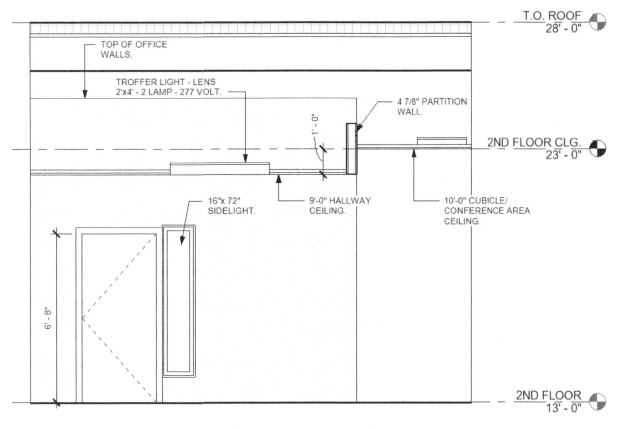

Hallway Ceiling Section View

13. Show the section mark in the second floor view.

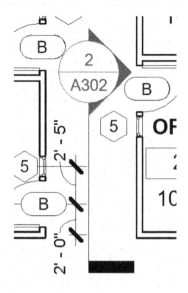

Section Mark at Second Floor View

14. Open the STOREFRONT ELEVATION view.

    The scale for the view is 1/4" = 1'-0".

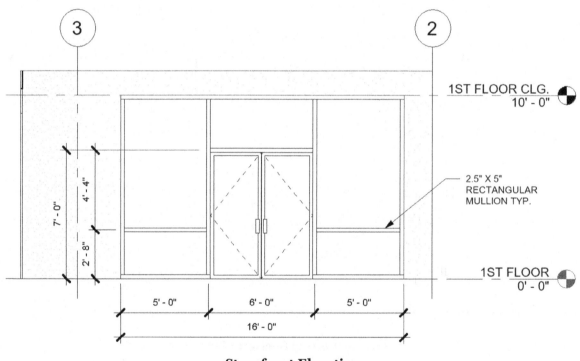

Storefront Elevation

15. Drag and drop the views onto your sheet.

    The scale for the longitudinal section view is 3/16" = 1'-0".

16. You may notice on the full sheet view that the hallway section does not have the edge of the view showing.

    This is because the crop window is turned off in the plotted view.

    If you would like to see the window you will need to turn off the "Hide crop boundaries" checkbox in the Print Setting dialog box.

    If you wish to leave this setting off, turn off the crop windows in the views that you do not to see the crop window in the plot.

    Another option would be to leave this setting off and draw a detail line at the edges of the view. If you use this option, the lines will need to be slightly to the inside of the edge of the cropped area.

Hide Crop Boundaries Checkbox

17. Add a detail line between the views.

18. Update the view titles to the 3/8" text version.

19. Fill in the sheet title in the properties for the view.

20. This is the end of Part 15. Save your file as CL8-15.

CL8-16   Sheet A400 – DESIGN OPTIONS

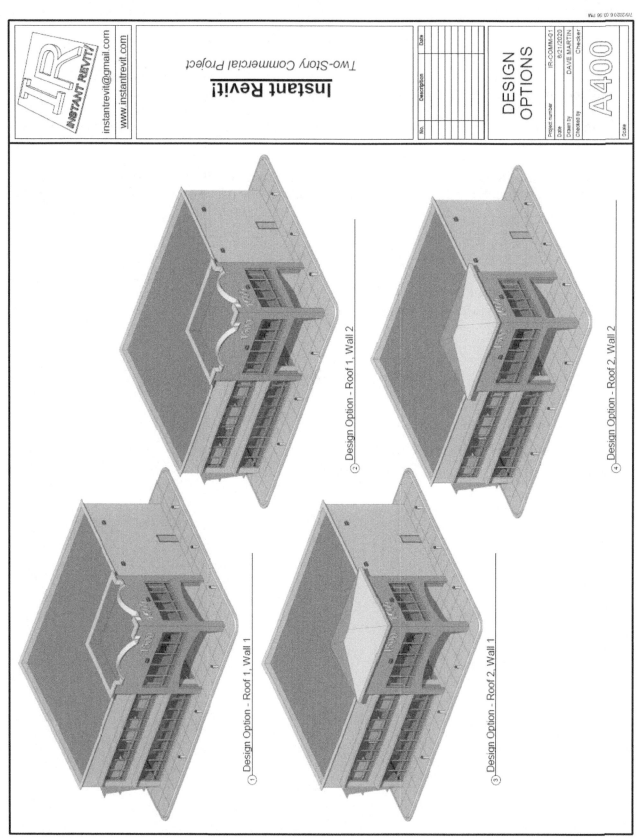

Design Options Sheet

1. Open the CL8-15 file, save the file as CL8-16.

2. Create a sheet named A400 – DESIGN OPTIONS.

3. Go to each of the Design Option 3D views and set the scale of the view to a custom scale.

4. Click on the View Scale setting at the bottom left of the view window.

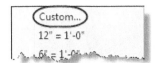

Custom... Setting

5. Select Custom at the top of the list.

6. Set the custom scale to 1:150.

7. Hide the cars, people, parking stalls, topography, and the block wall in the background.

Scale Set to 1:150

8. Return to the sheet view and drag and drop the views onto the sheet. Arrange as shown in the example.

9. For the view title, you will need to modify the family.

   Open the View Title – 3-16 Text family in the project browser.

10. Save the family as:
    View Title - 3-16 Text - No Scale.rfa.

    Remove the word Scale and the scale label below the view name.

① View Name

SCALE: Removed

11. Load the family into your project and create a new View Title style called:
    Title w Line - Design Options.

12. Update the four views with the new style.

13. This is the end of Part 15. Save your file as CL8-15.

CL8-17   Sheet A401 – RENDERINGS

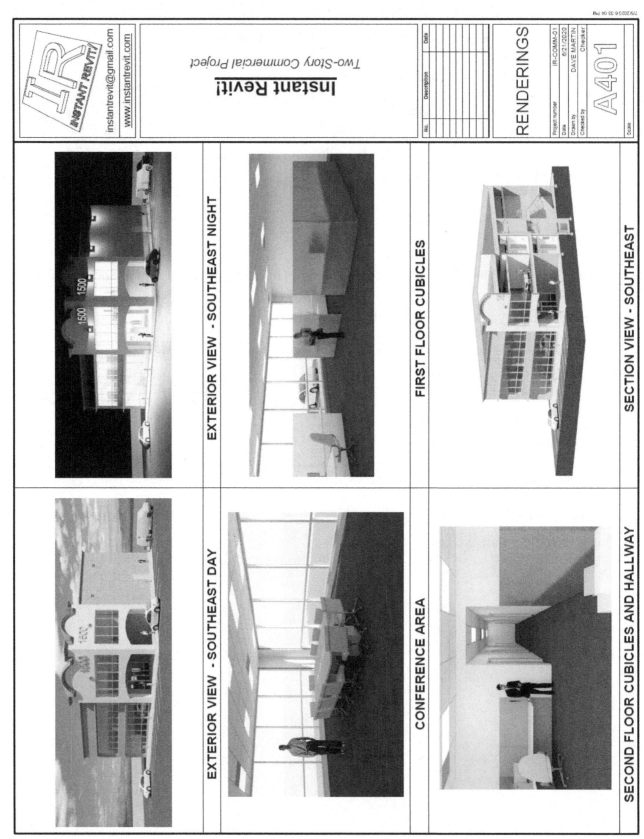

Renderings Sheet

1. Open the CL8-16 file, save the file as CL8-17.

2. Create a sheet named A401 – RENDERINGS.

3. Go to the Insert tab, Import panel, Image tool to insert the images.

   You may also drag and drop the renderings from the Renderings category if you used the Revit program to create your renderings. Turn off the titles for the viewports.

4. Use the handles on the corners to size the images.

5. Create equally spaced boxes in the border.

   You can use the dimension tool to equally space the lines.

6. Add boxes for the text. The lines are 1/2" above the bottom lines for the boxes.

7. Use the text tool to create captions for the views.

   The size of the text is 1/4".

   Center the text within the boxes.

8. Insert the Exterior View – Southeast Day rendering onto your A400 sheet.

   Insert the remaining views onto the sheet.

   Notes:
   You may position the images in any location that you wish.
   If you wish to crop the images you will need to use a bitmap editing program.

9. This is the end of Part 16. Save your file as CL8-16.

CL8-18   Assembling the PDF Portfolio

Now that you have finished creating the sheets, you will create a Sheet Index.
Follow this procedure to create the index.

1.   Open the CL8-17 file, save the file as CL8-18.

2.   Go to the Schedules tool in the View tab, Create panel and
     select the Sheet List tool.

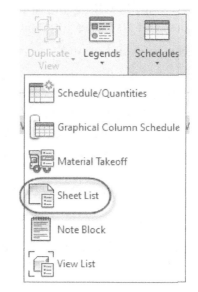

Sheet List Tool

3.   In the Sheet List Properties
     dialog box, add the Sheet
     Number and Sheet Name
     fields.

Sheet List Properties Dialog Box

4.   Set the font sizes using the Appearance tab and the Font tool in the appearance panel.

5.   For the Title of the Sheet Index use Arial Black, 1/4" and Bold.

     Change the title to SHEET LIST.

6. For the header text use Arial, 9/64", Bold, and Underlined.

   Change the text to all caps.

7. For the body text use Arial, 1/8".

   Change the Sheet Number column to Centered

8. Setup the columns as shown...

\<SHEET LIST\>	
A	B
SHEET NUMBER	SHEET NAME
A100	TITLE SHEET
A101	SITE PLAN
A300	GENERAL NOTES (STRUCT.)
A102	SCHEDULES & CALLOUT VIEW
A103	FIRST FLOOR PLAN
A104	SECOND FLOOR PLAN
A105	1ST FLOOR REFLECTED CLG. PLN.
A106	2ND FLOOR REFLECTED CLG. PLN.
A107	1ST & 2ND FLR. COLOR LEGENDS
A108	1ST & 2ND FLR. FURN. PLANS
A109	1ST & 2ND FLR. PATHS OF TRAVEL
A201	EAST/NORTH ELEVATIONS
A202	WEST/SOUTH ELEVATIONS
A301	SECTIONS & INT. ELEVS.
A302	LONG. & HALLWAY. SECTS.
A400	DESIGN OPTIONS
A401	RENDERINGS

Sheet Index Set Up

9. When finished setting up the Sheet Index, drag the schedule onto the Title Sheet in the lower right corner.

SHEET LIST	
SHEET NUMBER	SHEET NAME
A100	TITLE SHEET
A101	SITE PLAN
A300	GENERAL NOTES (STRUCT.)
A102	SCHEDULES & CALLOUT VIEW
A103	FIRST FLOOR PLAN
A104	SECOND FLOOR PLAN
A105	1ST FLOOR REFLECTED CLG. PLN.
A106	2ND FLOOR REFLECTED CLG. PLN.
A107	1ST & 2ND FLR. COLOR LEGENDS
A108	1ST & 2ND FLR. FURN. PLANS
A109	1ST & 2ND FLR. PATHS OF TRAVEL
A201	EAST/NORTH ELEVATIONS
A202	WEST/SOUTH ELEVATIONS
A301	SECTIONS & INT. ELEVS.
A302	LONG. & HALLWAY. SECTS.
A400	DESIGN OPTIONS
A401	RENDERINGS

TITLE
SHEET

Project number	IR-COMM-01
Date	6/21/2020
Drawn by	DAVE MARTIN
Checked by	Checker

A100

Scale

Sheet Index Placed

Next you will create a PDF portfolio of your project. Use the PDF ReDirect v2 program to create the PDF files of each sheet and merge them into one file.

You may download the program at www.exp-systems.com.

1. Click on the File menu and select the Print command.

Print Command in Quick Access Toolbar

Print Command

2. The Print dialog box opens.

    Match the settings as shown.

    Your folder location may be different.

Print Dialog Box

3. Click on the Select... button in the Print Range area.

Select... Button

4. The View/Sheet Set dialog opens.

    Uncheck the Views checkbox and select all the sheets as shown.

    Click the OK button.

    An alert box will appear asking you if you would like to save the settings for a future Revit session.

Save Settings   ✕

Do you want to save these settings for use in a future Revit session?

| Yes | No | Cancel |

Save Settings Alert Box

View/Sheet Set   ? ✕

Name: <in-session> ⌄   Save

☑ Sheet: A100 - TITLE SHEET
☑ Sheet: A101 - SITE PLAN
☑ Sheet: A102 - SCHEDULES & CALLOUT VIEW
☑ Sheet: A103 - FIRST FLOOR PLAN
☑ Sheet: A104 - SECOND FLOOR PLAN
☑ Sheet: A105 - 1ST FLOOR REFLECTED CLG. PLN.
☑ Sheet: A106 - 2ND FLOOR REFLECTED CLG. PLN.
☑ Sheet: A107 - 1ST & 2ND FLR. COLOR LEGENDS
☑ Sheet: A108 - 1ST & 2ND FLR. FURN. PLANS
☑ Sheet: A109 - 1ST & 2ND FLR. PATHS OF TRAVEL
☑ Sheet: A201 - EAST/NORTH ELEVATIONS
☑ Sheet: A202 - WEST/SOUTH ELEVATIONS
☑ Sheet: A300 - GENERAL NOTES (STRUCT.)
☑ Sheet: A301 - SECTIONS & INT. ELEVS.
☑ Sheet: A302 - LONG. & HALLWAY. SECTS.
☑ Sheet: A400 - DESIGN OPTIONS
☑ Sheet: A401 - RENDERINGS

Save As...
Revert
Rename...
Delete

Check All
Check None

Show
☑ Sheets   ☐ Views

| OK | Cancel | Help |

View/Sheet Set Dialog Box

5. Click the Setup... button
    at the bottom right corner
    of the dialog box.

Setup... Button

6. Match the settings in
    the Print Setup dialog
    as shown...

Print Setup

Printer: PDF reDirect v2

Name: <in-session>   Save

Paper   Orientation   Save As...
Size: ARCH C (18 x 24 in)   ○ Portrait   Revert
                                         ⊙ Landscape   Rename...
Source: <default tray>
                                                               Delete
Paper Placement   Hidden Line Views
⊙ Center   Remove Lines Using:
○ Offset from   Printer limit   ○ Vector Processing
  corner:
         0.0000" =x 0.0000" =y   ⊙ Raster Processing

Zoom   Appearance
○ Fit to page   Raster quality:
                                         High
⊙ Zoom: 100 ↕ % size
                                         Colors:
                                         Color

Options
☐ View links in blue (Color prints only)   ☑ Hide scope boxes
☑ Hide ref/work planes   ☑ Hide crop boundaries
☐ Hide unreferenced view tags   ☐ Replace halftone with thin lines
☐ Region edges mask coincident lines

                                         OK   Cancel

Print Setup Dialog

7. An alert box will appear notifying you
    that you will be printing the
    views/sheets as separate files.

    Click the Yes button to continue.

Printing Separate Files   ✕

You have chosen to print 17 views/sheets as
separate files. Do you wish to continue?

                                         Yes   No

Printing Separate Files Alert Box

8. Click the OK button to close the dialog box.

    Click OK in the Print dialog to begin creating the PDF files.

    It will take a few minutes as each file is created. Wait for each of the files to finish rendering.

    Select the folder for the PDF file.

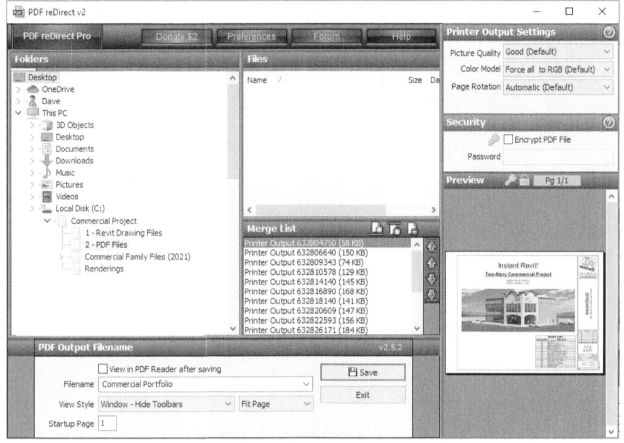

PDF ReDirect v2 Interface

9. Name the file Commercial Portfolio.pdf and set the View Style to Fit page.

10. Once completed with printing you will have 17 sheets.

11. This is the end of Part 18, Tutorial 8, and the Commercial Project. Save your file as RL8-18.

Congratulations on Completing the Commercial Project!

Appendix A   Adding the Stacked Walls and Wall Profiles

| **Part 1** | Creating the New Basic and Stacked Wall Types |
| **Part 2** | Updating the Model |

Note: All screenshots are from the Autodesk® Revit® software.

This tutorial may be completed after completing the Commercial Project.

In this section you will change the exterior walls from a Basic Wall type to a Stacked Wall type. Stacked walls are walls that consist of standard wall types that are stacked on top of one another.

You will add a wall type with a brick façade at the base of the wall. Once the stacked walls are added to the project, they will be modified to include wall profiles.

After modifying the walls, you will then update the entire model to show these changes.

There is a sample portfolio on the Instant Revit website that shows the project after the completion of Appendix A.

Beginning the Project

1. Open the last file in the Commercial Tutorial, CL8-18.

2. Save the file as, CLA-1.

CLA-1   Creating the New Basic and Stacked Wall Types

1. Before creating a stacked wall, you will need to create two additional Basic Wall types.

    Open the 1st Floor view. Click on the Wall tool.

2. Select the Exterior – Concrete on Mtl. Stud wall type.

    Click the Edit type button in the Properties window.

    Duplicate it and rename it: Exterior – Concrete on Mtl. Stud w/Brick Facade.

3. Add the two layers as shown in the example below.

    Change the Brick material cut pattern and surface pattern to light gray.

Basic Wall: Exterior – Concrete on Mtl. Stud w/Brick Facade Assembly

4. Click the OK button the save the wall type and close the dialog box.

    Press the OK button in the Type Properties dialog box to close this one as well.

5. Create a second wall type called: Exterior - Concrete w/Brick Facade.

    This wall will be used for the wall at the stairwell and the east exterior wall.

6.   Add the three layers as shown in the example.

Note: You may begin with the Exterior – Concrete on Mtl. Stud w/Brick Façade wall type and delete the interior layers.

Basic Wall: Exterior – Concrete w/Brick Facade Assembly

7.   Click on the Wall tool.

Select the Stacked wall called: Exterior Brick Over CMU w Metal Stud.

8.   Click the Edit Type button and duplicate the wall type.

Name the wall type: Exterior – Concrete on Mtl. Stud w/Brick Facade (Stacked).

Note: The stacked wall type is used to create a wall with other types stacked on top of one another. You cannot modify the layers of the walls within this wall type. To do this, you will need to return to the Basic Wall type and modify the layers there.

9. Add the additional wall types as shown. Click on the Variable button to make the wall height variable.

   Press OK to save the wall type.

   Note: The reason for the 1'-0" high bottom portion is for the part of the wall that extends below the first floor level to the top of the footer.

Stacked Wall: Exterior – Concrete on Mtl. Stud w/Brick Facade Assembly

10. Starting with the stacked wall type: Exterior – Concrete on Mtl. Stud w/Brick Façade (Stacked), create another stacked wall type called: Exterior – Concrete w/Brick Façade (Stacked).

    This is the same wall type as the other type except the gypsum board and metal studs have been removed.

    Change the wall types as shown.

Stacked Wall: Exterior – Concrete w/Brick Facade Assembly

11. Click OK twice to close the dialog boxes.

Changing the Exterior Walls to the Stacked Wall Type

In this section you will change the North, West, and East exterior walls. You will not change the South walls or the wall at the main entry.

1. Open the 3D view.

    Rotate the view to show the West exterior wall.

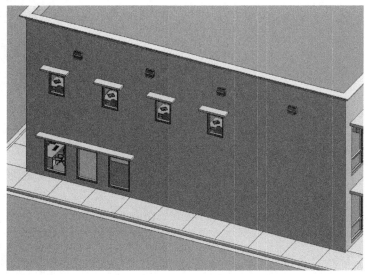

3D View of West Exterior Wall

2. Select the Exterior wall and change it to the Stacked Wall: Exterior – Concrete on Mtl. Stud w/Brick Façade (Stacked) wall type in the Properties window.

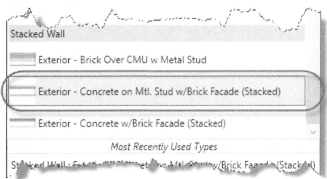

Stacked Wall Type

3. An error box may open. This may be because the wall has changed thickness, one or more dimension references have become invalid.

    If so, click the Remove Reference(s) button to accept the error and close the box.

4. A second error box will open.

    Click the Delete Dimension(s) button to delete the dimensions.

    You will add the deleted dimensions back into your drawing later.

5. The west exterior wall now has a brick façade at the lower 3'-6" of the wall.

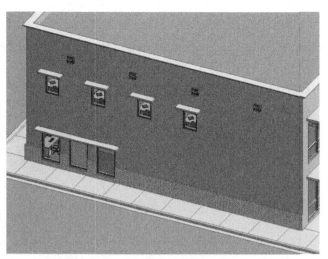

Brick Façade Added to West Wall

6. Repeat the process for the North exterior wall.

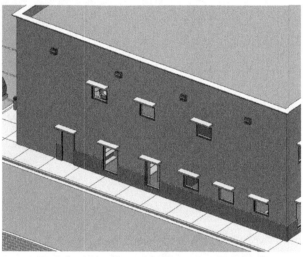

Brick Façade Added to North Wall

7. For the shorter North wall, use the Stacked Wall: Exterior – Concrete w/Brick Facade (Stacked) wall type.

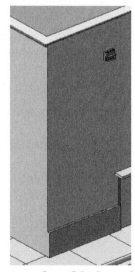

Brick Façade Added to Shorter North Wall

8. If you receive an error message regarding constraints, click the Remove Constraints button to clear the box.

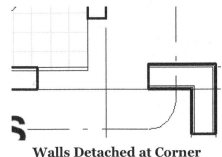

Constraints Error Message

9. Before changing the East exterior wall, you will need to detach the South wall and the East exterior wall at the restrooms at the corner.

   This will avoid an error in the model that will prevent changing the wall type.

   Open the 1st Floor view.

10. The order that you detach the walls is important.

    Click on the South exterior wall and drag the end to the left so that it is detached at the corner intersection.

    Repeat for the other two walls.

    To detach the tower wall you will switch to the 1 – Arched Opening design option.

11. Switch back to the Main Model.

    Change the East exterior wall to the Stacked Wall: Exterior – Concrete w/Brick Facade (Stacked) wall type.

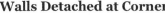

Walls Detached at Corner

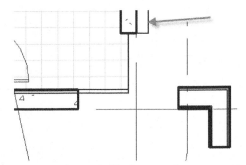

East Exterior Wall Changed to New Type

12. To rejoin the walls, you will need to first drag the end of the East wall down to the grid line.

   Then drag the end of the South wall to the intersection.

   Lastly, drag the end of the Tower wall to the edge of the East wall.

   A warning box will open. You may ignore it.

   The Men's Restroom will become a room again.

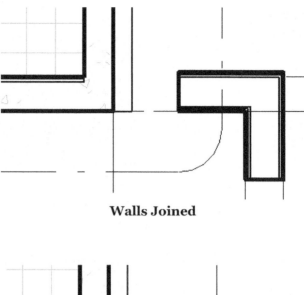

Walls Joined

13. Switch to the 1 – Arched Opening design option.

   Drag the Tower Wall end until it touches the East exterior wall.

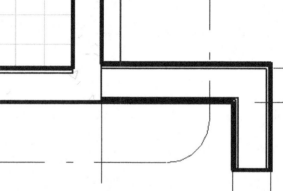

Tower Wall Joined

14. Switch back to the Main Model.

   The East exterior wall is now changed to the new stacked wall type.

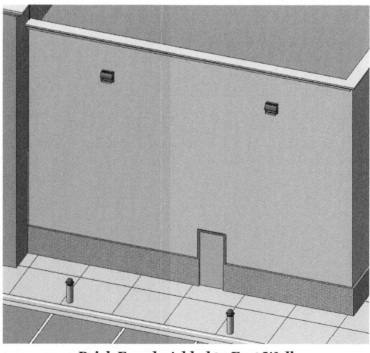

Brick Façade Added to East Wall

Adding Profiles for the Top of the Brick Façade and Curb at Base of the Wall

In this section you will update the new wall types with a profile for the transition between the brick and the concrete material.

You will also add a curb at the base of the wall.

1. Click on the Wall tool and select the Exterior – Concrete on Mtl. Stud wall.

2. Click the Edit Type button and duplicate the wall type. Name the new wall type Exterior – Concrete on Mtl. Stud w/Profile.

    The reason for the new wall type is so that the original wall types are not affected.

3. Edit the structure of the new wall.

    Click on the Sweeps button at the bottom of the Edit Assembly dialog box.

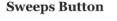

Sweeps Button

4. The Wall Sweeps dialog box opens.

    Click the Load Profile button to load the shape of the wall ledge.

Wall Sweeps Dialog Box

5. In the Load Family dialog box, open the custom families folder and select the Wall Ledge.rfa file.

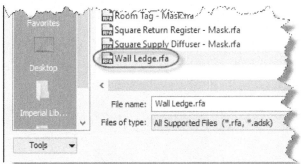

Wall Ledge.rfa File

6. Click the Add button to add the profile to the wall.

    Select the Wall Ledge :Ledge profile file in the
    drop down menu.

7. Click <By Category> in the Material column and
    change the material to Concrete – Lightweight.

    There are no other changes to make. Click the OK
    button to close the dialog box.

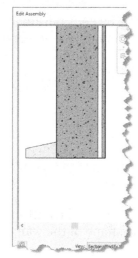

Wall Ledge Profile Selected

8. You will now see the profile added to the wall type.

    Click OK twice to save the wall type and close the
    dialog box.

Wall Ledge Profile Added

9. Before adding a curb profile to the Exterior - Concrete on Mtl. Stud w/Brick Façade wall type,
    you will need to create a profile.

    In the Families portion of the Project Browser, scroll down to the Profiles section and expand it.

10. Scroll down to the Wall Ledge profile and
    right-click on it.

    Select the Edit choice in the menu.

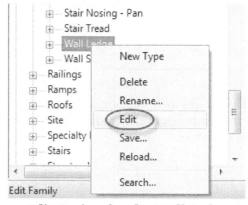

Edit Option for the Wall Ledge

11. The Wall Ledge profile family file opens.

    Save it in the Commercial Families folder as Curb-1.rfa.

    Note: A completed version of this file is in the Commercial Families folder. The name of the file is Curb.rfa. You may use this version instead of creating your own.

12. Zoom in on the profile in the drawing area.

    Use the sketch as a guide for the new shape.

    Use the Line tool in the Create tab, Detail panel to draw the lines for the edge of the profile.

    Do not include the dimensions as part of the profile.

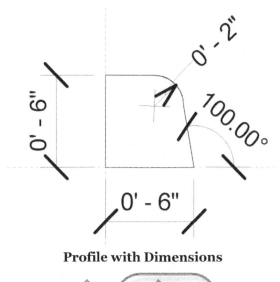

Profile with Dimensions

13. Save the file and click the Load Into Project and Close button.

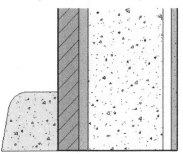

Load into Project and Close Button

14. Open the wall type: Exterior - Concrete on Mtl. Stud w/Brick Facade.

    Create a duplicate wall type called: Exterior - Concrete on Mtl. Stud w/Brick Facade w/Profile.

15. Add the Curb profile at the bottom edge of the wall profile.

    Set the material to Concrete – Lightweight.

    Click OK twice to save the wall type and close the dialog box.

Curb Profile Added

16. Open the wall type: Exterior - Concrete on Mtl. Stud w/Brick Facade (Stacked). You do not need to duplicate the wall type.

    Change the structure so that the top wall type is the new wall type: Exterior Concrete on Mtl. Stud w/Profile.

    Change the second wall type to: Exterior - Concrete on Mtl. Stud w/Brick Facade w/Profile.

    Click OK twice to save the wall type and close the dialog box.

    Note: If the doors and windows disappear around the outside wall, undo the change and then redo.

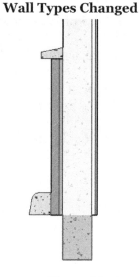

Types		
		TOP
	Name	Height
1	Exterior - Concrete on Mtl. Stud w/Profile	Variable
2	Exterior - Concrete on Mtl. Stud w/Brick Facade w/Profile	3' 6"
3	Exterior - Concrete	1' 0"

Wall Types Changed

Profiles Added

17. Repeat the process for the Exterior – Concrete w/Façade (Stacked) wall type.

    Add the Wall Ledge profile to the Exterior – Concrete wall type.

    Add the Curb profile to the Exterior – Concrete w/Brick Façade. Rename the new wall types.

    Use the same profile families.

18. The Exterior walls now have the profiles for the Wall Ledge and Curb added.

    You may notice a break in the profiles where the exterior wall changes type. This will be resolved in the next section.

Profiles Added to Exterior Walls

19. This is the end of Part 1. Save your file as CLA-1.

CLA-2   Updating the Model

This next part will give you a list of changes that you will need to do to the model. Some elements in the model will need to be changed due to the changes in the exterior wall type.

Some of these changes may not be needed on your project.

Repairing the Gap in the Profile and Adding Missing Dimensions

1. Open the CLA-1 file, save the file as CLA-2.

2. Open the 1st Floor view.

3. If you have a gap in the outside profile, zoom in on the upper right corner of the drawing and temporarily detach the wall separating the stairs from the hallway.

    When you detach the wall the profiles should join together.

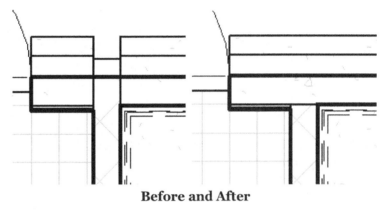

Before and After

4. The first floor carpet material may have reverted to the 8" tile material.

    If so, use the Remove Paint tool to change the 1st Floor floor material back to Carpet.

5. Some dimensions may have been deleted when the exterior walls were changed.

    Add the missing dimensions back in.

6. Open the 2nd Floor view.

7. Some dimensions may have been deleted during the wall type change.

    Add the dimensions back into the drawing.

    The missing dimensions are most likely located at the top left corner of the view.

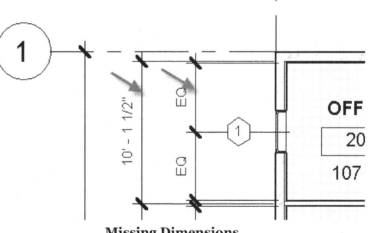

Missing Dimensions

Reattaching the Eyebrows

1. The Eyebrows will need to be reattached to the wall face.

    Open the North elevation view.

2. Click on one of the eyebrows to select the entire set.

    Click the Edit In-Place tool.

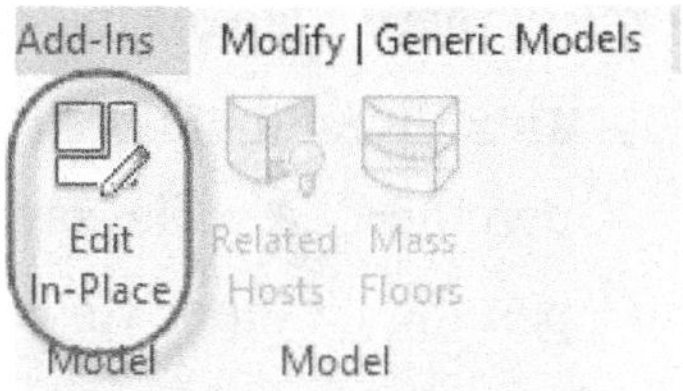

Edit In-Place Tool

3. Click on one of the eyebrows again and then the Edit Work Plane tool.

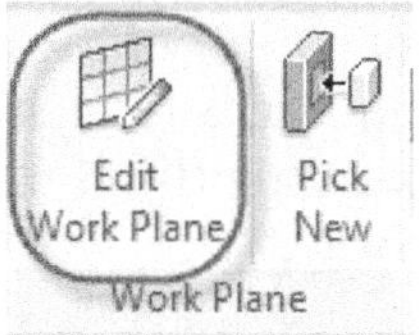

Edit Work Plane Tool

4. In the Work Plane dialog box, click the Pick a plane option.

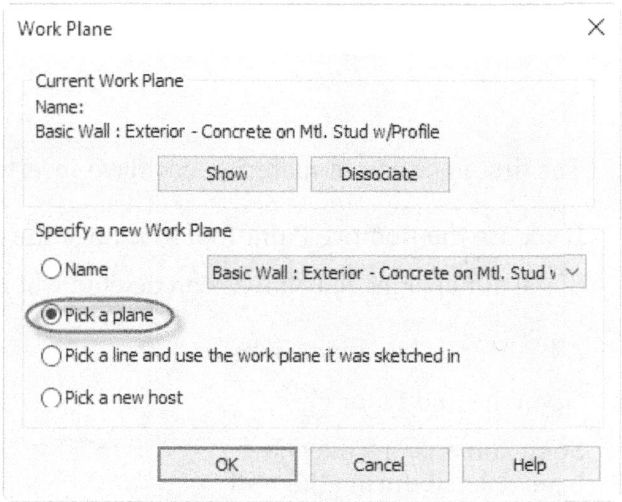

Pick a Plane Option

5. Pick the edge of the North exterior wall.
6. Click the Finish Model tool to complete the changes.
7. Repeat the process for the West exterior wall.
8. Open the 3D view to confirm the changes.

Realigning the Floors, Ceiling, and Roof Edges

1. Open the 1st Floor view.

2. Pick the edge of the floor.

   Click the Edit Boundary tool.

3. Realign the west, north, and east edges of the floor to the core of the wall.

   Answer Yes to the alert box regarding the joining of the floors to the walls.

4. If you receive a Warning message, click OK to accept it.

5. Use the Remove Paint tool to change the Carpet back to the correct surface pattern.

6. Repeat the process for the second floor edges.

7. Open the 1st Floor ceiling plan view.

   You might need to adjust the view range if you are having difficulties picking only one ceiling.

8. Click on the cubicle area ceiling and edit the boundary.

   Move the edges of the ceiling to the edges of the wall gypsum board.

9. Repeat for the Office, Storage, and Men's Room ceilings.

10. Open the 2nd Floor ceiling plan view.

11. Update the ceilings for the cubicle area, the offices along the west wall, hallway, break room, and men's restroom.

12. Adjust the upper cabinets in the break room to the edge of the gypsum board.

    Click on the cabinet and then the Pick New Host tool. Then click on the wall to reattach the cabinet to the gypsum board.

13. While in the 2nd Floor view, you may also need to update the wall joins at the northwest corner of the walls.

    You will use the Wall Joins tool to resolve this.

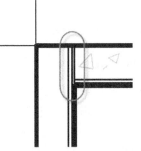

Gypsum Layer Inside Wall

14. Click on the Wall Joins tool in the Modify tab, Geometry panel.

Wall Joins Tool

15. Mouse over and click on the corner of the walls.

    Select the Miter button in the options bar.

    | Configuration | Previous | Next | ○ Butt ⦿ Miter ○ Square off | Display | Use View Settin ∨ | ⦿ Allow Join ○ Disallow Join |

    Miter Button

16. The walls are joined as an angled corner.

17. Open the T.O. Roof view.

18. Open the View Range dialog box.

    Change the settings temporarily to cut through the wall to adjust the roof edge to the wall core.

19. Hide the roof coping.

View Range			✕
Primary Range			
Top:	Associated Level (T.O. ROC ∨	Offset:	7 6"
Cut plane:	Associated Level (T.O. ROC ∨	Offset:	1' 0"
Bottom:	Associated Level (T.O. ROC ∨	Offset:	-1' 0"
View Depth			
Level:	Associated Level (T.O. ROC ∨	Offset:	-1' 0"
Learn more about view range			
<< Show		OK Apply Cancel	

    View Range Changed

20. Select the roof and click the Edit Boundary tool.

21. Adjust the edges of the roof so that they are aligned with the inside edge of the wall core.

    Answer Yes to the alert box.

    When finished, return to the original view range settings and unhide the roof coping.

22. Open the 3d view.

23. You will need to realign the edge of the roof coping.

    Click on the edge of the coping and click the Edit In-Place tool.

24. Click on the edge of the coping again and click the Edit Sweep tool.

25. Click on the black line that represents the path.

    Click the Pick Path tool. The lines will turn magenta.

26. Click VV to open the Visibility/Graphic Overrides dialog box.

    Uncheck the Roof visibility.

27. Select the new path at the outside corners of the walls. You will not be able to move the original lines.

    You may need to use the Pick 3D Edges to pick the corners of the walls.

    Delete the old path lines.

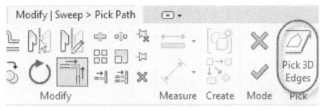

Pick 3D Edges Tool

28. Click the Green Check to complete the changes.

    Turn on the Roofs.

Painting the Inside of the Door and Window Openings

For this next section, you will paint the inside surface of the door and window insets with a brick surface material.

1. Open the 3D view.

2. Set the display to Shaded.

3. Click on the Paint tool and set the material to Brick, Common.

4. Zoom in to where the windows and door intersect the brick façade.

    Using the Paint tool, click on the surfaces at the inside to paint them with the brick pattern.

Surfaces Changed to Brick Material

5. For the South wall, you will need to use the Split Face tool to create a separate surface.

    Split the face at the southwest corner.

South Wall with Split Face

6. Add the Brick material to the face.

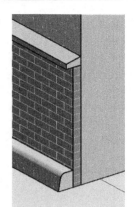

Brick Material Added

Adding a Curb Around the Remaining Walls

In this section you will use the sweep tool to add the curb profile at the base of the remaining walls. You will use the same profile as you used for the base of the brick façade wall type.

1. Continue in the 3D view.

    Hide the people and cars (if applicable).

    You need to create three separate sweeps.

2. Zoom in on the entry area.

3. Click on the Component, Model In-Place tool.

    Choose the Generic Models category for the new family.

    Name the family, Curb 1

4. Click on the Sweep tool.

    Set the Work Plane to the top surface of the concrete walkway. You will use this plane for the three curbs.

5. Click on the Pick Path or the Pick 3D Edges tool and click the corners of the wall/floor intersections as shown.

    You will need to switch to the Wireframe display style to pick the inside corners of the wall.

    Shorten the line at the entry so that the curb does not cover the front door or windows.

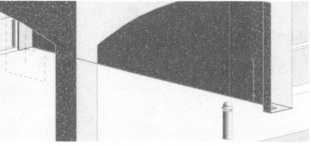

Path Lines Picked

6. Click the Green check to complete the path.

7. Select the Curb profile when selecting the profile.

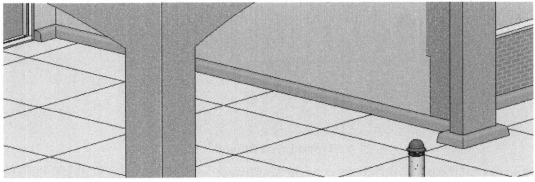

Curb Profile Selected

8. Click the Green Check to place the curb.

9. Change the material of the curb to Concrete – Lightweight.

10. Click the Green Check to finish the model.

The curb is placed.

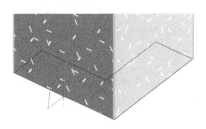

Curb Placed

11. Repeat the process for the south east corner of the tower walls.

Name the sweep: Curb 2

You may need to flip and rotate the sweep profile.

Path and Profile Located

12. Click the Green Check to place the curb.

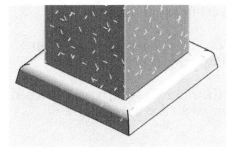

Curb Placed

13. Add one more curb for the South wall at the curtain wall.

    Wrap the curb around the south west corner of the tower to the left side of the main entry.

    Stop the path at the edge of the brick on the southwest corner of the building.

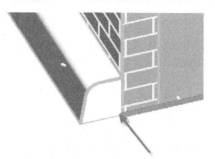

End of Path at Southwest Corner

Third Curb Placed

14. You will see that the curbs do not meet at the southwest corner.

    You will create a curved sweep profile for this last portion.

    Zoom in on the southwest corner.

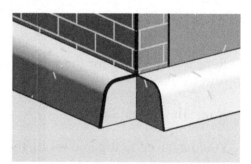

Curb Gap at Southwest Corner

15. Load a new profile into your drawing called Curb – Corner from the custom family folder.

    This profile uses the same shape, but the origin has been flipped to the outside corner.

    The width has also been shortened from 6" to 5 15/16" to allow it to be swept around a small arc.

Shape of the Curb – Corner Profile

16. Start a new sweep using the Component, Model In-Place tool.

    This time the sweep path will be a 90 degree, 6" radius arc.

    Name the family: Curb, Corner

    When placing the sweep path, the center will be at the intersection of the two curbs and the radius will be 6".

Sweep Path

17. Use the Curb – Corner profile for the profile shape.

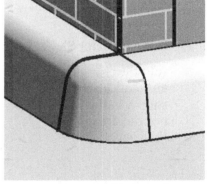

Profile Shape Placed

18. Click the Green Check to place the curb.

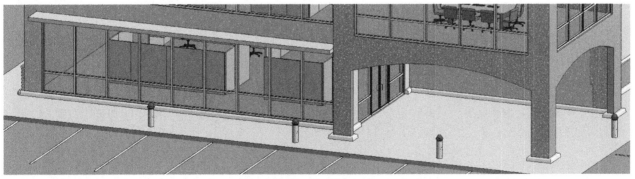

Corner Curb Placed

19. This concludes the model updates.

All Curbs Placed

Updating the Section Views

1. Open the Exterior Wall Section view.

2. Add the three annotations as shown.

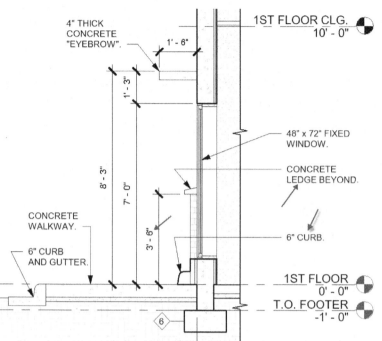

Additional Annotations Added

3. Open the Elevator Shaft Section wall section.

    1. Add the annotations as shown to the bottom area of the view.

2.

3. Additional Annotations Added

4. Open the Exterior Footing Detail.

    Move the break line to the right to expose the curb.

    You will not be adding any annotations.

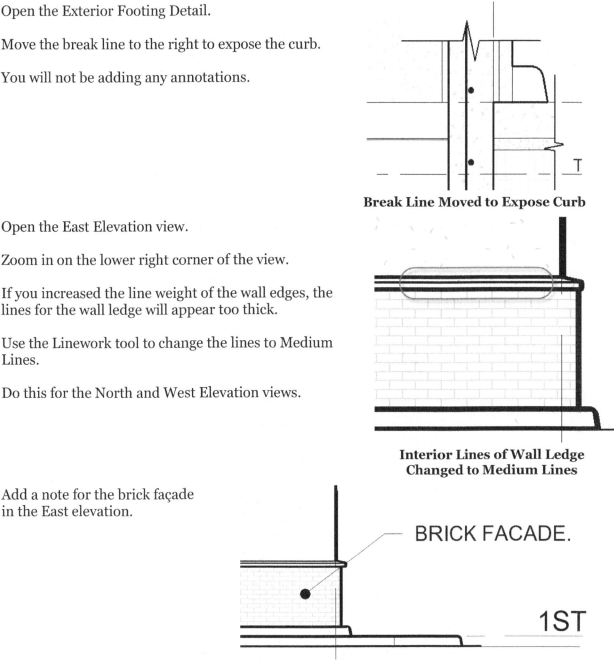

Break Line Moved to Expose Curb

5. Open the East Elevation view.

    Zoom in on the lower right corner of the view.

    If you increased the line weight of the wall edges, the lines for the wall ledge will appear too thick.

    Use the Linework tool to change the lines to Medium Lines.

    Do this for the North and West Elevation views.

**Interior Lines of Wall Ledge
Changed to Medium Lines**

6. Add a note for the brick façade in the East elevation.

BRICK FACADE.

1ST

Note Added

7. You will need to re-render the Exterior View – Southeast Day, Exterior View – Southeast Night, and Section View – Southeast views and place them on the Renderings Sheet.

Updating the Wall Schedule

In the previous version of the project you were able to show the wall types as all capital letters. This was done by adding a text column called Name on Schedule. In this section you will modify the Wall Schedule. This needs to be done because some of the walls will not be able to have text added in the column.

1. Open the Exterior Wall Section view and label the two exterior wall types based on the updated Wall Schedule below.

2. Open the Elevator Shaft Section and label the other two wall types.

3. Open the Wall Schedule.

4. Unhide the Family and Type column.

5. Fill in the WALL TYPE column for the remaining four wall types.

    As was done with the original, you may wish to export the schedule to a text file. You can use software such as Microsoft Word® to change the text to all capitals.

6. After naming the new wall types, hide the Family and Type Column.

7. Open sheet A102 and adjust the size and location of the wall schedule on the sheet.

WALL SCHEDULE

MARK	WALL TYPE
1	EXTERIOR - CONCRETE ON MTL. STUD
2	EXTERIOR - CONCRETE
3	EXTERIOR - 9 1/2 PARTITION
4	EXTERIOR - STUCCO ON MTL. STUD
5	EXTERIOR - STUCCO ON MTL. STUD W/GYP BD INTERIOR
6	FOUNDATION - 1'-8" WIDE
7	GENERIC - 8 MASONRY
8	INTERIOR - 4 1/4" WET WALL
9	INTERIOR - 4 7/8" PARTITION (1-HR)
10	INTERIOR - 5 1/2" PARTITION (1-HR)
11	CURTAIN WALL
12	EXTERIOR - CONCRETE ON MTL. STUD w/BRICK FACADE w/PROFILE
13	EXTERIOR - CONCRETE ON MTL. STUD w/PROFILE
14	EXTERIOR - CONCRETE w/BRICK FACADE w/PROFILE
15	EXTERIOR - CONCRETE w/PROFILE

Updated Wall Schedule with New Wall Types Named

8. This is the end of Part 2 and the Appendix A Tutorial. Save your file as CLA-2.

Note: You may wish to re-print your Commercial Project at this time.

Appendix B   Adding Keynotes to the Project

Part 1	Adding Element Keynotes to the Project
Part 2	Adding User Keynotes to the Project

Note: All screenshots are from the Autodesk® Revit® software.

This tutorial may be completed after completing the Commercial Project or Appendix A. For this tutorial, you will begin after completing the Commercial Project.

In this section you will add Keynotes to the project. Revit has three different types of keynotes: Element Keynotes, Material Keynotes, and User Keynotes. Key notes are used to replace textual notes on the drawing. Instead of adding lines of text to describe an element, a numbered note is used instead. This helps to remove "clutter" from the drawing and make it easier to read.

We will not be using the Material Keynote tool. You may wish to try the Material tag tool in the Annotate tab, Tag panel to tag materials on your project.

When adding Element Keynotes, the Revit software utilizes the MasterSpec® system of categorizing the different elements of an architectural project. More information about this system may be found on the MasterSpec website at: http://www.masterspec.com.

You will be adding two different types of keynotes to the sheets on your project. Typically, keynotes are only used on large plan, section, or elevation views. You will not be adding keynotes to the detail or wall section views.

As with Appendix A, you may wish to re-print your portfolio after the changes are made. There is a sample portfolio on the Instant Revit website that shows the project after the completion of Appendix B.

Beginning the Project

1. Open the last file in the Commercial Tutorial, CL8-18.

2. Save the file as, CLB-1.

CLB-1   Adding Element Keynotes to the Project

You will begin by adding Element Keynotes to the drawing. For this project you will add keynotes to the Site Plan, 1st Floor Plan, and the Restroom Callout View.

Updating the Keynote Text File

1. Open the 1st Floor view.

    Before adding keynotes, you will load a new keynote text file.

    Click on the Keynoting Settings tool under the Keynote tool in the Annotate tab, Tag panel.

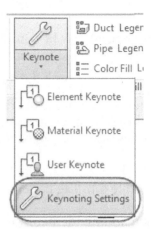

Keynoting Settings Tool

2. The Keynoting Settings dialog box opens.

    You will see that the text file that is loaded is called: RevitKeynotes_Imperial_2004.txt. You will update this to the 2010 version.

Keynoting Settings Dialog Box

Note: At the bottom of the dialog box there are two buttons to select the Numbering Method. If you were not using element keynotes you would use the "By sheet" method. This would place sequential numbers in the tags. Since you are using element keynotes that reference the MasterSpec numbering system, you will use the "By keynote" method.

3. Click on the Browse button.

    In the Browse for Keynote File dialog box, select the RevitKeynotes_Imperial_2010.txt file.

4. You will see an alert box indicating the is loaded successfully.

> Reload Successful   ×
>
> Keynote table reloaded successfully.
>
>   OK

Reload Successful

5. Click OK to close the dialog box.

<u>Adding the Keynote</u>

1. Open the Site Plan view.

2. You will add an Element Keynote for the bollard light.

   Click in the down arrow beneath the Keynote tool in the Annotate tab, Tag panel.

   Click on the Element Keynote tool.

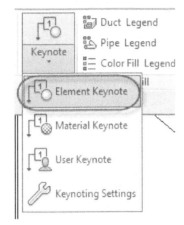

Element Keynote Tool

3. Click on the edge of one of the bollard lights.

   The Keynotes window will open.

   Scroll down to Division 26, Section 26 56 00 – Exterior Lighting.

   Click OK to accept the Key Value and close the Keynotes window.

Keynotes - [C:\ProgramData\Autodesk\RVT 2021\Libraries\English-Imperial\RevitKeynotes_Im... ×

Key Value	Keynote Text
Division 12	Furnishings
Division 13	Special Construction
Division 14	Conveying Equipment
Division 21	Fire Suppression
Division 22	Plumbing
Division 23	Heating, Ventilating, and Air-Conditioning (HVAC)
Division 25	Integrated Automation
Division 26	Electrical
26 00 00	Electrical
26 20 00	Low-Voltage Electrical Transmission
26 30 00	Facility Electrical Power Generating and Storing Equipment
26 50 00	Lighting
26 56 00	Exterior Lighting
Division 27	Communications
Division 28	Electronic Safety and Security
Division 31	Earthwork
Division 32	Exterior Improvements
Division 33	Utilities
Division 34	Transportation
Division 35	Waterway and Marine Construction
Division 40	Process Integration
Division 41	Material Processing and Handling Equipment

Keynote Text:

Exterior Lighting

OK   Cancel   Help

Keynotes Text Window

4.   The keynote is placed.

     Note: This will change all bollard
     lights to this keynote value.

     To change the value, double-click on
     the keynote number text. This will
     allow you to choose a different value.

5.   Change the leader arrowhead style to
     Arrow Filled 30 degree.

Keynote Placed

Leader Arrowhead Value Changed

6.   Open the 1st Floor view

7.   Add an Element Keynote to
     the mullion at the main
     entry.

     Use the Keynote value
     shown.

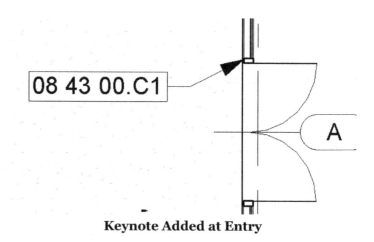

Keynote Added at Entry

Updating the Keynote Text File

The information for the keynotes is contained in a text file (.txt) located in the English-Imperial folder on the hard drive. This is the same folder that contains the family files that are loaded when the Revit software is installed.

Unless the path has been changed, the folder path of this file is:
C:\ProgramData\Autodesk\RVT 2021\Libraries\English-Imperial

To see the ProgramData folder on the hard drive you will need to have the Hidden Folders turned on. In Windows® 10, this is done in the Control Panel under Appearance and Personalization, File Explorer Options, Show hidden files and folders.

Also uncheck the "Hide extensions for known file type" checkbox to show the file extension for text files.

In this section you will make a copy of this file and update it to include changes that have been made to the MasterSpec system.

In a later tutorial you will also modify this file to include your own keynotes.

File Explorer Options

1. Open the Keynoting Settings dialog box by clicking on the Keynoting Settings tool in the Keynote tool.

Next, you will make a copy of the text file and modify it.

The text file for the keynotes is known as a tab-delimited file. The different sections are separated by tabs. This file may be edited using the Notepad application or you can create an Excel spreadsheet file.

2. In the Keynoting Setting dialog box, click the Browse button.

3. Right-click on the RevitKeynotes_Imperial_2010.txt file and select Copy.

4. Right-click in the same folder and
    select Paste.

    This will make a copy of the file.

RevitKeynotes_Imperial.txt
RevitKeynotes_Imperial_2004.txt
RevitKeynotes_Imperial_2010.txt
RevitKeynotes_Metric.txt
UniformatClassifications.txt
UniformatClassifications_2010.txt
RevitKeynotes_Imperial_2010 - Copy.txt

File name: RevitKeynotes_Imperial_2010 - Copy.txt
Files of type: Delimited text (*.txt)

Text File Copied

5. Right-click on the file and select rename.

    Rename the copied file: RevitKeynotes_Imperial_2010 - Modified.txt

6. Right-click on the file again and select
    Properties.

    Check the Attributes of the modified file to
    see if it is set to read-only. If it is, uncheck
    the box.

    This will allow you to make changes to the
    text file and save it.

RevitKeynotes_Imperial_2010 - Modified.txt Properties   ✕

General Security Details Previous Versions

RevitKeynotes_Imperial_2010 - Modified.txt

Type of file: Text Document (.txt)

Opens with: 📄 Notepad   Change...

Location: C:\ProgramData\Autodesk\RVT 2018\Libraries\US

Size: 212 KB (217,142 bytes)

Size on disk: 216 KB (221,184 bytes)

Created: Today, April 30, 2017, 1 minute ago

Modified: Tuesday, December 20, 2016, 9:22:12 AM

Accessed: Today, April 30, 2017, 1 minute ago

Attributes: ☐ Read-only   ☐ Hidden   Advanced...

OK   Cancel   Apply

Text File Properties

7. Right-click on the file and select Edit.

   On most systems, this will open the modified text file using your Notepad application.

RevitKeynotes_Imperial_2010 - Modified.txt - Notepad   —   □   ✕

File Edit Format View Help

```
Division 00        Procurement and Contracting Requirements

Division 01        General Requirements
01 50 00           Temporary Facilities and Controls        Division 01
01 53 00           Temporary Construction   01 50 00
01 53 13           Temporary Bridges        01 53 00
01 53 16           Temporary Decking        01 53 00
01 53 19           Temporary Overpasses     01 53 00
01 53 23           Temporary Ramps 01 53 00
01 53 26           Temporary Runarounds     01 53 00

01 70 00           Execution and Closeout Requirements      Division 01
01 73 00           Execution        01 70 00
01 73 23           Bracing and Anchoring    01 73 00
01 73 23.A1        Bracing 01 73 23

Division 02        Existing Conditions
02 40 00           Demolition and Structure Moving Division 02
```

Keynote Text File Open in Notepad

8. Scroll down to Division 14.

   This is the division for conveying equipment such as Elevators.

   You will be inserting a new section for Electric Traction Elevators. This is the type of elevator you are using on your project. The current keynote file does not have a section for this type.

   Note: Information regarding the MasterFormat® Numbers & Titles are available from various locations in the internet. One of the web addresses that contains this information is at: https://www.arcat.com/divs/building_products.shtml. This file contains a list of recent additions to the MasterSpec system as of 2020. A 2016 version of this information is also available in PDF format in the Commercial Family Files (2021)/Appendix B Files folder.

   To access the developers of the MasterSpec content and software visit: https://avitru.com/specifications/masterspec/. This system was originally developed in 1969 by the American Institute of Architects (AIA) and is currently distributed by Avitru (formerly ARCOM).

9. In the text file, click in front of the line, 14 24 00   Hydraulic Elevators   14 20 00.

   Press the Enter key to insert a new line.

   Type in: 14 21 00(tab)Electric Traction Elevators(tab)14 20 00

   Note: The (tab) indicates that there is a tab separating the text. The 14 20 00 text at the end of the line will place the new subsection under the 14 20 00   Elevators section.

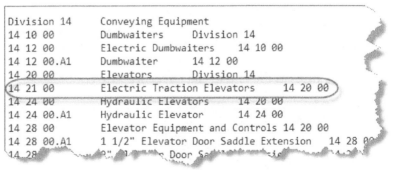

```
Division 14        Conveying Equipment
14 10 00           Dumbwaiters      Division 14
14 12 00           Electric Dumbwaiters     14 10 00
14 12 00.A1        Dumbwaiter       14 12 00
14 20 00           Elevators        Division 14
14 21 00           Electric Traction Elevators       14 20 00
14 24 00           Hydraulic Elevators      14 20 00
14 24 00.A1        Hydraulic Elevator       14 24 00
14 28 00           Elevator Equipment and Controls 14 20 00
14 28 00.A1        1 1/2" Elevator Door Saddle Extension    14 28 00
14 28            2"  ... Door Sa...
```

Line Added in Text File

10. Save and close the text file.

11. While still in the Keynoting Settings dialog box, click the Browse... button in the dialog box and select the updated text file (RevitKeynotes_Imperial_2010 – Modified.txt).

12. Click Open to reload the modified text file into your drawing.

    Once again you will see an alert box indicating that the file was reloaded successfully.

13. Click the View button to view the text file.

14. Scroll down to Division 14.

    You will see a new subsection for Electric Traction Elevators.

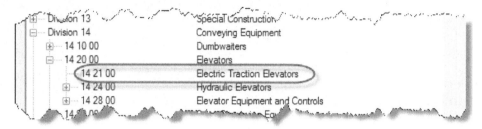

New Subsection

15. Click OK to close the Keynoting Settings dialog box.

16. Click on the Element Keynote tool.

17. Place a keynote for the elevator as shown.

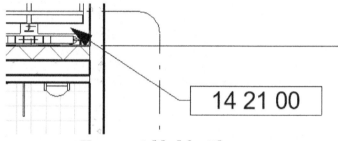

Keynote Added for Elevator

18. Place a keynote for the metal stairs.

    To do this, you will need to edit the keynote file again. You will need to add a new subsection called 05 50 00 Metal Fabrications and a subsection under that called 05 51 13 Steel Pan Stairs.

    Add the lines at the end of the Division 05 section.

Two Lines Added for Steel Pan Stairs

19. Update the revised keynote text file and add the keynote as shown.

Note: If you were in the middle of the Element Keynote tool when you edited the text file, you will need to exit the command, reload the file and then add the element keynote to the stairs.

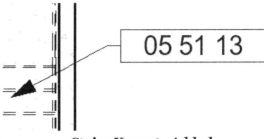

Stairs Keynote Added

Adding the Remaining Keynotes

1. Open the 1st Floor Restroom Callout view.

2. Add the keynotes in the Men's and Women's Restrooms as shown.

   For some of the keynotes you will need to use the Keynote Tag Keynote Number – Boxed – Large family type due to the number of characters.

   Change the arrowhead type for this one as well.

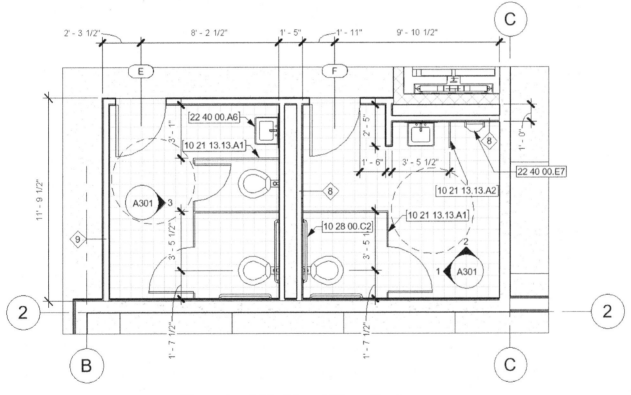

Keynotes Added to 1st Floor Restrooms

3. You may need to add additional lines to the keynote text file depending on what other elements you are noting.

    Note: The 36" Grab Bar spec is under Division 10 20 00 and is already included.

```
Keynotes - [C:\ProgramData\Autodesk\RVT 2021\Libraries\English-Imperial\RevitKeynotes_Im...   ✕

 Key Value                          Keynote Text                                          ∧
 ⊟  Division 10                      Specialties
    ⊟  10 10 00                       Information Specialties
       ⊞  10 11 00                     Visual Display Surfaces
       ⊞  10 13 00                     Directories
    ⊞  10 14 00                       Signage
    ⊞  10 17 00                       Telephone Specialties
    ⊟  10 20 00                       Interior Specialties
       ⊞  10 21 00                     Compartments and Cubicles
       ⊟  10 28 00                     Toilet, Bath, and Laundry Accessories
           10 28 00.A1               Paper Towel Dispenser
```

```
           10 28 00.                 Toilet Seat Cover Dispen
           10 28 00.B1               Shower Curtain Rod
           10 28 00.B2               Towel Bar
           10 28 00.B3               Shower Door
           10 28 00.C1               Grab Bar
           10 28 00.C2               36" Grab Bar
           10 28 00.C3               42" Grab Bar
    ⊞  10 22 00                       Partitions
    ⊞  10 26 00                       Wall and Door Protection
    ⊞  10 40 00                       Safety Specialties
       10 50 00
```

<u>Creating the Keynote Legend and Placing it on the Sheet</u>

This is the last section of this tutorial. Now that you have added keynotes to the project, you will create a schedule that provides names for the numbering. The schedule will be placed on the title sheet.

1. Click on the arrow beneath the Legends tool in the View tab, Create panel.

    Click on the Keynote Legend tool.

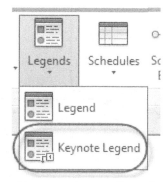

Keynote Legend Tool

2. Keep the name of the legend as: Keynote Legend

```
New Keynote Legend                                   ✕

 Name:
 ┌─────────────────────────────────────────┐
 │ Keynote Legend                          │
 └─────────────────────────────────────────┘

     ┌──────────┐   ┌──────────┐   ┌──────────┐
     │    OK    │   │  Cancel  │   │   Help   │
     └──────────┘   └──────────┘   └──────────┘
```

New Keynote Legend

3. The Keynote Legend Properties dialog box opens.

   This is like the other schedules. The main difference is the you will not be able to add additional fields to the schedule.

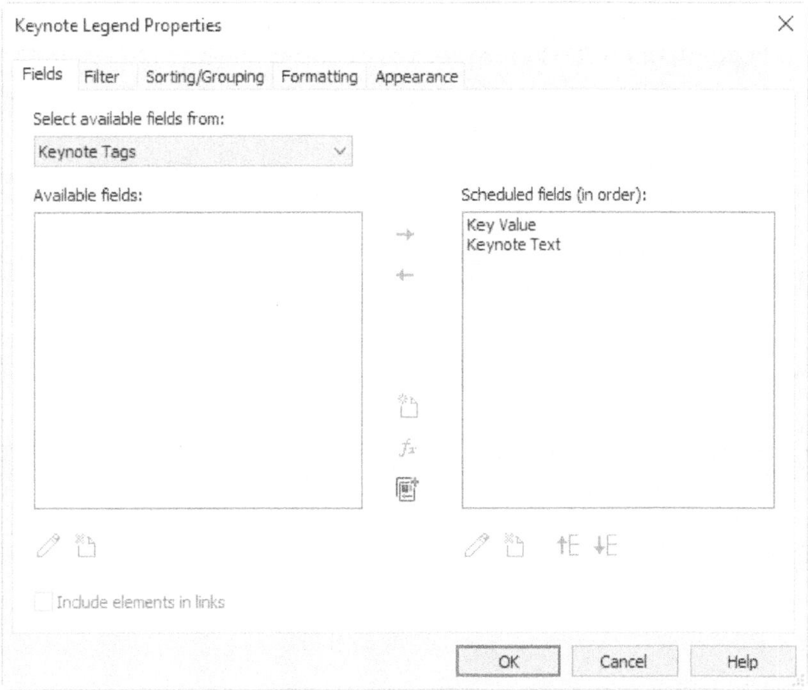

Keynote Legend Properties

4. Click on the Sorting/Grouping tab.

   The Sort by: setting should be set to Key Value.

5. Click on the Appearance tab.

   Uncheck the Grid Lines checkbox. Uncheck the "Blank row before data" checkbox.

   Click OK to close the dialog box.

6. Set the font properties for the title of the schedule to: 1/4", Arial Black, Bold.

   Set the font properties for the text to: 1/8", Arial.

   Set the font properties for the headers to: 9/64", Arial, Bold, Underlined.

   Change the Title and Headers to all caps and justify the text to the left.

<KEYNOTE LEGEND>	
A	B
KEY VALUE	KEYNOTE DESCRIPTION
05 51 13	Steel Pan Stairs
08 43 00.C1	Storefront Mullion
10 21 13.13.A1	Toilet Partition
10 21 13.13.A2	Urinal Screen
10 28 00.C2	36" Grab Bar
14 21 00	Electric Traction Elevators
22 40 00.A6	Wall Mount Sink
22 40 00.E3	Toilet
22 40 00.E7	Wall Mount Urinal
26 56 00	Exterior Lighting

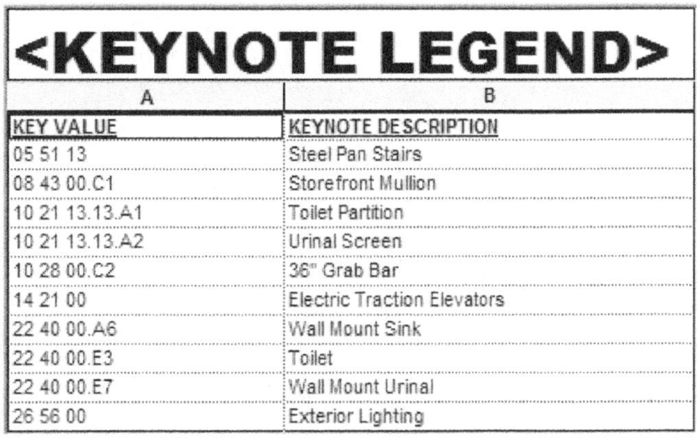

Keynote Legend Formatted

7. While still in the Keynote Legend, open the Filter tab.

   Uncheck the Filter by sheet checkbox.

   Filter by: Key Value and contains then add a space in the box to the right. This will ensure that only Key Values with a "space character" in them will appear.

   Note: This will become important in the next tutorial part.

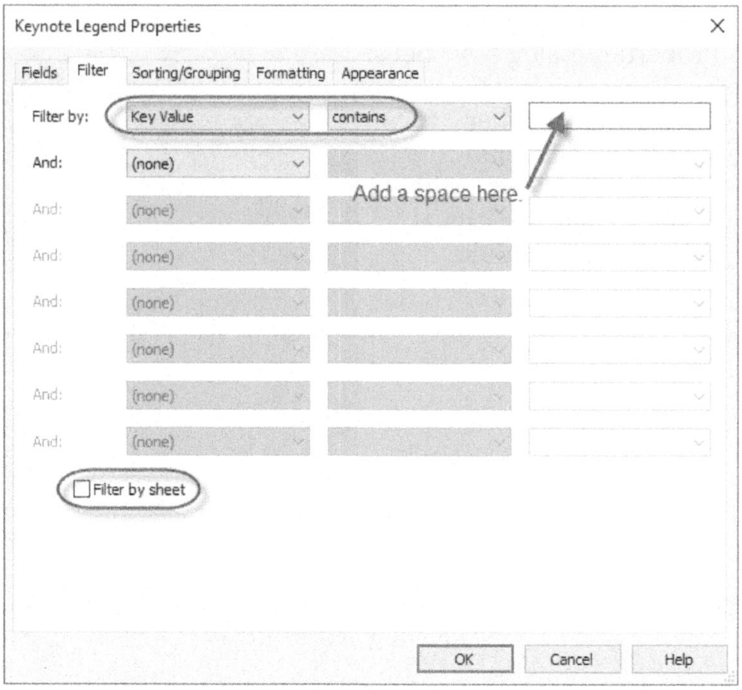

Keynote Legend Properties

8. Open the Title Sheet.

   Drag and drop the legend next to the Sheet Index.

KEYNOTE LEGEND

KEY VALUE	KEYNOTE DESCRIPTION
05 51 13	Steel Pan Stairs
08 43 00.C1	Storefront Mullion
10 21 13.13.A1	Toilet Partition
10 21 13.13.A2	Urinal Screen
10 28 00.C2	36" Grab Bar
14 21 00	Electric Traction Elevators
22 40 00.A6	Wall Mount Sink
22 40 00.E3	Toilet
22 40 00.E7	Wall Mount Urinal
26 56 00	Exterior Lighting

SHEET NUM…
A100
A101
A102
A103
A104
A105
A106
A107
A108
A109
A201
A202
A301
A302
A400
A401

Keynote Legend Placed

9. Duplicate the Keynote Legend and name it Restroom Legend.

   Open the Filter tab and check the Filter by sheet checkbox.

10. Open the Schedules & Callout View Sheet.

Drag and drop the Restroom Keynotes legend to the right of the callout.

Only the keynotes that are on the sheet will shown.

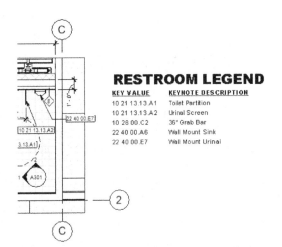

11. This is the end of Part 1. Save your file as CLB-1.

CLB-2   Adding User Keynotes to the Project

In this tutorial, you will be adding custom keynotes to the project. You currently are using textual notes to note the furniture, lighting types, ceiling materials, HVAC components, and exterior materials.

You will replace these text notes with numbers and list the keynotes on a sheet-by-sheet basis.

As stated in CLB-1, you are using the "By keynote" numbering method. If you were using the "By sheet" method, you would still need to have a unique number for each user keynote in the modified text file. At the end of this tutorial, you may want to try switching between the two numbering methods to see the difference.

Beginning the Project

1. Open the last file in the Appendix B Tutorial, CLB-1.

2. Save the file as, CLB-2.

Updating the Keynote Text File

1. Before adding keynotes, you will need to update the modified text file that you created in tutorial CLB-1.

   Click on the Keynoting Settings tool in the Keynote tool.

   Note: A completed version of the modified text file is available in the Support Files available on the Instant Revit! website. You may choose to use this file instead of typing in the information yourself. If you use this file for the remaining notes, replace it within the folder on the C:\ Drive.

   The location for the file is at: C:\ProgramData\Autodesk\RVT 2021\Libraries\English-Imperial

2. Click the Browse button and then right-click on the modified text file and select the Edit option.

3. The text tile opens in the Notepad application.

   You will start by adding a new section at the top of the text file for the Furniture Plan notes.

4. Add the notes as shown.

Place a tab between the text number, name, and referencing section.

Note: The Revit program requires that the keynotes have unique numbers. For the Furniture Plan notes you will place the letters FP in front of the note number. For the other sheets you will create a different numbering system.

```
RevitKeynotes_Imperial_2010 - Modified.txt - Notepad

File  Edit  Format  View  Help
00          Furniture Plan Notes
FP1         Workstation Cubicle        00
FP2         Storage Cabinets           00
FP3         Desk     00
FP4         Task Chair and Computer 00
FP5         Coalesse E-Table Conference Table        00
FP6         36" Diameter Table         00
FP7         Floor Copier     00
```

New Section in Keynotes File

5. When finished, save the file, and reload it into the drawing.

Adding the Keynotes to the 1st and 2nd Floor Furniture Plans

1. Open the 1ST FLOOR – FURNITURE PLAN view.

2. Before adding the keynotes, you will load a custom tag.

This tag will show the keynote value inside of a hexagon with the letter/number value.

Click the Load Family tool in the Insert tab, Load from Library panel.

3. Select the Keynote Tag – Hexagon.rfa file from the Custom Families, Annotation folder from the website.

4. Click the User Keynote tool in the Key tool.

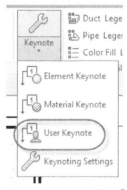

User Keynote Tool

5. In the type selector, select the family type Keynote Number – Hex w/Arrow.

    Click the Edit Type button to modify the properties.

Keynote Number – Hex w/Arrow Type

6. Set the Leader Arrowhead value to Arrow Filled 30 Degree.

    Repeat the process for the Hex w/Dot type. Use the Filled Dot 1/16" value for the Leader Arrowhead.

    Click OK to save the changes and close the Type Properties dialog box.

Leader Arrowhead Value Changed

7. Click on the edge of the desk in the Office and choose note number FP3 for the keynote.

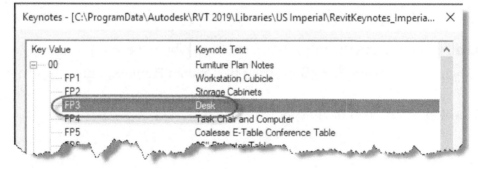

Note FP3 Selected

8. Note the Workstation Cubicle, Task Chair and Computer, and Storage Cabinets.

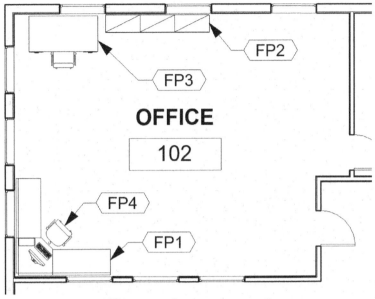

Office Furniture Keynoted

9. Open the 2ND FLOOR – FURNITURE PLAN view.

10. Add the keynotes in the Cubicle/Conference Area and Break Room as shown.

Also add a keynote for the conference room table.

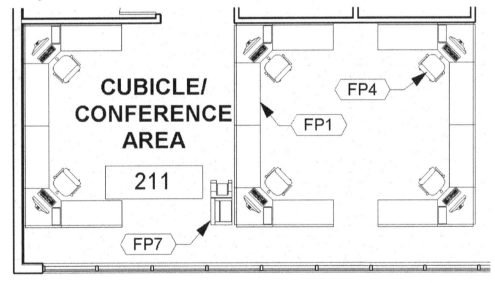

Keynotes in Cubicle/Conference Area

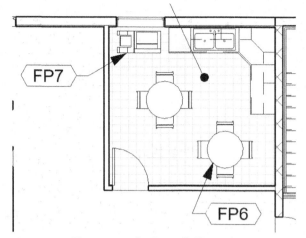

Keynotes in Break Room

<u>Adding the Reflected Ceiling Plan Keynotes</u>

1. Open the modified text file for the keynotes.

2. Add the keynotes to the text file for the Reflected Ceiling Plan sheet.

    Save and reload the file when finished. Do this after modifying the notes for each sheet.

```
01        Reflected Ceiling Plan Notes
CP1       2' X 2' Acoustic Tile Ceiling      01
CP2       2' X 4' Acoustic Tile Ceiling      01
CP3       Troffer Light - Lens 2' X 2' - 4 Lamp - 277 Volt        01
CP4       Troffer Light - Lens 2' X 4' - 4 Lamp - 277 Volt        01
CP5       5/8" Gypsum Board Ceiling on Metal Stud 01
CP6       Downlight - Recessed Can - 8" Incandescent 277 Volt     01
CP7       Stairway Floor Above      01
CP8       Square Return Register 12" X 12"        01
CP9       Square Return Register 24" X 24"        01
CP10      Square Supply Diffuser 12" X 12"        01
CP11      Square Supply Diffuser 24" X 24"        01
```

Reflected Ceiling Plan Notes

3. Add the keynotes on the 1st and 2nd Floor Reflected Ceiling Plan views as shown.

    Remove the text notes on the 1st FLOOR Reflected Ceiling Plan view.

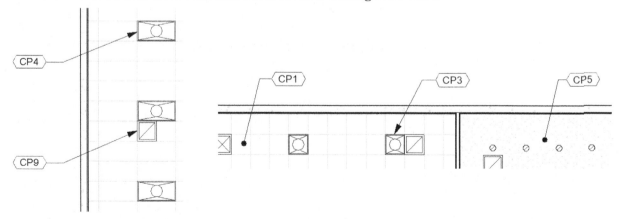

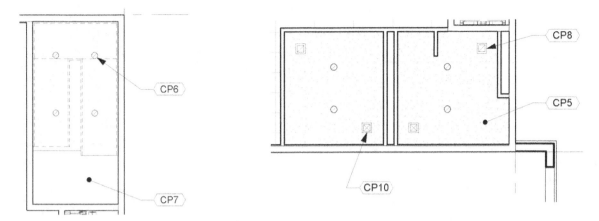

Keynotes for 1st Floor Reflected Ceiling Plan

Keynotes for 2nd Floor Reflected Ceiling Plan

Adding the Site Plan Keynotes

1. Open the modified text file for the keynotes.

2. Add the keynotes to the text file for the Site Plan sheet.

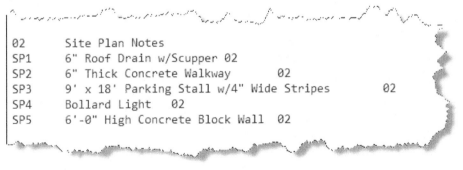

```
02        Site Plan Notes
SP1       6" Roof Drain w/Scupper 02
SP2       6" Thick Concrete Walkway          02
SP3       9' x 18' Parking Stall w/4" Wide Stripes         02
SP4       Bollard Light     02
SP5       6'-0" High Concrete Block Wall   02
```

Site Plan Notes

3. Open the Site Plan view.

    Delete the text notes that duplicate the key notes to be added.

4. Add the keynotes on the Site Plan view as shown.

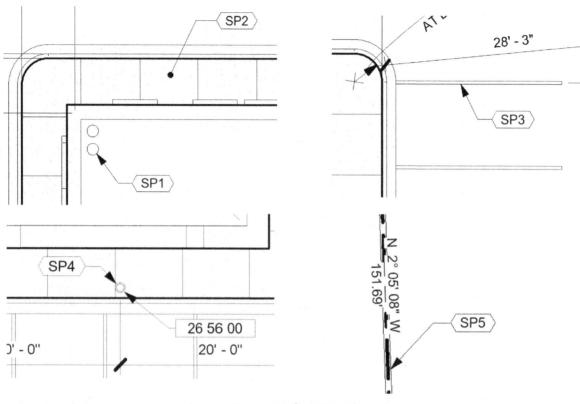

Keynotes for Site Plan

Adding the East/North Elevation Keynotes

1. Open the East and North Elevation Views.

    Delete the text notes that duplicate the key notes to be added in each view.

2. Open the modified text file for the keynotes.

3. Add the keynotes to the text file for the East/North Elevation sheet.

```
03        East/North Elevation Notes
EN1       Wallpack Light 120 Volt 03
EN2       Illuminated Signage      03
EN3       Stucco over Metal Studs 03
EN4       8" Concrete Cast-In-Place Walls 03
EN5       Bollard Light      03
EN6       Concrete "Eyebrow" Window Shading      03
EN7       Concrete Roof Coping      03
```

East/North Elevation Notes

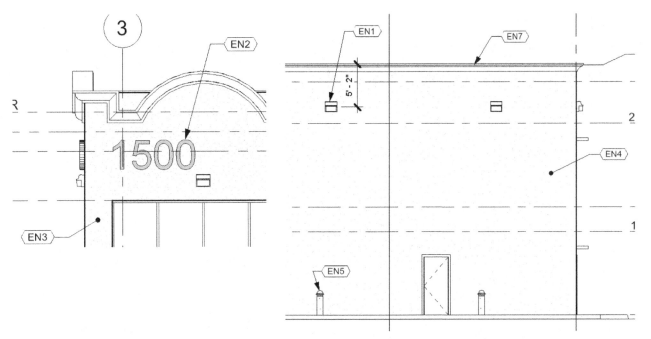

Keynotes for East Elevation View

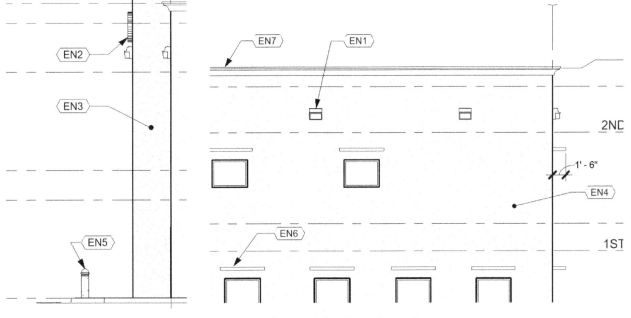

Keynotes for North Elevation View

Adding the West/South Elevation Keynotes

1. Open the West and South Elevation Views.

    Delete the text notes that duplicate the key notes to be added in each view

2. Add the keynotes to the text file for the West/South Elevation sheet.

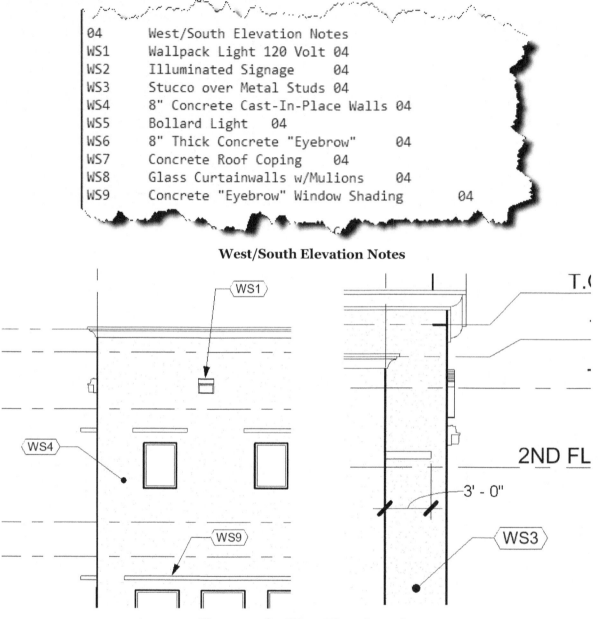

```
04        West/South Elevation Notes
WS1       Wallpack Light 120 Volt 04
WS2       Illuminated Signage        04
WS3       Stucco over Metal Studs 04
WS4       8" Concrete Cast-In-Place Walls 04
WS5       Bollard Light    04
WS6       8" Thick Concrete "Eyebrow"      04
WS7       Concrete Roof Coping      04
WS8       Glass Curtainwalls w/Mulions     04
WS9       Concrete "Eyebrow" Window Shading      04
```

West/South Elevation Notes

Keynotes for West Elevation View

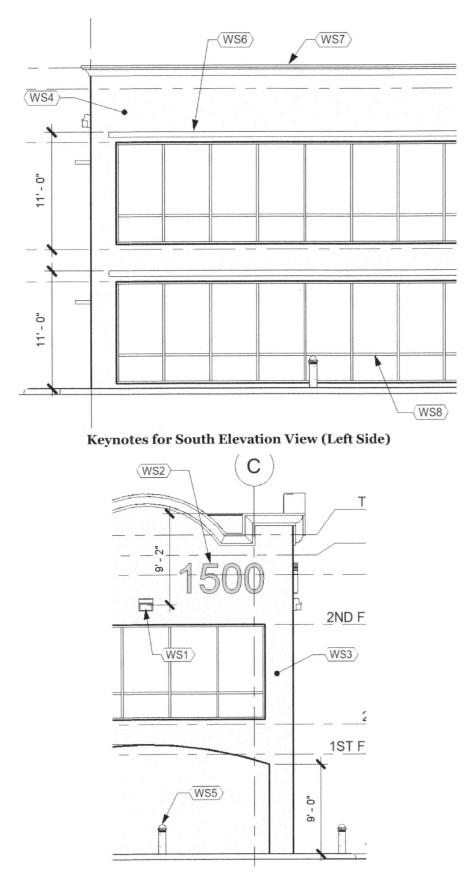

Keynotes for South Elevation View (Left Side)

Keynotes for South Elevation View (Right Side)

<u>Setting up the Keynote Legends and Adding them to the Sheets</u>

In this last section, you will create Keynote Legends for each of the sheets with keynotes.

1. Click on the Keynote Legend tool in the View tab, Create panel.

2. Name the legend, SITE PLAN KEYNOTES.

New Keynote Legend

3. The Keynote Legend Properties dialog box opens.

    Click OK to close the dialog box.

    The legend is create showing all the keynotes in the project.

A	B
\<SITE PLAN KEYNOTES\>	
Key Value	Keynote Text
05 51 13	Steel Pan Stairs
08 43 00.C1	Storefront Mullion
10 21 13.13.A1	Toilet Partition
10 21 13.13.A2	Urinal Screen
10 28 00.C2	36" Grab Bar
14 21 00	Electric Traction Elevators
22 40 00.A6	Wall Mount Sink
22 40 00.E3	Toilet
22 40 00.E7	Wall Mount Urinal
26 56 00	Exterior Lighting
CP1	2' X 2' Acoustic Tile Ceiling
CP2	2' X 4' Acoustic Tile Ceiling
CP4	Troffer Light - Lens 2' X 4' - 4 Lamp - 277 Volt
CP5	5/8" Gypsum Board Ceiling on Metal Stud
CP6	Downlight - Recessed Can - 8" Incandescent 277 Volt

Site Plan Keynotes

4. Click on the Edit... button next to Filter in the Properties box.

    This will filter out only the keynotes that contain the letters SP.

    Check the "Filter by sheet" checkbox.

Filter Settings

5. The legend will now only show keynotes for the Site Plan.

<SITE PLAN KEYNOTES>	
A	**B**
Key Value	Keynote Text
SP1	6" Roof Drain w/Scupper
SP2	6" Thick Concrete Walkway
SP3	9' x 18' Parking Stall w/4" Wide Sripes
SP4	Bollard Light
SP5	6'-0" High Concrete Block Wall

Only Site Plan Keynotes Visible

6. Use the following settings to set up the text sizes and appearance:

Title: Arial, 3/16", Bold, Underline, Left Justified
Keynotes: Arial, 1/8", Left Justified

In the Appearance tab:
Remove blank row before data.
Turn off the Grids lines and Outline.
Uncheck the Show Headers checkbox.

<SITE PLAN KEYNOTES>	
A	**B**
SP1	6" Roof Drain w/Scupper
SP2	6" Thick Concrete Walkway
SP3	9' x 18' Parking Stall w/4" Wide Sripes
SP4	Bollard Light
SP5	6'-0" High Concrete Block Wall

Final Legend Appearance (Site Plan)

7. Duplicate the Site Plan legend and rename it: CEILING PLAN KEYNOTES.

   Filter the notes to only show the ones that contain the letters CP.

8. Repeat the process and create legends for the 1st Floor sheet, East/North Elevation sheet, West/South Elevation sheet, and the Furniture Plan sheet.

9. When finished you should have eight legends.

   This includes the original Keynote Legend created earlier.

Legends Created

10. Open the Keynote Legend.

    Because of the additional
    legends, the keynote
    legend now shows all of
    the keynotes in the
    project.

    Use the Filter by: setting
    to only show the element
    keynotes.

Filter Settings for the Keynote Legend

Note: If you completed
this step at the end of
tutorial CLB-1, verify the
settings that were made.

Set the Filter by: setting to Key Value, contains, (Space) character.

Use only a single space character. This works because there are spaces in each of the key values
for the element keynotes. Also, keep the "Filter by sheet" checkbox unchecked.

11. Open the 1st Floor Keynotes legend.

    Use the same filter settings as the Keynote legend but leave the "Filter by sheet" checkbox
    checked.

12. Open the Furniture Plan Keynote legend.

    Filter the notes to only show the ones that contain the letters FP.

13. Open the East/North Keynote legend.

    Filter the notes to only show the ones that contain the letters EN.

14. Open the West/South Keynote legend.

    Filter the notes to only show the ones that contain the letters WS.

15. The keynote legends are prepared.

    Next, you will add the keynote legends to their respective sheets.

    Open the A101 – SITE PLAN sheet.

16. Drag and drop the Site Plan keynotes to the lower right corner of the sheet.

    You may need to move the Site Plan view up slightly.

    Widen the columns as needed.

SITE PLAN KEYNOTES

SP1	6" Roof Drain w/Scupper
SP2	6" Thick Concrete Walkway
SP3	9' x 18' Parking Stall w/4" Wide Stripes
SP4	Bollard Light
SP5	6'-0" High Concrete Block Wall

Site Plan Keynotes Legend Placed

17. Repeat the process for sheets:

    A103 – First Floor Plan, A105 – 1st Floor Reflected Ceiling Plan,
    A106 – 2nd Floor Reflected Ceiling Plan, A108 – 1st & 2nd Flr. Furniture Plans,
    A201 – East/North Elevations, and A202 – West/South Elevations.

    Place the keynote legends at the lower right corner of the sheet.

    On some of the sheets you will need to move the views to position the legend.

18. This is the end of Part 2 and the Appendix B Tutorial. Save your file as CLB-2.

    Note: You may wish to re-print your Commercial Project at this time.

Glossary of Terms and Tools

Note: All screenshots are from the Autodesk® Revit® software.

Add-Ins	Programs that may be added to be used within the Revit® software.
Align(ed)	Elements that line up with one another. The Align tool in the Modify tab is used for this. Also used for the Aligned Dimension dimension style.
Annotation(s)	Elements such as: text, dimensions, or symbols that are placed in 2D or 3D views.
Autodesk®	The company the makes the Revit® software.
Callout	A portion of the view that shown in a separate view at a finer scale to show more detail. The tool is located in the View tab.

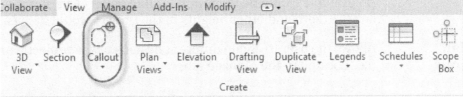

Callout Tool

Camera View	A three-dimensional view of that structure that is in perspective projection. The view is created by using the Camera tool in the 3D View tool located in the View tab, Create panel.
Cascade (Windows)	Arranging and opening views/windows so that all they are of equal size and overlapping one another.
Component	This tool is used to add an existing family or create a Model in the project using the Model In-Place option.
Contextual Tab	A tab above the ribbon panel that appears while using a tool. Contains tools that are specific to the current command. The tab is green in color and will disappear when the command is completed.

Contextual Tab (Place Door Tab Shown)

Core	The inner portion of an element. Usually is used as structural support. Example: The structural core of a wall.
Curtain Wall	A type of wall that does not provide support for the structure. Usually made of glass panels with mullions.

Curtain Grid   Used with Curtain Wall elements. A curtain grid is a system of lines that is used to separate a larger panel. These are required to add mullions to a curtain wall.

Cut   To remove material where two elements intersect.
(Geometry)   Located in the Modify tab.

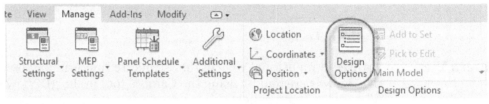

Cut Tool

Cut Plane   This is a portion of the plan view that is visible in section. By default this is set to 4'-0" above the floor level but may be raised or lowered depending on the desired result. This setting is changed in the Properties dialog box in the View Range setting.

Datum   A base or reference surface than provides a location reference for other elements. An example would be the first floor line on an elevation view. This height would be set to zero and other heights in the project would be measured from it.

Design   Allows the user to create different designs of the project within the same Revit
Options   file. Located in the Manage tab.

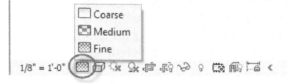

Design Options Tool

Detail   Elements that are placed in two dimensional views. A detail line would only be visible in the view in which it was placed. A level is a type of datum.

Detail Level   The level of detail that is shown in the view. The settings are: course, medium, and fine. This is adjusted at the bottom of the screen in the View Control Bar.

Detail Level Tool

Drafting View   A two-dimensional view. May be used for structural details or other annotative elements.

Element   A single object within the project. A line of text would be considered a text element.

Export   To take elements from the file (or the entire file) and convert them to another format so that it may be opened in a different application. The Export tool is located in the Application menu.

Extrusion   When a flat shape is extended (or extruded) into a solid. This method of creating elements is used in the Roof tool, Modeling components, Slab edges, and others.

Face   The outside surface or edge of an element. The Face of Core option may be used when placing dimensions to locate wall locations.

Family(ies)   A single element or collection of Revit elements that may be added to the project as a group. Examples include doors, windows, and cabinetry. These files have the .rfa file extension.

Footprint   An area or shape that is created to define the size and shape of an element such as a floor or roof. This is done while in Sketch Mode. The lines that make up the edge of the footprint are magenta in color.

Grid(s)   Lines that are added to the project to aid in locating walls or columns. Usually used on larger or commercial projects. The Grid tool is located in the Datum panel in the Architecture tab. Grids may also refer to lines that divide a curtain wall.

Group   A collection of elements that are made part of a single group. This is done so that the group of elements may be modified as one. Located in the Modify tab.

Create Group Tool

GUI   Graphics User Interface. The interface of the Revit program.

Host   An element that provides a place for another component to become a part of it. A Stair would be considered a host for the railings.

Import   To bring in elements from another file.

Info Center   Used to access the help file, sign in to Autodesk 360, and access other resources.

Info Center

Join (Geometry)   To merge two elements together to eliminate seam lines. Located in the Modify tab.

Join Tool

Keynote   A type of note that shows the MasterSpec® value for a material, component, or other aspect of the project. Element Keynotes and User Keynotes may be added to the project.

Legend   A key that defines the meaning of diagrams or notes. The tool is located within the Create panel in the View tab. A legend would be used to show the meaning of electrical symbols.

Level
A key height within the project. Floor, roof, and footers may all be assigned a level within the project. Levels may also be used to generate views.

Mass
A type of three-dimensional element that can be converted to a roof, wall, or floor.

MEP
Mechanical, Electrical, and Plumbing.

Model (Elements)
A three-dimensional structure or collection of elements that are placed in a three dimensional view.

Mullion
A separator between two panels of a curtain wall. A curtain grid must be placed before adding a mullion.

Object Styles
A dialog box that sets the line weight, color, pattern and material of different categories and types of elements. Located in the Settings panel in the Manage tab.

Offset
Tool used to move or copy an element in a parallel direction to the existing element at a set distance. Located in the Modify tab.

Offset Tool

Options Bar
This bar appears when the program needs information about a particular command. The bar will turn off when the command is ended.

Portion of the Place Wall Options Bar

Paint
A tool that is used to override a surface of an element with a different material. Located in the Modify palette.

Property Line
A line the shows the legal boundary of the property. This line is typically shown on the Site Plan view. The line may be sketched or added using distances and bearing (direction) values. The Property Line tool is located in the Massing & Site tab.

Reference Plane
A three dimensional plane that is used to provide a location in the project for other elements to be anchored or dimensioned. May be used as a construction line within the project.

Quick Access Toolbar
The tool bar located at the top of the screen. Contains commonly used tools such as Open, Save, Undo, and other tools.

Quick Access Toolbar

Ribbon   The entire collection of panels and tools that appear when the tab is selected. Also known as a Tab.

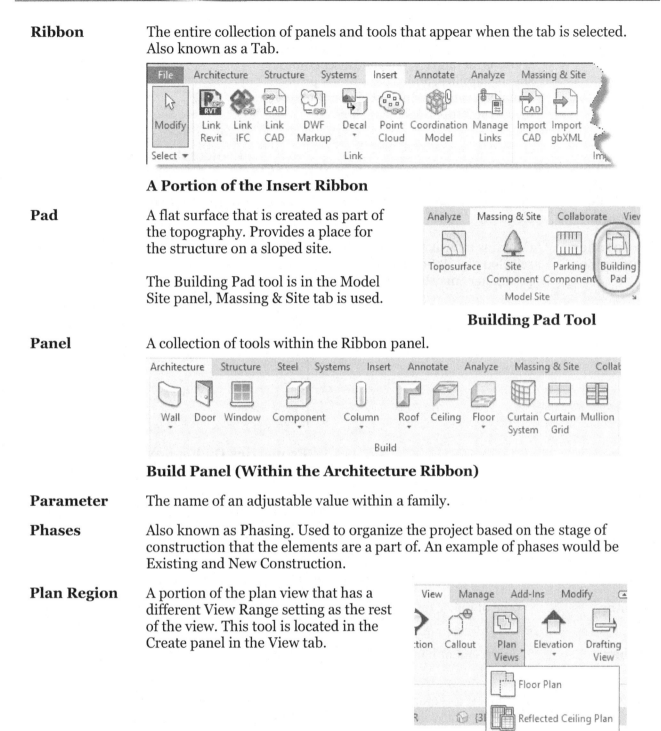

A Portion of the Insert Ribbon

Pad   A flat surface that is created as part of the topography. Provides a place for the structure on a sloped site.

The Building Pad tool is in the Model Site panel, Massing & Site tab is used.

Building Pad Tool

Panel   A collection of tools within the Ribbon panel.

Build Panel (Within the Architecture Ribbon)

Parameter   The name of an adjustable value within a family.

Phases   Also known as Phasing. Used to organize the project based on the stage of construction that the elements are a part of. An example of phases would be Existing and New Construction.

Plan Region   A portion of the plan view that has a different View Range setting as the rest of the view. This tool is located in the Create panel in the View tab.

Plan Region Tool

Project Browser	Shows a tree-type view of the plan views, 3D views, elevations (exterior and interior), sections, detail views, legends, schedules, sheets, families, and groups of the project. Usually located on the left side of the screen below the Properties dialog box.	

Project Browser

Properties (Type and Instance) — The parameters of an element, component, or family. Type Properties affect all instances of the element within the project. Instance Properties only affect one element.

Properties Dialog Box — Contains information about the selected object. Some of the parameters may be modified.

Properties Dialog Box
(Showing Floor Plan View Properties)

PDF — Portable Document File. A file format developed by the Adobe® corporation that is used as a file format for images of Revit drawings. This format is free to use. The file has a .pdf file extension. The PDF redirect v2 program is used in the book tutorials to convert files to this format.

Purge — As in to remove (purge) unused elements from the drawing.

Raster — A type of image or output of a Revit file that consists of pixels instead of lines and shapes (vector elements). Images and shaded views are printed in this way.

Rebar — Reinforcement bar. Used to strengthen concrete slabs and walls and to reduce cracking.

Render — To convert a vector or shaded view into a raster image file. This may be done within the software or by using the Autodesk® 360 Cloud Rendering service.

Revision — A change that is made to the project. The change may be documented in a Revision Block.

Separator — Used to separate a space such as a room into two separate spaces that may be labeled separately. The Room Separator tool in the Architecture tab is used to do this.

Room Separator Tool

Schedule   A tabular element that shows information about a type of element. Doors, Windows, and Rooms may have schedules created for them. This helps to eliminate notes on the drawing by placing the information in the schedule. Schedules may be created by using the Schedules tool in the View tab.

Schedules Tool

Sheet   A view of the project that contains one of more view windows. Typically includes a title block. Located in the View tab.

Sheet Tool

Sketch &   The preliminary process in creating a solid from a shape. When beginning a roof,
Sketch Mode   the first step is to create a roof sketch. When the program is in sketch mode, most of the tools are grayed out and the contextual (green) tab is active. To leave sketch mode the green check or red "X" is clicked.

Sketch Path   A line that is drawn to indicate the location and length for railing element.

Slab   A flat surface with thickness. This is usually applied to floor slabs.

Snap   Assists in locking a new element to an existing element. Elements may be locked to the endpoint, midpoint, nearest, center, tangency, and other locations. Located in the Manage tab.

Snaps Tool

Split Face   A tool used to create separate faces on one face. Used to change the major material of a large surface such as bathroom tile with the floor of a building. Located in the Modify tab.

Split Face Tool

Status Bar   Gives information and prompts for the current tool and process. Located at the bottom left side of the screen.

Click on Wall to place Door (Space Bar to flip the instance left/right)

Status Bar (Prompt for Door Tool Shown)

Structural   These are elements of the model that provide support. Examples: Columns, Structural Walls, and Beams.

Subregion   A portion of the toposurface that is separate from the major region. This is done to change a portion of the toposurface to a different material. The Subregion tool is in the Model Site panel, Massing & Site tab.

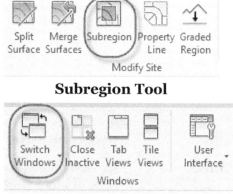

Subregion Tool

Switch Windows   Allows the user to switch from one open file/view to another by selecting from a list of views. Tool is located in the View tab.

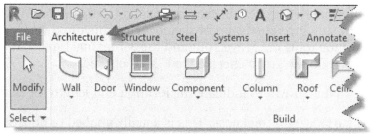

Switch Window Tool

Tab   Located at the top of the Revit interface. By clicking on a tab the ribbon will be visible. Example: Architecture Tab (see graphic). The term "Ribbon" and "Tab" are interchangeable.

Architecture Tab

Tag   A label that is attached to a family or space such as a door, window, or room. The tag may be attached when the element is added to the projects or later in the project.

Template File   A file that is used when beginning a new drawing file. Has the extension of .rte. Example: Residential-Default.rte.

Tile (Windows)   Arrange open views/windows so that all are of equal size and completely visible.

Title Block   A portion of the border that contains information about the project. May be loaded from a title block family file or included in the template file.

Topo surface   A surface that is created when adding topography to the project. A toposurface may be created from points place in the view or from imported drawings or files.

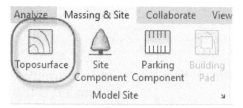

Topo surface Tool

The Topo surface tool is in the Massing & Site tab, Model Site panel.

Type Selector   Located in the Properties dialog box. This allows the user to select different types of elements within the same family such as: door and window types.

**Type Selector
Showing a Door Type**

Vector   A type of file where the elements consist of lines and shapes instead of individual pixels. Revit construction documents are usually printed in this format.

View   A plan (top) or elevation (side) image of the object taken at a particular height or level.

View Control Bar   Shows view-related tools such as: view scale, detail level, view display, sun settings, shadow toggle, crop window settings, and temporary visibility settings.

View Control Bar

View Range   The top and bottom of the view. The view is setup so that only objects are visible that are between the upper and lower range.

This is adjusted in the View Properties dialog box.

View Range Edit... Button

Walkthrough   A collection of rendered images that simulate traveling around or through a project.

Wall Join   A tool used to override the automatic joining of two walls.

Wall Join Tool

Witness Lines   The extension line of a dimension.

Conclusion

Congratulations on Completing the Project!

You should now have an excellent understanding of the techniques required to create a two-story commercial building using the Autodesk Revit 2021 design software. Feel free to continue to modify this project with additional elements such as additional parking, exterior lighting, additional site elements, and other elements.

I hope that you have enjoyed the project and will recommend this book to others. Please feel free share your experiences that you have had while working through the project and feel free to offer any suggestions to improve the book.

Once again, congratulations and good luck in your future study of Revit and Architecture!

Sincerely,

David Martin
instantrevit@gmail.com
instantrevit.com

June 2020 and March 2021

Index

Made in the USA
Las Vegas, NV
09 March 2023